This book provides a general introduction to the history of Bulgaria and the Bulgarians. The text and illustrations trace the rich and dramatic story from the days when Bulgaria was the centre of a powerful mediaeval empire, through the long centuries of Ottoman rule, to the cultural renaissance in the nineteenth century and the political upheavals of our own century.

Independence, when achieved, posed its own problems. The most persistent – that of the frontiers and territorial dissatisfaction – led Bulgaria into three wars during the twentieth century. In all three Bulgaria emerged as a loser, yet defeat did not always bring dishonour: for example, Bulgaria managed to save its Jews from deportation to the gas chambers during the second world war. Communist domination seemed to merge Bulgaria into the Soviet orbit but, as the post-communist years have shown, Bulgaria and the Bulgarians have a sturdy sense of national pride and identity which derive from their rich and varied history.

CAMBRIDGE CONCISE HISTORIES

A Concise History of Bulgaria

CAMBRIDGE CONCISE HISTORIES

This is a series of illustrated 'concise histories' of selected individual countries, intended both as university and college textbooks and as general historical introductions for general readers, travellers and members of the business community.

Titles in the series:

A Concise History of Germany
MARY FULBROOK

A Concise History of Greece
RICHARD CLOGG

A Concise History of France
ROGER PRICE

A Concise History of Britain, 1707–1975
W. A. SPECK

A Concise History of Portugal
DAVID BIRMINGHAM

A Concise History of Italy
CHRISTOPHER DUGGAN

Other titles are in preparation

A Concise History of Bulgaria

R. J. CRAMPTON

Professor of East European History,
and Fellow of St Edmund Hall, University of Oxford

CAMBRIDGE
UNIVERSITY PRESS

Published by the Press Syndicate of the University of Cambridge
The Pitt Building, Trumpington Street, Cambridge CB2 1RP
40 West 20th Street, New York, NY 10011–4211, USA
10 Stamford Road, Oakleigh, Melbourne 3166, Australia

First published 1997

Printed in Great Britain at the University Press, Cambridge

A catalogue record for this book is available from the British Library

Library of Congress cataloguing in publication data
Crampton, R. J.
A Concise History of Bulgaria / R. J. Crampton.
p.   cm. – (Cambridge concise histories)
Includes index.
ISBN 0 521 56183 3. – ISBN 0 521 56719 X (pbk.)
1. Bulgaria – history. I. Title. II. Series.
DR67.C72 1997
949.77 – dc20   96–7778 cip

ISBN 0 521 56183 3 hardback
ISBN 0 521 56719 X paperback

WD

For my cousin

ROBERT GRAY

with affection and in
commemoration of our childhoods of
long, long ago

CONTENTS

ILLUSTRATIONS

PLATES

MAPS

PREFACE

The crowded departure lounge at Gatwick airport on a busy summer Sunday morning may not seem the obvious place to encounter the effects of recent changes in Eastern Europe, but to see young British couples with their children queuing not to go on holiday but to go and work near the Black Sea coast assembling British cars for sale in the Balkans is something which would have been unthinkable ten years ago; it would have been even more of a fantasy in 1967 when I first went to Bulgaria. Even if the Rover venture has tragically collapsed Bulgaria has opened itself to European and American culture and business.

This being so it is reasonable to assume that there is a growing need in the west for a concise history of a country which for the last fifty or so years has seldom attracted much attention. It is hoped the present volume will go some way to showing western readers that Bulgaria has at least as much to offer in terms of historic interest as it does in financial reward.

All too often in the west we tend to blur the distinction between the nation and the state; when the Portuguese delegate suggested to the first meeting of the League of Nations that the organisation would be better called the League of States he was told that the difference was too insignificant to bother about. No-one who had any connection with the Balkans would make that mistake. And if this book is called *A Concise History of Bulgaria* it is also to some degree a concise history of the Bulgarians after they had arrived in the Balkans in the seventh century. For the most part the book concentrates on the various Bulgarian states but it cannot ignore the fate of the Bulgarians during the 500 years when they were part of the Ottoman empire and there was no Bulgaria. Even when a Bulgarian state re-emerged in 1878 there still has to be a distinction between Bulgaria and the Bulgarians. Many who considered themselves to be Bulgarians lived outside Bulgaria; even more numerous were those outside Bulgaria whom the Bulgarians inside Bulgaria described as Bulgarian. Indeed, the difference between the territorial definitions of Bulgaria and the lands inhabited by the Bulgarians is one of the main themes of modern Bulgarian history.

It is on modern history that this book concentrates, though an attempt is made to illustrate how the Bulgarian nation and the Bulgarian state emerged in the second and third quarters of the nineteenth century. In that process the rebirth of Bulgarian literature and the revivifying of its culture played a vital part. In a general book limited to 70,000 words it has not been possible to explore these phenomena to the extent that they deserve, but it is hoped that this short introduction will excite further interest and lead to further exploration of these fascinating processes.

For anyone writing on Balkan or East European history there are difficulties with nomenclature, dates and transliteration. In general, when English forms do not exist, I have used the modern Bulgarian name for towns or geographic features. There are however some exceptions. Istanbul seems inappropriate usage before the Ottomans took the city in 1453 and therefore I have preferred Byzantium or Constantinople; in the short chapter on the pre-Bulgarian period I have generally used classical rather than present-day names, though an obvious exception to this is 'Balkan' which is a post-classical term. Readers already familiar with Bulgaria might be surprised at the use of 'Tûrnovo' rather than 'Veliko Tûrnovo'; the adjective has been omitted for the sake of brevity and because no mention is made in the text of Malko Tûrnovo. I have, I hope, been more consistent with dates. I have used the Gregorian or western calendar rather than the Julian used by Orthodox Christians; the footnote on p. 134 gives more information on this point.

It would be impossible to thank directly all those, in Britain and Bulgaria, who have helped me formulate the ideas and amass the information presented in these pages. The librarians of the Bodleian Library in Oxford and the Kiril i Metodi Library in Sofia have made my life much easier, and Sasho and Daniella Shûrbanov and Andrei Pantev have provided human companionship and endless hospitality when I have been in Bulgaria. In Britain teaching with Michael Hurst has been an enormously rewarding experience. I have also learnt much from my students, particularly Kyril Drezov, Ivan Krûstev, Marietta Stankova and Naoum Kaytchev; in addition to intellectual stimulation they have provided the dual satisfaction of seeing intelligent young Bulgarians making their way in a difficult world, and proving that Bulgarian scholarship is amongst the finest in that world. Aglika Markova and Ivan Stancioff transformed the official image of Bulgaria in Britain and for this I thank them, as well as for making it so easy to deal with Bulgaria. Sasho Shûrbanov and Aglika Markova provided invaluable and indefatigable help in the search for the cover illustration and Vanya Stoyanova unearthed the gruesome photograph on page 112. To all of them I offer my heartfelt thanks. Sheila Kane cast an expert and perceptive eye over the text and is responsible for many improvements in it. William Davies' gentle, civilised guidance made my task immeasurably easier; he is that rare and priceless phenomenon: the ideal editor. But above all I have to thank my wife for over thirty years of patience, understanding and unstinting support.

A NOTE ON TRANSLITERATION

а	a	п	p
б	b	p	r
в	v	c	s
г	g (always hard)	т	t
д	d	y	u
е	e (or é at the end of proper nouns)	ф	f
ж	zh (but дж has been transliterated ('dj')	x	h (but 'kh' in Russian and proto-Bulgarian words)
з	z	ц	ts
и	i	ч	ch
й	i	ш	sh
к	k	щ	sht (but 'shch' in Russian words)
л	n	ъ	û
м	m	ю	iu
н	n	я	ya
о	o		

The Bulgarian lands: main rivers and mountains

I

The Bulgarian lands from prehistory to the arrival of the Bulgarians

The lands which now constitute the state of Bulgaria were amongst the first in Europe to witness the emergence of organised, social life. Settlements existed in these lands as early as the middle palaeolithic period, from *c.* 100,000 to 40,000 BC. In neolithic times the population gradually forsook their caves for the plains where they began to work the land. By the third millennium BC they were cultivating non-food crops such as flax and had become adept at metal-working. In the sixth millennium BC an unknown people were producing objects of great originality and which experts consider to be the products of a spontaneously generated rather than an imported culture. This culture, in which the chief object of veneration appears to have been the mother goddess, reached its zenith in the fourth millennium BC.

By the end of the third millennium BC the lands to the east of the Morava–Vardar valleys were falling under the cultural influence of the Thracians. An Indo-European people, the Thracians lived in a loosely organised tribal society. They were masters of metal-working, particularly with silver and gold. Many spectacular hoards have been unearthed in present-day Bulgaria at sites such as Panagiurishte, Velchitrun and Vratsa, and many more remain to be excavated. In addition to a high level of proficiency in metal-working the Thracians were renowned for their horsemanship. Music too was an essential feature of Thracian culture for Orpheus himself was an early Thracian king who managed to unite the disparate tribes of Thrace and Macedonia for a short period. This

Map 1.1 Ancient sites in present-day Bulgaria

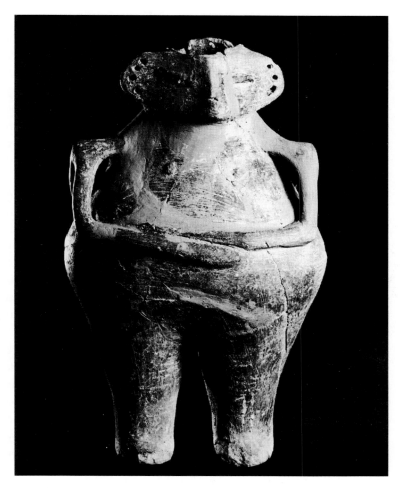

Plate 1.1 A Mother Goddess figure produced by the
unidentified people who thrived in the Bulgarian lands during
the sixth millennium BC

was a considerable feat in that the Thracians showed little disposition towards political cohesion and cooperation, Herodotus
once noting that if the Thracians could only unite and subordinate
themselves to one leader they would be invincible. As is so often the
case in the Balkans, it was external pressures rather than internal
inclinations which brought about political unity.

These pressures came from the Greeks who established mercantile centres and colonies along the Black Sea coast. The Greeks held the Thracians in low esteem, unjustifiably so because not only were the Thracians their equal in crafts – and horsemanship – they also began minting coins at much the same time as their haughty southern neighbours. The Persian invasions of the Balkans in the sixth and fifth centuries BC were a much more serious threat than Greek cultural arrogance. This external danger brought about the Odryssian kingdom which united the Thracian tribes of the central Balkans.

The Persian storm was weathered but in the fourth century BC another threat appeared, this time from within the Balkan peninsula. The powerful new Macedonian state soon clashed with the Thracians. The latter's cultural achievements continued but they suffered chronic political weakness; they accepted Macedonian domination, and Thracian archers and horsemen formed a significant proportion of the army which Alexander the Great took to the frontiers of India. After the disappearance of the Macedonian danger came one much more ominous.

Landing first in the west of the Balkans to suppress pirates in the third century BC, the Romans spread inexorably inland. By the first century AD the entire peninsula south of the Danube was under their control. For a while they allowed a truncated Thracian kingdom to continue as a client state but eventually that too disappeared. The Thracian language survived in remote areas until the fifth century AD and their worship of the horse was continued by later inhabitants of the area; and some scholars still see the 'mummers' found in parts of the south-west of present-day Bulgaria as a relict of Thracian culture.

Roman rule was inevitably efficient and strict, giving the Balkan peninsula a unity and stability enjoyed neither before nor since. Under Roman law and the firm grip of the legions the provinces of Moesia, the area between the Balkan mountains and the Danube, and Thrace, from the Balkans to the Aegean, prospered. The new system of roads bound the Balkans together on both a north–south and an east–west axis. At the crossroads of important diagonal routes across the peninsula was to be found the city of Serdica, the site on which Sofia now stands. Other cities flourished, not least

Plate 1.2 A one-handled vase from the Vratsa treasure,
between 380 and 350 BC. The vase, 9 cm in height, illustrates
the Thracian prowess in horsemanship

Trimontium, now Plovdiv, whose magnificent Roman theatre was
discovered only in the 1970s when a new road was being built.

With Roman rule, eventually, came Christianity and when the
empire was divided in 395 Moesia and Thrace became part of
the eastern empire focused on Constantinople (Byzantium). For the
next millennium and a half the city was to play a hugely important
role in the history of the Bulgarian lands.

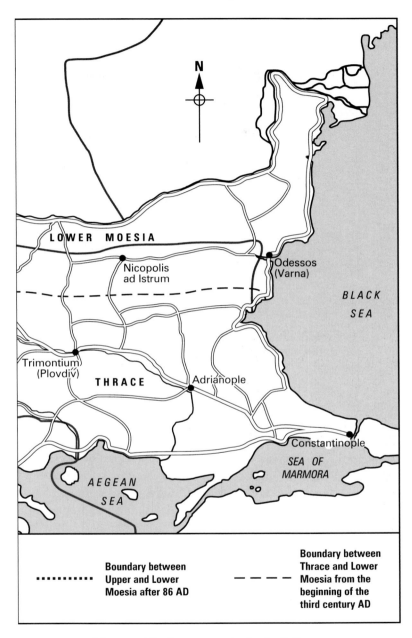

Map 1.2 The Roman empire in the Balkans

Plate 1.3   The Roman theatre in Plovdiv which came to light
only in the 1970s during the construction of a new inner city
road

By the fourth century Roman power was weakening. Internal
problems were compounded when tribes from the Asiatic steppes
raided the north-east of the Balkans. In the following century
ultimately fatal damage was inflicted on the Roman body politic by
a series of such invaders who included the Alani, the Goths and
the Huns, all of whom were enticed by the prospect of looting the
fabled wealth of Byzantium. They failed in that aspiration and soon
moved out of the Balkans in search of fresh plunder, but if these
invaders were transient, the Slavs who also first appeared in the fifth
century, were not. They were settlers. They colonised areas of the
eastern Balkans and in the seventh century other Slav tribes
combined with the Proto-Bulgars, a group of Turkic origin, to
launch a fresh assault into the Balkans. The Proto-Bulgars
originated in the area between the Urals and the Volga and were a
pot-pourri of various ethnic elements, the word *Bulgar* being
derived from a Turkic verb meaning 'to mix'. What differentiated

the Proto-Bulgars from the Slavs was that they had, in addition to a formidable military reputation, a highly developed sense of political cohesion and organisation. In 680 their leader, Khan Asparukh, led an army across the Danube and in the following year established his capital at Pliska, near what is now Shumen. A Bulgarian state had appeared in the Balkans.

2

Mediaeval Bulgaria, 681–1393

Two main problems confronted the new Bulgarian state at the end of the seventh century: the need to establish clearly defined and secure borders; and the need to weld together the two main human components of the state, the Proto-Bulgarian conquerors and the conquered Slavs. The second of the these two problems was eventually to be resolved, but the first was seldom out of consideration for more than a few years; this problem was to be a persistent feature of Bulgarian states, modern as well as mediaeval.

The new state commanded a powerful position. From Pliska it could control the north–south routes through the eastern passes of the Balkan mountains and along the narrow lowland coastal strip. In the north, however, its extensive territories beyond the Danube inevitably led it into conflict with both the tribal groups milling around in the plains to the north-east, and with the succession of states which were established on the north-western borders. For the leaders of mediaeval Bulgaria, however, the most persistent and pressing problem was defining Bulgaria's relations with the great power to the south. The first mediaeval Bulgarian state was to be destroyed by Byzantium; the second was to fall to Byzantium's successor, the Ottoman empire.

BULGARIA UNDER THE KHANS, 681–852

After its foundation in 681 the new state enjoyed almost a century of growth. Initial tensions with Byzantium were contained and regulated in a treaty of 716 which awarded northern Thrace to Bulgaria and was unusual in the mediaeval era in that it contained purely economic clauses. Immediately after the treaty the Bulgarian state assisted Byzantium in the latter's conflict with the Arabs in Asia Minor. By the middle of the eighth century part of the Morava valley had been added to Bulgaria which then included much of what is now southern Romania and parts of present-day Ukraine.

By this time the Black Sea was a virtual Byzantine lake, and in this sector it went virtually unchallenged by Bulgaria because Bulgaria never developed a sizeable sea-going force. Even if the strategic need for a such a force had been recognised it is doubtful if anything effective could have been done to act upon that need; the Bulgarian state had a relatively low technological base and the degree of planning and coordination needed to produce a navy would have been difficult to achieve in an economy which did not even mint its own coins, preferring instead to rely on Byzantine currency.

The lack of a navy ruled out expansion along the Black Sea coast either to the north or the south, just as the chaos of the steppe area made impossible any territorial gains to the north-east; the natural direction of movement for the Bulgarian state was therefore to the north-west and the south-west. In the north-west the collapse of the Avar kingdom created a vacuum into which Bulgaria's rulers gladly advanced, thus taking their frontier up to the river Tisza; Transylvania too became part of Bulgaria. Expansion to the south and south-west was not so easy. Some of Macedonia had been taken late in the eighth century but only at the cost of losing part of Bulgaria's possessions in Thrace. Khan Krum (803–14) determined to remedy this. In 811 he took the recently fortified Sredets (now Sofia) from the Byzantines, went on to seize Nesebûr on the Black Sea coast, and then marched as far as the walls of Byzantium itself. This was a characteristically vicious war in which, in 811, the Byzantine Emperor Nicephorus, became the first of his rank for almost 500 years to lose his life on the battlefield; Krum encrusted his deceased enemy's skull in silver and used it as a drinking goblet.

In 814 his successor, Khan Omurtag (814–31), concluded a peace which gave Bulgaria some territory in the Tundja valley, and later in his reign he was able to add Belgrade (Singidunum) and its surrounding district to his kingdom. In the second quarter of the ninth century Bulgaria, taking advantage of Byzantium's preoccupations with the iconoclast controversy and with threats to its power in Asia Minor, expanded into Macedonia, a predominantly Slav area which welcomed this alternative to Greek, Byzantine domination. By the middle of the century Ohrid and Prespa were incorporated into Bulgaria as was much of southern Albania; Byzantine power in Europe was now confined to western Albania, Greece, the southern Vardar valley and Thrace.

Omurtag, however, was not merely a warrior. He continued Krum's work in introducing a proper legal system into Bulgaria and he was an avid builder, his most notable achievement in this regard being the reconstruction of Pliska after the city had been burnt in 811. There are more extant inscriptions to Omurtag than to any other mediaeval Bulgarian ruler.

THE REIGN OF BORIS I (852–888) AND THE CONVERSION TO CHRISTIANITY

The celebration of Omurtag is perhaps surprising in view of the achievements of Boris I who in his three and a half decades of power was to impose huge and portentous changes on his realm and its inhabitants.

Boris was no less a warrior than his famous predecessors but his most important act was to impose Christianity upon Bulgaria. He did this in part to escape immediate military embarrassments and in particular to relieve pressure from the Byzantine armies, but there were also other long-standing causes, both domestic and external, for his decision.

In the first place, almost the entire civilised world was by now Christian, with only distant tribes such as the Letts and the Finns outside the Christian community; if Bulgaria were to be accepted as an equal amongst the powerful states of Europe, east and west, it would have to become part of their cultural and religious community. Even more importantly, conversion, it could reasonably be hoped, would help bridge the gap between the two main ethnic groups in Bulgaria, the Proto-Bulgarians and the Slavs. This gap still existed although the languages had merged into a Slavo-Bulgarian in which the Slav tongue of the conquered masses predominated.

Map 2.1 Bulgaria's borders during the first kingdom,
681–1018

Christianity had taken root in the Balkans during the later period of the Roman empire, and when they entered the area and colonised it the Slavs to a large degree adopted the Christian religion of those whom they had subdued. This was much less true of the Proto-Bulgarians, especially the nobility and the rulers, who for decades remained steadfastly pagan. It was not that its Christian Slav subjects had presented any threat to the Bulgarian state. On the contrary, they had provided the bulk of the armies which fought against Christian Byzantium, and they continued to guard the passes through the Balkan mountains, this being a vital service because if Byzantine forces had penetrated the Balkan range they could have strangled a Bulgarian state based on Pliska. The problem was potential rather than actual; the difference between Christian and pagan could provide a dividing line which might be exploited by an external enemy, and which might deepen dangerously in times of internal difficulty. This problem had been compounded by the wars of expansion waged during the eighth and ninth centuries. The acquisition of territory south of the Balkans and in Macedonia had greatly increased the number of Slavs and Christians within the state, thus making the Proto-Bulgarians quite obviously a minority. Also the wars, especially under Krum, had brought into Bulgaria thousands of prisoners of war, most of whom were Christians. Given the slavery and misery into which most of these unfortunates were plunged they had but little alternative than to take refuge in whatever consolations their faith could offer them. This set an impressive example to many of their captors. Omurtag was not one of them; he continued to persecute the Christians, primarily in order to preserve the faith of his predecessors, but he was fighting a losing battle. Christianity continued to spread and reached even his own family, with one of his sons taking the new faith.

Omurtag had attempted to centralise the Bulgarian state, increasing the power of the ruler and diminishing that of the overwhelmingly Proto-Bulgarian boyars or nobility. Meanwhile, Byzantine Christianity was associated with a centralised, autocratic state. This truth was not lost on Boris and was one of the factors leading him to his decision in 864 to accept Christianity for himself and for all his subjects. A number of nobles reacted violently, stressing the decentralised traditions which were associated with paganism. Fifty-two of them were executed.

The conversion did not bring entirely satisfactory results for Boris. Bulgaria was made part of the Byzantine church and was denied the right to have its own, Bulgarian, patriarch or to appoint its own bishops. This strengthened existing fears in Bulgaria that, because in the empire the church was seen as an arm of the state, the church in Bulgaria would become an arm of the Byzantine state and would be used to interfere in the internal affairs of Bulgaria. Fears of potential subversion via the Byzantine church led Boris to ask if Byzantium's religious rival, Rome, would offer better terms. Emissaries were dispatched to enquire whether the pope would allow Boris to nominate the Bulgarian bishops and appoint a Bulgarian patriarch. At the same time, Boris requested clarification of certain points of doctrine and religious regimen: could, he asked, the Bulgarian tradition of the ruler eating alone, with his wife and followers relegated to separate, lower tables, continue? on what days was it permitted to hunt? and could sexual intercourse be allowed on Sundays? The answers to these specific questions, including the latter, were comfortingly indulgent, but on the critical political issue of the appointment of a patriarch and of subordinate bishops, they were not. Rome was as adamant as Byzantium in its refusal to allow the nomination of bishops by the secular power; nor would Rome permit the Bulgarians to have their own patriarch, though the pope did consent to their having an archbishop, who would, however, be nominated by the pope. These terms were no better than those offered by the emperor in Byzantium and Boris therefore remained with the devil he knew. In 870 a council regulated the organisation of the church in Bulgaria which was to be headed by an archbishop chosen by and dependent upon the patriarch in Constantinople.

The conversion caused other difficulties. The masses needed to be educated in their new faith, and though the Greeks sent missionaries to accomplish this task, they were too few in number. Furthermore, Slav and Proto-Bulgarian alike had been accustomed for the last two centuries to regard the Greeks as cunning but implacable enemies and therefore treated their new instructors with some suspicion. Nor did the indigenous population take kindly to the fact that the vast majority of the new clergy, especially its upper echelons, were Greek. With so many of the locals suspicious and/or ignorant of the new doctrines they were required to profess, it was hardly surprising that heresies rapidly gained a strong foothold in the Bulgarian lands. Some of them were to play a formative part in the later history of these lands. Nevertheless, despite these problems, the conversion to Christianity was a watershed in the history of Bulgaria. Despite the many difficulties which it created it did facilitate the merging of the two constituent elements in the population. The Slavs could now more readily accept the state because it was Christian, and the Proto-Bulgarians had nothing to fear from Christianity because it was no longer divorced from the state and because it was no longer predominantly Slav or Greek. Thanks largely to the conversion, by the tenth century there were 'Bulgarians' as opposed to Slav and Proto-Bulgarian subjects of the Bulgarian state.

In a development which was parallel to the conversion in time, and its equal in importance, an alphabet for use in the Slavonic languages emerged in the mid to late ninth century. The origin of this development is thought to be a request in 862 from the ruler of Moravia for an alphabet for use amongst his own people so that the influence of the Franks and Germans could be contained. Little is known of the origins of the Cyrillic alphabet, and what is known is extremely contentious, but its creation is generally acknowledged to be the work of two Salonika born monks, Cyril and Methodius.

The introduction of the Cyrillic alphabet was of enormous importance. More than any other development it prevented the absorption of the Bulgarians by the Greeks to their south or the Franks to their west. It enabled the Bulgarians to create their own literature. And this they did with great rapidity. Kliment of Ohrid (Kliment Ohridski), who died in 896, and after whom Sofia university is named, established a thriving school of learning which embraced theological and many other studies and which attracted over 3,000 students in its first 7 years. The new language also facilitated the production of important secular texts such as a legal code, *Zakon Sudnii Liudim*; and without an alphabet it is difficult to imagine how the Bulgarian state could have carried out administration in the Slavo-Bulgarian language. Above all, however, the new alphabet enabled the Bulgarian church to use Slavo-Bulgarian as the language of the liturgy, and had it not been able to do this it would have been impossible for the Bulgarian church to escape total Greek domination.

That Slavo-Bulgarian, or as we shall call it henceforth, Bulgarian, should become the language of the state and the Bulgarian church was decreed by an assembly of notables in 893.

THE REIGN OF SIMEON THE GREAT (893–927)

The assembly which decreed that Bulgarian should be the language of the state and the church, also accepted as ruler Simeon, who had come to power by a palace coup. In that he was not exceptional in the history of mediaeval Bulgaria, but he was the only monarch in those centuries to be accorded the epithet 'the Great'.

Simeon, who was brought up in Constantinople, originally intended to pursue a religious life and had been tipped as a prime candidate for the leadership of the church in Bulgaria. Despite his association with Constantinople Simeon spent much of the early part of his reign at war with the empire and with his other neighbours. He extended the boundaries of Bulgaria westwards to the Adriatic, south to the Aegean and north-westwards to incorporate most of modern Serbia and Montenegro. Twice he led his armies to the walls of Constantinople itself; on the second occasion he was forced to raise his siege only because of pressure from the Magyars in the north, where in fact Simeon witnessed the loss of almost all Bulgarian territory beyond the Danube. In 896 he concluded a peace with the empire which agreed to accept the independence of the Bulgarian church. Thirty years later, at the end of further wars, a second treaty confirmed this and recognised Boris as *basileus*, that is, king or tsar; the only other monarch to whom Constantinople extended such recognition was the Holy Roman Emperor.

Simeon made a further significant change when he moved the Bulgarian capital from Pliska to the nearby Preslav. In the new capital the pagan tradition would be less strong. Preslav saw Bulgarian art and literature flower with unprecedented brilliance, Simeon having for long surrounded himself with men of letters such as the Monk Hrabr, John the Exarch and Konstantin of Preslav.

That flowering of literature was helped by the twenty years of peace and prosperity which followed the treaty of 896 with Constantinople. The prosperity of those golden years was based to a considerable degree on close and healthy commercial relations with the empire, though trading links with Venetia and the west were also developing. The good times could not last, however, and the final years of Simeon's reign were again clouded by war, primarily against Constantinople.

THE END OF THE FIRST EMPIRE, 896–1018

Simeon died in 927, having nominated his second son, Petûr, as his successor. Petûr's reign was of exceptional duration – he remained king until 970 – but these were years of decline for Bulgaria. As usual, there were wars to be fought, though these were now defensive rather than expansionist, the chief threat being the Magyars in the north. There were also continuing clashes with the imperial power to the south. This almost constant warfare inevitably weakened the state.

There were also important internal explanations for the decline of Bulgarian power. Throughout the country there had been if not the expectation then at least the hope that the new reign would bring about a return to the golden days of peace. This illusion was shattered by the Magyar invasions. The disappointed nobility dreamed of a return to the old days, whilst the increasingly Byzantinified court harboured is own solutions. The church, meanwhile, fell to corruption and self-enrichment.

The latter development had a profound effect amongst the silent masses of the population. The tenth century saw a steady increase in the economic and social power of the landowner, partly because the central authority of the state was not as great as it had been under Boris and Simeon. One landowner whose property had been greatly extended was the church. Whilst the few grew rich, times became ever harder for the poor. Inevitably alienation set in.

Since the conversion to Christianity many Bulgarians had been left insufficiently educated in and therefore insecurely committed to their new church. It was no longer possible to revert to paganism, even if that had been desired, but this did not mean that unques-

Plate 2.1 Tsar Simeon defeating the Byzantines, a miniature from the Madrid manuscript of the Chronicles of Ivan Skilitsa

tioning obedience had to be given to the official church: if the alienated could not revert to paganism they could at least escape into heresy. Heresy had entered Bulgaria with Christianity itself. First among the unofficial doctrines to arrive were those brought by Syrians and Armenians, and very soon hermitism became popular amongst the religiously committed; Bulgaria's national saint, Ivan Rilski (John of Rila), was a hermit who was born between 876 and 880 and died in 947. Hermitism obviously indicated a willingness to withdraw from the world and its problems, and this sense of 'internal migration' or dissociation from the temporal world was further encouraged by the greatest and most lasting of the heresies to enter Bulgaria: bogomilism.

The bogomils argued that the entire visible world, including mankind, was the creation of satan; only the human soul was created by God who sent his son, Christ, to show humanity the way to salvation. The bogomils believed the gratification of all bodily pleasures to be an expression of the diabolic side of creation, and therefore they preached a formidable asceticism which enjoined poverty, celibacy, temperance and vegetarianism. The few peripatetic 'Holy Ones' who lived up to these exacting precepts were greatly respected by the general body of the population, who were painfully aware of the contrast between these 'Holy Ones' and the official clergy. The bogomils also questioned the social order by preaching that man should live in communities where property was shared and individual ownership unknown, and in which all men would be levelled by an equal participation in agricultural labour. The bogomils had no formal priesthood, though each district or area had a *dyado* or elder (literally a 'grandfather'), and there were loose links between different regions.

The bogomils satisfied a spiritual hunger amongst the peasant masses. There was a need amongst the recently converted for an explanation of the increasingly harsh conditions in which they found themselves. The teachers and priests of the official church were neither as able nor as committed as the ones brought in by Boris and Simeon, and the many who felt abandoned by a clergy apparently more interested in self-enrichment than in the well-being of its flock naturally found more to respect in those who practised the exacting doctrine they preached. Because bogomilism was very much a reaction to mounting social pressures its popularity increased in times of hardship. This was understandable; in such times it was easier than ever to believe that the temporal world was entirely the creation of the Evil One.

Bogomilism has been unfairly criticised for causing all or most of the misfortunes which befell mediaeval Bulgaria, but bogomilism, in declaring all institutions irredeemably evil, did implicitly condemn any effort to improve those institutions as in the long run irrelevant. For this reason bogomilism was essentially negative and did not give rise to any reformist movement or pressures, nor did it stimulate the creative intellectual revolution which the questioning of the Catholic church produced in the west.

The end of the tenth century saw the first Bulgarian kingdom decline rapidly to a tragic end. Wars continued with clashes with Kievan Rus in the north and, inevitably, resumed conflict with Constantinople in the south. In 971 Preslav was taken as the empire

Plate 2.2 Hermitism was strong in mediaeval Bulgaria: the arrow indicates the entrance to the monastery church of Gospodev Dol near the village of Ivanovo in the Rusé district

conquered much of eastern Bulgaria. The Bulgaria of Krum, Boris and Simeon was finished. The capital moved between a number of western centres, Byzantine influence having always been less noticeable in that part of Bulgaria. It finally settled in Ohrid. In the 980s the Bulgarian kingdom enjoyed a brief resurgence with its armies retaking much of the territory it had lost south of the Danube. Under the leadership of Tsar Samuil (997–1014) Bulgaria expanded further into present-day Albania and Montenegro, but it was a false dawn. Bulgarian successes had come about primarily because Constantinople was again preoccupied with the Arab threat to its possessions in Asia Minor. A military victory in 1001 freed Constantinople of this concern and the emperor, Basil II, could turn his full attention to the Bulgarian problem; his efforts in this direction were to earn him the grim title, 'the Bulgar-slayer'.

The end for the first Bulgarian state came when the Bulgarian and imperial armies met in Macedonia in 1014. On the slopes of Mount Belassitsa 15,000 Bulgarian troops were captured; 99 out of every 100 were blinded; the remainder were left with one eye to guide their comrades back to their leader. The loss of the army, despite the hideous treatment meted out to the survivors, was not the fatal blow; armies had been lost before and were to be lost again. What destroyed Bulgaria was the loss of leadership. Samuil died three days after first beholding his blighted troops. Four years later the state collapsed and was incorporated into the Byzantine empire.

The first Bulgarian empire had achieved much. It had created a Bulgarian nation from the Proto-Bulgarians and the Slavs. As in the merging of the Normans and the Anglo-Saxons to produce the English, the process was neither easy nor rapid, yet by the beginning of the eleventh century there was a nation, a state, a language, a literature and a church, all of which were clearly Bulgarian. But the kingdom, despite the brilliance of a few of its rulers, also suffered grave weaknesses. The introduction of Christianity, and the consolidation of boyar power which followed soon afterwards, required Bulgaria to undergo a fundamental reordering of its values and beliefs, and to adapt to far-reaching social changes. The Bulgarians were required to absorb in a few decades processes which in other lands lasted centuries, and inevitably the strains and fissures ran deep and far. The bogomils grew strong on such strains and fissures, and their dismissive attitude to the temporal world hardly encouraged full-scale commitment to the state in danger. The first Bulgarian state was also in some respects surprisingly backward. Not only did it fail to produce a navy but it failed to see the dangers of geography. Given its position in the Balkans, the Bulgarian kingdom was exposed to threats from the south, the north-east and the north-west. There was perhaps *folie de grandeur* in the assumption that all these enemies could for ever be contained, and it was certainly a mistake, albeit an understandable one, to assume, as many Bulgarian leaders did, that danger could be circumvented by playing one enemy off against another. This *folie de grandeur* was all the greater when one takes into account that the kingdom was always heavily influenced by Byzantium and by Byzantine practices. The Bulgarian aristocracy aped that of its southern neighbour; the state and church administrations were similar to those of the empire, as was the tax system; the kingdom used mainly Byzantine currency; and even the vocabulary of administration, commerce and much of public life were derived from the empire.

BULGARIA UNDER BYZANTINE RULE, 1018–1185

In his treatment of the defeated Bulgaria Basil was as moderate in victory as he had been implacable in battle. Most importantly for the Bulgarians, the Bulgarian church was allowed to continue as a separate national institution. Headed by a patriarch in Ohrid, the Bulgarian church included much of present-day Bulgaria, Serbia, Albania and Macedonia. Basil's moderation, however, did not survive him. The Ohrid patriarchate increasingly fell under Greek influence, and the Bulgarian bishops were no longer allowed to elect their patriarch from amongst themselves. The tax system changed for the worse. Before, taxes had been levied mainly in kind but now, to feed the army, the government had to have recourse to forced purchases at fixed prices with taxes then being paid in cash not kind. A new form of land-holding was introduced: the *proniya*. The holders of this land had the right to its produce but could not pass it on by inheritance; they therefore worked it and its peasants for all they could get out of it in the time available; many of them were absentee landlords who used bailiffs who in turn took their share of the profits. In 1040 Petûr Delyan, a descendant of Samuil, collected an army and took the chief Bulgarian town, Skopje, and soon came to dominate Thrace, Epirus and Macedonia. His revolt was not a nationalist movement but a protest against worsening social conditions, and it was joined by some oppressed Greeks. In 1041 Delyan was betrayed by his allies, blinded, and later captured by Byzantine troops amongst whose ranks were Varangians under the command of Harald Hardrada, later prince of Norway and the founder of Oslo.

Bulgaria remained an integral part of the Byzantine imperium until the late twelfth century. There had been a few outbreaks of unrest, mainly social in origin, and it was clear that a sense of Bulgarian cultural identity and separateness survived. Ironically, this was in part due to bogomil influence. Bogomil ideas tended to be absorbed more easily by the Slavs than the Greeks and this hindered the assimilation of the former by the latter. It also prevented any commitment to the ruling state or church.

THE SECOND BULGARIAN EMPIRE, 1185–1393

In the 1180s the Normans, who had already dislodged the Byzantines from Sicily, attacked imperial territory in Greece and along the Adriatic. In retaliation to this and other threats the imperial government was forced to increase taxation and conscription levels. It was more than many Bulgarians could bear. In 1185 two landowners from near Tûrnovo, Petûr and Asen, requested an alleviation of the new burdens along with concessions for themselves. Not only were they refused, one of them had his faced slapped by a Byzantine courtier. News of this humiliation helped feed the already healthy fires of revolt and soon most of eastern Bulgaria had taken to arms and Petûr had been proclaimed tsar in Tûrnovo.

The second Bulgarian kingdom, based on Tûrnovo, was to last for two centuries. Like its predecessor it fluctuated in size but it was seldom free either from external dangers or crippling internal divisions. It was stabilised by Tsar Kaloyan who ruled from 1197 to 1207. Much of his reign was spent in warfare. His first military achievement was to drive the Magyars out of north-west Bulgaria and in 1202 he concluded a much needed peace with Constantinople. By now, however, a new factor had disturbed the delicate balance of power in the Balkans: the Crusaders. In 1204 they took Constantinople and proclaimed the Bulgarians their vassals. This effrontery Kaloyan demolished the following year in a fierce battle near Adrianople, the present-day Edirne. By 1207 Kaloyan had reconquered most of Macedonia but he was to be betrayed and murdered that year when laying siege to Salonika.

Unlike many Bulgarian rulers Kaloyan backed his military might with skilful diplomacy. That he was able to defeat the Crusaders was in no small measure due to an agreement he concluded in 1204 with the pope which did much to guarantee Bulgaria's western frontier. The essence of the agreement was that the Bulgarians would recognise the supreme authority of the bishop of Rome, though there was little actual papal interference in Bulgarian

Map 2.2 Bulgaria's borders during the second kingdom, 1185–1393

ecclesiastical affairs. Bulgaria, in fact, despite its endless political and territorial disputes with Constantinople, remained part of the Orthodox Christian east which had finally broken with the Catholic west in the schism of 1054.

In the disturbed years at the end of the twelfth century bogomilism had flourished and in 1211 a council in Tûrnovo, having heard the bogomil case, condemned the heresy and initiated severe persecution of it. This was relaxed when Bulgaria again found relative security and stability in the reign of Ivan Asen II (1218–41). Ivan Asen II reduced the Magyar threat to Bulgaria but his main achievement was to destroy the power of the despot of Epirus, Theodore Angelus Comnenus, who sought to drive the Crusaders from Constantinople. In 1230 at the battle of Klokotnitsa, near the present-day Haskovo, Theodore Angelus was captured and his extensive territories incorporated into Bulgaria, which now spread from the Black Sea to the Aegean and the Adriatic.

Like Kaloyan, Ivan Asen II was an adept diplomat. In concluding a treaty with them against the Crusaders he was prepared to allow the Greeks the lion's share of any conquests that might be made, and in return he insisted upon only one condition: that the independence of the Bulgarian church and its patriarch be recognised by the Greeks. Having secured this, Ivan Asen successfully negotiated with Rome for the complete restoration of the independence of the Bulgarian church in 1235.

Ivan Asen II took the second Bulgarian kingdom to its greatest geographic extent and to the height of its power. He also did much to develop its capital, Tûrnovo. The kingdom went on to produce one of the masterpieces of mediaeval Balkan art: the frescoes in Boyana church near Sofia, begun in 1259, which are now a UNESCO protected monument and which deserve to be numbered amongst the greatest artistic attainments of the Slavonic world.

The political situation did not reflect the artistic world. In the early fourteenth century Bulgaria was forced for a while to acknowledge Tatar tutelage, and the Magyars were once again a danger, having taken Vidin in 1261, the year in which the Greeks finally drove the Crusaders out of Constantinople. Internally no

Plate 2.3 The Christ child, detail from the frescoes at Boyana near Sofia which is now a UNESCO World Heritage site. The frescoes, which date from 1259, are remarkable for their sophistication and realism

strong monarch appeared and by the end of the thirteenth century the kingdom was on the point of disintegration, not least because of incessant feuding among its nobility. It was also beset by another debilitating heresy, hesychism, whose adherents called for the rejection of all social activity and for a life devoted to *hesychia*, or silent contemplation and prayer; this, its adherents argued, was the

Plate 2.4 Tsar Ivan Alexander and his family from the Ivan
Alexander Gospels. The tsar is holding the sceptre and is
surrounded by his sons, Ivan Shishman who reigned from
1371 to 1395, and Ivan Asen. The tsar's wife, the Tsaritsa
Theodora, is described as the 'Newly Enlightened', a
reference to her conversion to Christianity from Judaism. The
tsar is described as 'Autocrat of all Bulgarians and Greeks'.
To the tsaritsa's right are: Duke Constantine, the tsar's son-
in-law; the tsar's eldest daughter, Kera Thamara, the wife of
Constantine; Keratsa, another daughter of the tsar; and
Desislava, the tsar's youngest daughter

only condition in which God's true light could be perceived. Maybe
it was, but it did little to help repel invaders.

In the fourteenth century two new invaders added to Bulgaria's
difficulties: the Serbs from the west and the Ottomans from the
south. There were flashes of recovery, as when Tsar Mihail
Shishman (1323–30) contained the Serbian threat for a while before
losing his life on the battlefield near Kiustendil. The last monarch to
achieve any form of stability was Ivan Alexander (1331–71). He
recovered some lost territory whilst his lands enjoyed a welcome
economic recovery caused in part because the landing of Ottoman

forces on the Aegean coast had pushed trade routes northwards into the Bulgarian lands, and in part because he was able to improve relations with Serbia. It was during Ivan Alexander's reign that Bulgaria produced another of the great treasures of Slavonic art: the four gospels which bear his name and are now in the British Museum. Commissioned in 1355 the gospels, with their 367 miniatures, were completed in the extraordinarily short period of one year.

Despite this, however, the costs of Ivan Alexander's wars were high and taxes had to be raised. At the same time his preoccupation with external affairs meant that the tsar could not check the seepage of political power from the centre to the landowning aristocracy. Once again the main victims were the peasantry.

After the death of Ivan Alexander, Bulgaria was no longer the master of its own fate. This would be settled by the looming contest between the two major Balkan powers: Serbia and the Ottoman Turks. In the 1360s the latter had taken Adrianople, whence they began to push up the Maritsa valley. In 1389 the issue was decided when the Serbs were broken in the battle of Kosovo Polje. Bulgaria's defeat came shortly afterwards. After a three-month siege Tûrnovo capitulated in July 1393. The patriarch was shut up in a monastery, the dynasty deposed, the great aristocrats dispossessed and the state dissolved. Resistance continued in Vidin for three more years but it too was eclipsed in 1396. Bulgaria as a state was not to exist for almost half a millennium.

3

Ottoman rule in the Bulgarian lands

The vigorous but self-righteous Christians of the Victorian era created the impression that their co-religionists under Ottoman domination had suffered continual persecution for 500 years. It was not so. Ottoman history is certainly not free from terrible incidents of hideous outrage, but in Europe these were occasional. Many, if not most, followed acts of rebellion and if this does not excuse the excess it perhaps goes some way to explain it. Other outbursts were spontaneous, localised and random, the result usually of a peculiar combination of personal, political, social or economic factors. It would be unwise to imagine the Ottoman empire as some form of lost, multi-cultural paradise, but on the other hand it would also be wrong to deny that at some periods in its history the empire assured for all its subjects, irrespective of religion, stability, security and a reasonable degree of prosperity.

OTTOMAN SOCIETY AND ADMINISTRATION

If the Christians of the empire at times enjoyed the blessings of peace and relative prosperity they were never given equality of status with Muslims. The Ottoman empire was a theocracy. Its head of state, the sultan, was also caliph, or the representative of God on earth and the supreme Muslim religious authority; he was pope as well as emperor. Non-Muslims were discriminated against in a variety of ways: they paid higher taxes than Muslims; Christian churches could not be as high as mosques; Christians could not wear the sacred colour green; no attempt could be made to proselytise amongst Muslims; at times, Christians had to dismount from their horses when a Muslim passed the other way; Christians could not carry arms; they could not become tanners because that was Mohammed's trade; and, most importantly, Muslim law was always superior to any other.

Because temporal society and the state had, in the Muslim conception, so obvious a religious nature most of the imperial administration was placed on a religious basis. Under a system introduced in 1454, the year after Constantinople had fallen to the Ottomans, the population was divided according to creed. Each separate religious group, or *millet*, was allowed to regulate its internal affairs. This meant not merely the organisation of their own religious life but also such issues as education, property law and family law. The head of a *millet* was the head of the religious group in question and he represented that community before the sultan and the Sublime Porte, or Ottoman government. The head of a *millet* was held responsible by the latter for the good behaviour of his flock who would be expected to pay their taxes and, where necessary or appropriate, to provide troops for the army or navy. In larger settlements which included different religious communities the different *millets* continued to operate, so Ottoman rule therefore accepted separate jurisdictions within the same territorial unit. Originally there were four *millets*: the Muslim, the Orthodox, the Armenian Christian and the Jewish, the latter functioning from 1454 but not being officially recognised until 1839. Others were added later and to be awarded the status of a separate *millet* was a major achievement for any group. Although the non-Muslim *millets* enjoyed internal self-administration, they were subordinate to the Muslims; any law dispute involving a Muslim had to be tried by Muslim law.

The *millet* system meant for the most part that Christian communities did not suffer pressures to convert to Islam, and although conversions, some of them involuntary, did take place, religious intolerance of the sort which plagued most of western and central Europe in the reformation and counter-reformation never became official policy in the Ottoman empire. Nor, at least in the early centuries of Ottoman rule in Europe, did official policy-

Map 3.1 The Bulgarian lands under Ottoman rule

makers recognise any concept of ethnicity. This created difficulties because the administrators did not recognise that their system of categorising people by religion was not shared by others. They did not realise that all Orthodox Christians were not 'Greeks', that the Bulgarians and the Serbs had had their own national churches with a fully developed system of ecclesiastic administration and their own distinctive forms of liturgy and religious art. Because the Greeks for much of the period of Ottoman rule dominated the Orthodox church the non-Greeks were in effect second-class citizens in a second-class *millet*.

In its heyday the military power of the empire was based on the *timar*. This was land held from the sultan in return for which the *spahi*, or tenant, was required in time of need to provide men for the imperial armies, the number of men varying directly with the amount of land held. The *spahi* also held various local government responsibilities. Land not held as *timars* could be in the hands of the sultan, his family or of a few influential members of the empire, and on this so-called *hass* land the tenants, Christian or Muslim, were free from most or sometimes all forms of taxation. Another crucially important category of land was the *vakûf*. *Vakûf* land was that whose income had by bequest been allotted to a charitable foundation. Initially this had been primarily to secure the upkeep of mosques or Islamic schools, but in later years Christian churches and monasteries could also hold *vakûf* land.

For those Christians not living in villages which enjoyed tax privileges the main levies were the poll tax and a tax levied in lieu of military service. There was also the *devshirme*. The *devshirme* was levied at intervals of between one and seven years, and it brought in not cash but Christian boys aged between seven and fourteen. The boys were chosen for their physical and mental ability and were taken from their families and villages to be converted to Islam and then given a rigorous education and military training, after which they entered the ranks of the janissary corps. For almost two centuries after the conquest of Constantinople the janissaries, forbidden to marry, formed the highly trained and totally disciplined élite of the Ottoman army. They also played an important part in the imperial administrations; at times they remembered and favoured their home villages, and there are even records of villages requesting that the *devshirme* be levied on them in the hope that in future years such favours would be paid, but for the most part this tax in human kind was a dreaded feature of Ottoman rule until the late seventeenth century; the last full levy in the Bulgarian lands was in 1685.

THE BULGARIAN POPULATION UNDER OTTOMAN RULE

Shortly after the Ottoman conquest the Christian Bulgarians formed about a third of the total population of the empire in the Balkans, though precise figures are impossible to obtain because Christians living in privileged villages or on *hass* estates were not recorded because they did not pay taxes. By the beginning of the sixteenth century, Christian Bulgarians were only about 8 per cent of the total population. There were four main reasons for this relative decline. The first, and by far the most important, was that the empire expanded into the remainder of the Balkans and into Hungary thus greatly increasing the total population without adding many Bulgarians to its number. The second was persecution, especially following outbreaks of political or social unrest. The third was disease and pestilence. The fourth was the conversion of some Christian Bulgarians to Islam.

This has long been a contentious issue. There is no doubt that pressures for conversion were stronger amongst the Bulgarians than amongst other Balkan Christians, because Bulgaria was more densely settled by Ottoman/Muslim elements than anywhere else; furthermore, the Bulgarians were at the very centre of the European section of the Ottoman empire, commanding the military and trade routes into central Europe and the defensive ring around Constantinople itself. Nor is there any doubt that some Bulgarian landowners accepted the faith of the conquerors in order to retain their property. The great aristocrats had been dispossessed immediately after the conquest but the lower nobility remained, merging gradually into the ranks of the *spahis*. Some Christian communities may also have been tempted into Islam by the prospect of easier tax burdens and the privileges which belonging to the dominant religion could offer. There were additional cases where Christian villages were enticed into Islam by being offered the freedom to loot *khriſten kinder daraus man die Janirſcharn macht*

Plate 3.1 Christian children taken under the *devshirme* and turned into janissaries

and pillage local church or monastic property. Finally there were
cases of enforced, violent conversion. There were a number of such
instances in the third quarter of the seventeenth century in the
Rhodope mountains. The motivation for this sudden outburst of
militancy amongst the Muslims is unclear. This was a time when
Islam seemed to be resurgent with the sultan's armies soon to press
forward to Vienna itself, and the conversions could in part be
explained by the exhilaration which this resurgence bred. A more
sober explanation might be that the Ottoman military planners
were anxious not to leave the passes through the Rhodopes in the
hands of non-Muslims in view of the critical nature of the forthcoming campaigns; but this seems a risky strategy as the forcibly
converted might be less reliable than Christians left in peace, besides
which to forcibly convert relatively large areas to Islam would
reduce the number of taxpayers, and this at a time when the
imperial government was desperately short of revenue.

Of those who did convert, some, especially the landowners, were
absorbed into the Muslim world and became entirely Islamicised
and Turkified. Many converted villages, on the other hand, retained
their Bulgarian language, folk traditions and costumes. The
Bulgarian-speaking Muslims became known as pomaks.

Most Bulgarians, Muslim or Christian, lived in villages. Most of
these villages were small with between 150 and 200 inhabitants.
Larger settlements were known, Kotel, for example, having over
2,500 in 1648, but these were rare. Villages were run by the family
elders who chose from amongst themselves officials such as the
local village headman, called in Bulgarian *kmet* (mayor) or sometimes even *knyaz* (prince), names which represented a continuum
with the pre-conquest officials; by the nineteenth century many
local *prominenti*, many of whom had recently acquired wealth and
property, were known by the somewhat pejorative and Turkish-
based, *chorbadjiya* (soup-provider). Ottoman officials seldom
visited villages other than to collect taxes, including, of course, the
devshirme. A number of communities, the so-called privileged
villages, were granted freedom from taxation and left to order their
own affairs in return for providing specified services to the sultan or
his officials. A number of such villages were made responsible for
guaranteeing safe passage for troops and traders through local

Plate 3.2 Bulgarian peasants

mountain passes. Other tasks were more unusual. Some had to procure birds for the sultan's falconries and one, Dedovo, was required to provide two barrels of water per day from its spring for the nearby city of Plovdiv. The experience gained by these villages in self-administration were, centuries later, to be useful in organising the schools and other institutions which so helped the Bulgarian national revival.

In the seventeenth century only about one in fifty Christian Bulgarians lived in towns. This was in part because in the early and frequently violent days of the Ottoman occupation urban Bulgarians had fled or had been driven from their homes; villages, especially the remoter ones in the mountains, provided relative security and greater opportunities to continue living a Christian, Bulgarian life. As Ottoman society evolved its trade became dominated by the Greeks, Jews and Armenians, though in the seventeenth century Bulgarian traders were active as far afield as Transylvania, even if many of them were described as or even called themselves 'Greek'.

The centres of Ottoman towns were generally occupied by administrative or military buildings, but in the surrounding areas were the *mahalla* or small urban districts. These were frequently based on ethnic identity, sometimes on occupation, and infrequently on both: in some larger towns, therefore, there would be a Christian shoe-makers' and a Muslim shoe-makers' district. In the *mahalla* the streets were narrow and the houses faced inwards onto courtyards rather outwards onto the street.

In urban economic activity the *esnaf*, or guild, played a dominant role. The structure of the *esnaf*, with its ranking of apprentice, journeyman and master, and its ruling council elected by and from local masters, was similar to the structure of guilds in western Europe, and like those in the west they provided welfare for their members, but in the Ottoman empire the *esnaf* was subject to a great deal of interference from local officials of the central government; there was little of the fierce independence which frequently characterised western guilds. Many, but not all, *esnafs* had both Christian and Muslim members. After the initial decades of Ottoman rule Christian guilds encouraged the building or repair of many churches and other religious institutions, the church of Sveta

Petka in Sofia, for example, being redecorated by the local saddle-makers' *esnaf*. Bulgarians were prominent in the textile guilds, those in Sofia being famous for dress-making and the production of hooded cloaks.

Although many Bulgarian guilds flourished under Ottoman rule the conquest had been a cultural as well as a political disaster for the Bulgarian nation. Not only did the state disappear and the church fall subject to the domination of Constantinople, but Bulgarian language and literature seemed also to die. Bulgarian had once ranked with Greek, Latin and Arabic as the major tongues of the civilised European world, and it had produced a flourishing literature of secular as well as sacred works. But when, in the second half of the eighteenth century, Catherine the Great compiled her samples of 279 languages and dialects, included in which were some North American Indian tongues, Bulgarian was not mentioned, nor was Joseph Dobrovsky, 'The Father of Slavicists', familiar with it, whilst the treatment of it in Šafařík's history of the Slavic languages and literature, published in 1826, is cursory and flawed.

Yet the language remained alive during the years of Ottoman rule and eventually its literature was to be reborn. The language survived primarily because most Bulgarians lived in their small, isolated and usually ethnically homogenous villages. In such communities there was no need to adopt Greek for everyday economic or commercial transactions, nor to use Turkish when dealing with government officials. The villages therefore preserved the Bulgarian language and with it Bulgarian names, Bulgarian folk tales and legends, Bulgarian forms of family organisation and Bulgarian festivals and holidays.

THE BULGARIAN CHURCH UNDER OTTOMAN RULE

The festivals and holidays which the small Bulgarian villages preserved were primarily religious and the church's role in keeping alive a separate sense of 'Bulgardom' was critical. In 1394, the year after the fall of Tûrnovo, the Bulgarian patriarchate was dissolved and the Bulgarian church subjected to the authority of the patriarch in Constantinople. The patriarchate of Ohrid, however, continued to be known as 'Bulgarian', although in fact most of its prelates were Greek and were nominated by the Greek patriarch in Constantinople. Despite the Ohrid patriarchate, therefore, the church in both eastern and western Bulgaria was subjected to Greek domination, more especially at its higher levels. At the parish level, however, many Bulgarian priests were still nominated and at least until the eighteenth century the liturgy was still usually held in Bulgarian if the congregation so desired. In many communities the parish priest provided guidance in every aspect of life as well as spiritual leadership, and it was significant that, particularly in the seventeenth century and afterwards, priests often came from the most affluent section of the local population; they were the only ones who could afford the increasingly stiff bribes required to secure a parish appointment. Had the church not played this role, however, the survival of the Bulgarian language would have been much more difficult.

In the early years after the conquest the Ottomans generally abided by the letter of their law forbidding the building or rebuilding of churches. Later this was relaxed but even then the process of building or rebuilding Christian places of worship was a slow one, and one greatly demanding of money, time and patience. Yet a long pocket and careful organisation on the part of the village council and the priest could secure the necessary permission and thus, as in Poland under the communists, church building and restoration assumed more than a mere spiritual significance: it became a contest with the dominant non-Christian authority and victory could bring a great sense of pride and achievement. It could also mean that Bulgarian iconographers and painters could go to work and thus keep alive Bulgarian traditions in religious art.

The Bulgarian monasteries too helped keep alive religious art. Immediately after the conquest they had fallen upon very hard times. By the end of the fourteenth century many of them were destroyed or in a state of sad decline, but thereafter a slow regeneration began. Many were re-established far from the main routes used by the Ottoman armies, and some lucky ones were able to transform their properties into *vakûf* lands and thereby secure their income. The great foundation at Rila near where Ivan Rilski had spent his life as a hermit, was repopulated and rebuilt by three brothers from near Kiustendil and in 1469 it received an enormous boost when the remains of Ivan Rilski were brought back from Tûrnovo. Severe taxation was to threaten it once again in later years but the foundation survived, and with it its great library. Rila also helped to sponsor the flourishing school of religious painting to be found in the Sofia area in the seventeenth century and thereafter.

Monasteries also played a vital role in maintaining the rudiments of education. Mount Athos had provided refuge for a number of Bulgarian writers and other men of letters immediately after the fall of Tûrnovo, and when political conditions stabilised in the Bulgarian lands pilgrims were able to visit the holy mountain. Those monasteries on Athos, and others in the Bulgarian lands, which had retained their properties sent out monks to collect revenue and maintain contact with the inhabitants of those properties. The itinerant monks, or *taxidiots* as they were known, played an essential role in linking village and monastery. This was extremely important when monasteries began to develop 'cell schools' in which a small number of young men would be trained for service in the church or in monastic orders. In the fifteenth century refugees from Tûrnovo founded a large Slav school in Zograf on Mount Athos which later became a model for others throughout the Bulgarian lands, the villages having encouraged the *taxidiots* to arrange for the establishment of such schools. These schools were relatively few in number and they did not produce either the questioning religious minds of the reformation and counter-reformation or anything resembling an intelligentsia, but they did keep literacy alive. They also facilitated the merging of the old Bulgarian language with more vernacular usages, a process which produced in the seventeenth century what philologists have called 'new Bulgarian'.

Some monks copied old hagiographies, one of which was that compiled by Patriarch Evtimii in Tûrnovo shortly before the conquest and which gave great prominence to Bulgarian saints and martyrs. However, one should not be tempted into making this process into anything approaching a modern national revival, or even a precursor of it: of the 261 extant Bulgarian manuscripts dating from the seventeenth century only 46 contain mention of specifically Bulgarian saints. What the monasteries and the scriptoria did was to preserve that basic sense of ethnic separateness without which a national revival would have been impossible.

Protest against Ottoman rule was not a Christian monopoly. In 1416, for example, there was a rising by the Muslim Bedreddin order. In later centuries, however, political and social protests were predominantly Christian and when they came were usually based on the hope, always dashed, that Christian powers were about to inflict defeat upon the Ottoman empire. The 'long war' fought by the Habsburgs and their Transylvanian and Wallachian allies against the Turks at the turn of the sixteenth century, created the belief that a campaign south of the Danube was imminent, the agents of Vienna and Rome using the Dubrovnik merchants who were so powerful in the Balkans to encourage such beliefs. The result was a rising in the Tûrnovo region in 1598. It was suppressed with the customary brutality, but further to the west, in the mountains near Sofia, there remained armed groups of so-called *haiduks* who were more than mere robbers, if less than the nationalist heroes depicted by some later historians.

Almost a century later, in 1686, there was another rising around Tûrnovo, this time prompted by expectations of a Russian invasion. Two years later a larger outburst occurred around Chiprovets in the north-west of the Bulgarian lands. The Chiprovets area was unusual. It was rich in mines which had originally been worked by Serbs imported in the thirteenth century and then by Saxons whom the Ottomans settled there. The Orthodox Serbs were rapidly assimilated into the local Bulgarian population but the Saxons, though they became Bulgarian-speaking, retained their Catholicism. When it was learned that Habsburg armies were approaching from the north a rebellion was organised and the flag raised when it was believed the Christian forces were but a day's march away. Some rebel units managed to fight their way through to join the Habsburg soldiers but the latter gave no assistance to the rising which was crushed with exceptional severity. The town of Chiprovets was destroyed and some estimates put local fatalities at two-thirds of the population. Many of those who survived fled to

Plate 3.3 Christ Sabaoth and Christ Pantocrator (below) from the church of Sveti Iliye, Boboshevo village, Struma district. Executed in 1678 these represent, in the words of the leading western scholar of the subject, 'one of the most complete and best preserved ensembles of Bulgarian painting from the Ottoman period'. Machiel Kiel, *Art and Society of Bulgaria in the Turkish Period*, p. xviii

the Banat of Temesvar, now in Romania, where their descendants still live as one of Eastern Europe's lesser known minority groups.

THE DECLINE OF THE OTTOMAN EMPIRE

The Habsburg advance into the Balkans in the 1680s had followed the failure of the Ottomans to take Vienna in 1683. By this date the sultan's empire was in obvious decline. The *timar* system no longer functioned adequately. Too many properties had been allowed to convert to *vakûf* status with their inhabitants naming their descendants as the testamentary beneficiaries. This had a number of results. In the first place it made easier the emergence of estates which were worked purely for revenue rather than to equip the sultan's forces, and on the new properties the peasants were subjected to much greater exploitation. The decline of the *timars* also meant that too few soldiers were recruited from the *timar* lands thus forcing the government to rely more upon the janissaries as the mainstay of the army. But the janissaries were not the force they had once been. They were no longer as exclusive, as élitist, or as disciplined as in the first days of Ottoman power in Europe. They had long since been allowed to marry, then they had been allowed to admit their own children to their ranks, and finally other Muslim children had also been allowed to become janissaries.

Another effect of the decline of the *timar* system was the disappearance of the *beglerbeg*, the official who had once been the commander in chief of the *spahis* in his area and at the same time entrusted with the civil governance of that area. He was replaced by the *vali*. The *vali*'s main task was the collection of tax revenue in his allotted district and there were few restrictions on the way he could go about achieving this objective. The appearance of the *vali* was in part a consequence of the intensifying financial crisis which faced the Ottoman empire in the sixteenth and seventeenth centuries. The burden was in large measure the consequence of the almost constant state of war in which the empire found itself, but this burden was made less easy to bear because as the European–Asian trade routes shifted from land to sea the empire lost revenue levied on goods in transit. Nor did it benefit from the opening of western Europe's links with the Americas, not least because it suffered greatly from the inflation which followed. Increased military expenditure without a concomitant increase in revenue merely compounded the inflationary problem. The government naturally did all it could to maximise revenues and the tax burden which in the beginning of the seventeenth century had been approximately a third of the average value of family property in the Bulgarian lands was by the end of the century over four-fifths of that value.

A minor but useful source of revenue for the Sublime Porte was that derived from the bribes which those appointed to important offices were expected to donate to the government. The highest religious dignitaries were state appointees and they paid handsomely to assume their posts, no-one more so than the head of the Orthodox church, the patriarch of Constantinople. In the financial crisis of the seventeenth century the Porte would use any excuse to remove a patriarch and thus raise another bribe from his successor. By the end of the century only the wealthiest Greek families could afford high office; most of these Greeks were resident in the Phanar district of Constantinople, then, much in contrast to the present day, one of the wealthiest districts in the city. The 'Phanariots' thus came to dominate the patriarchate. Because ecclesiastic appointments in the provinces also required financial sweeteners, the policy whereby wealthy locals, again usually Greeks, came to dominate the church was repeated. Each cleric expected to recoup his expenses from those below him and this process percolated down until the burden fell eventually upon the ordinary villager and town-dweller. So onerous were church taxes in the seventeenth century that Orthodox bishops frequently used Ottoman troops to help collect them.

The sale of office and therefore the concentration of high posts in the hands of the financially capable also affected the civil administration. Here again it was the Greeks of the Phanar who could pay the most and it was they in the eighteenth century who came to dominate the Ottoman administrative system as well as the Orthodox church. But not even the undoubted ability of the Phanariots could save the Ottoman empire from decline. The pace of that decline accelerated during the eighteenth century and from it eventually emerged the seeds of the Bulgarian national revival.

4

The national revival
and the liberation

The *vûzrazhdane*, or national revival, is a phenomenon in which the Bulgarians take considerable and justifiable pride. As a historic process the revival was long and complicated with economic, social, cultural and psychological factors interweaving in intriguing and complex patterns. The first calls for a cultural revival were made by a small number of 'awakeners' in the eighteenth and very early nineteenth centuries, but though they saw the need for a revival they had no concept of what form it might take. The cultural revival, when it did take place, was made possible by the profound economic, social and political changes which overcame the Ottoman empire in the eighteenth and early nineteenth centuries. The manner in which the cultural revival was transformed into a national revival with its own institutions, first ecclesiastical and then political, was the work of the activists who emerged from the economic recovery and the cultural revival.

The seminal work of the Bulgarian national revival was that of Paiisi, a monk in the monastery of Hilendar on Mount Athos. Paiisi Hilendarski was born in the town of Bansko in 1722. In 1745 he entered Hilendar where after a few years he became a *taxidiot* and as such travelled around the Bulgarian lands on monastery business. His travels left a deep impression of the tribulations of the ordinary people and of the inferior status of the Bulgarians *vis-à-vis* the Greeks. As a natural scholar Paiisi seems to have become almost obsessed with the contrast between the present low standing of Bulgarian culture and its glorious past, a past with which he had become familiar through his avid reading of history; Paiisi is known to have travelled in 1761 as far as Sremski Karlovac in the Habsburg monarchy where he consulted copies of Russian manuscripts. In 1762, exhausted and ill, he moved from Hilendar to the nearby monastery of Zograf, where he consulted an earlier history of the Bulgarians. All this experience and learning he poured into his own great work, *A Slavonic-Bulgarian History of the Peoples, Tsars, Saints, and of all their Deeds and of the Bulgarian Way of Life.* Written in Old Church Slavonic but with the enlivening addition of some contemporary spoken forms, the book recalled the lost and great days of the mediaeval Bulgarian state and church. The work looked both backwards and forwards because together with his evocation of past greatness Paiisi warned of the dangers for the future posed by the Bulgarians' capitulation to hellenisation and he called upon his contemporary co-nationals to change their attitudes, to stand firm against Greek influences, and to 'keep close to your heart your race and your Bulgarian homeland'. He pointed out why there was reason to be proud of that homeland:

of all the Slav peoples the most glorious were the Bulgarians; they were the first who called themselves tsars, the first to have a patriarch, the first to adopt the Christian faith, and they it was who conquered the largest amount of territory. Thus, of all the Slav peoples they were the strongest and the most honoured, and the first Slav saints cast their radiance from amongst the Bulgarian people and through the Bulgarian language.

Given this glorious past, said Paiisi, the Bulgarians need not feel inferior to the Greeks, quite the contrary:

But, they say, the Greeks are wiser and more cultured, while the Bulgarians are simple and foolish and have no refined words. That is why, they say, we had better join the Greeks. But ... There are many peoples wiser and more glorious than the Greeks. Is any Greek foolish enough to abandon his language and his teaching and his people as you abandon yours ... ? Bulgarian, do not deceive yourself, know your own nation and language and study in your own tongue.

Map 4.1 The national revival

In the mid-1760s Paiisi took to the roads again, this time primarily to propagandise his manuscript which had been, he said, written 'for the ordinary Bulgarian' and for 'the benefit of the whole Bulgarian nation'. In 1765 in Kotel he met Sofroni Vrachenski (of Vratsa) who was so impressed with the *History* that he had it copied and placed in his church. Paiisi's work was much copied in subsequent decades and at least fifty copies are now extant, but knowledge of its author faded. When a printed version of the great text appeared in 1844 in Budapest, it was as an anonymous work; not until 1871 did Marin Drinov, Bulgaria's first modern professional historian, reidentify Paiisi as the author.

Until Drinov's identification of Paiisi the most notable of the awakeners was Yuri Venelin, a Habsburg subject and pioneer Slavicist who did much to rediscover the Bulgarian language and bring it to the notice of foreign scholars. Born in 1802 in Ruthenia, Venelin had been schooled in theology in Hungary but this he abandoned for history which he read at the University of Lemberg (Lvov). In 1829 he published *The Ancient and Present-Day Bulgarians in their Political, Ethnographic and Religious Relationship to the Russians. Historical-Critical Researches*. The main purpose of the book was to argue that the Bulgarians were of Slavic rather than Turkic origin. This argument gained as few supporters as his call for Bulgarian to be made into a virtual dialect of Russian.

The importance of Paiisi and his fellow awakeners lay not so much in their roles as creators of the national revival as in the fact that they provided *post facto* explanations for it. By the time Paiisi was widely read, let alone reidentified as the author of the *History*, the cultural revival was well under way. What prompted Bulgarians to call for more recognition of their cultural identity was not so much a consciousness of the past gained from reading Paiisi or one of the other awakeners, but contact with the world outside the Bulgarian lands, a contact gained through commerce, through education abroad, through the seepage of modern ideas into the Balkans during and after the French Revolution, and through participation in or knowledge of the Serbian and Greek revolts against rule from Constantinople. And few if any of these developments would have taken place without the upheavals experienced in the Ottoman empire in the late eighteenth and early nineteenth

Plate 4.1 A page of Paiisi's great history. The original of the manuscript was returned to Bulgaria after the revolution of 1989, since when mystery surrounds its whereabouts

Plate 4.2 Sofroni Vrachenski, a self portrait

centuries, upheavals which both delayed the spread of the awakeners' ideas and yet brought about the profound economic, social and political changes without which those ideas could not have been translated into action.

ECONOMIC, SOCIAL AND POLITICAL CHANGE IN THE OTTOMAN EMPIRE

As the Ottoman empire contracted it became more open to trade with the rest of Europe. The treaty of Passarowitz allowed Habsburg subjects to use the Danube for commercial purposes and in the 1740s Britain and France were given trading concessions. By the third quarter of the eighteenth century Russia was becoming an increasingly important factor in Balkan affairs. The treaty of Kutchuk Kainardji of July 1774 gave Russia control of the northern Black Sea littoral, but more importantly it allowed Russian trading vessels to operate in the Black Sea and to pass through the Straits into the Mediterranean. The treaty also sanctioned the opening up of the Danube to Russian traders.

Even more important than its commercial provisions were those clauses of the treaty of Kutchuk Kainardji which gave permission for the construction of a Russian Orthodox church in Constantinople, and which extended to the ruler of Russia vaguely defined rights to protect Orthodox Christians in the Ottoman empire. The 'Eastern Question' which so plagued nineteenth-century European diplomacy had been born; in it the emergence of a new Bulgarian nation and eventually of a new Bulgarian state was to play an integral part.

The Ottoman empire's reduced international power was inextricably linked with a decline in its internal cohesion. Throughout the century the quality of Ottoman administration deteriorated. Tax farming spread to the detriment of the peasant; the janissaries became less and less disciplined as their numbers increased; and in some areas commercial agriculture appeared with the production of cash crops such as cotton, and in these areas the exploitation of the peasants increased considerably. The most serious problem, particularly in the second half of the century, was the failure of the central government to control the *ayans*. The *ayans* were overmighty subjects. In origin they could be local officials who had simply turned their area of responsibility into a personal fiefdom – the pasha of Salonika, for example, collected the sum of 360,000 groschen in one year from his territory; they could be janissaries who had done much the same; they might be local figures who had accumulated sufficient wealth through agriculture, usury or trade to establish political as well as economic domination in an area; or they might be members of a traditionally influential clan or family. The most famous amongst them were Ali Pasha of Janina, who ruled over southern Albania and northern Greece, and Osman Pasvantoglu, who controlled over 200 villages in the Vidin region, but there were many others such as Ismail Trestenikioglu in Rusé and Ikilikioglu in Silistra. The rise of the *ayans* led to a virtual breakdown in central government in the Balkans, a period known in Bulgarian as the *kûrdjaliistvo*. Its effects on the villagers of Vilitsa in southern Macedonia in the 1780s were described by the English traveller E. D. Clarke:

They are at present in a most wretched condition, owing to the extortions of *Ali Pasha*, or of those who have plundered in his name. In the short space of six months, they had paid to his tax-gatherers, as they told us, eighty purses, a sum equivalent to forty thousand piastres. Poverty is very apparent in their dwellings . . . Nor can it be otherwise, where the wretched inhabitants are so oppressed by their lords. The whole of the earnings of the peasant is here taken from him; he is scarcely allowed any means of subsistence. Add to this the frequent calamities of sickness and fire, and 'plague, pestilence and famine' will be found to have done their work. This village has been twice burned within one year by *banditti* . . .

The beginnings of the *kûrdjaliistvo* can be seen in the 1770s but it reached its culmination in the 1790s and 1800s. In 1791 Sultan Selim III attempted to introduce a reform programme which would reestablish central authority but the *ayans* proved too strong for him, and his failure merely intensified the process he had endeavoured to check. In 1792 there were large numbers of inadequately controlled Ottoman soldiers milling around in the Balkans at the conclusion of the war of 1787–92 against Russia; and in 1793 a rebellion took place in the Rhodope area under the leadership of Mehmed Sinap. In 1804 it was the conduct of local *ayans* which precipitated the revolt by various clan and village elders in Serbia, a revolt which was to lead eventually to an autonomous and eventually an independent Serbia. In subsequent years the disorders were more noticeable to the north of the Balkan mountains but they were still disturbing much of Thrace in the 1800s whilst most of the Plovdiv district was under the sway of Kara Mustafa in 1810–12; even as late as 1816 much of the Adrianople area was beyond the reach of the central government and around Burgas the only effective authority was a band of brigands some 300 strong.

The upheavals of the late eighteenth and early nineteenth centuries, and especially the wars, had a profound effect on the demographic composition of the Bulgarian lands, and on the distribution of the Bulgarian peoples.

The eighteenth century had seen an increase in the Bulgarian population in the towns. Some scholars in the past have attributed this to declining levels of health amongst the Turks, and one traveller believed that abortion, a widespread practice amongst Muslims in the seventeenth century, was a major reason for the enfeeblement of the Turks. In fact, there is little hard evidence that the absolute as opposed to the relative number of Turks in the towns did fall. More Bulgarians came into the towns because trade and manufacturing were expanding and, in some cases, because life in the countryside was beginning to become insecure. The *kûrdjaliistvo* speeded up this process but it did so selectively. The *kûrdjaliistvo* affected mainly the plains – the word derives from a Turkish one meaning fields or plains – and those threatened by it therefore sought refuge in the small mountain towns which were less likely to receive the unwelcome attention of the *ayans* and their hangers-on. This was an important development because the mountain towns were predominantly Bulgarian whereas those in the lowlands were much more likely to be subject to strong Greek cultural pressures. The flight to the mountains therefore tended to save Bulgarians not only from the unruly Muslim *ayans* but also from the hellenising forces which had been operating in many towns in the eighteenth century. At the same time, the insecurity of the lowland settlements increased the economic potential of those towns which remained less affected by the disorders, i.e. the Bulgarian mountain towns. They were to become of great importance when peace and security returned after the 1820s.

Some Bulgarians, however, fled much further afield than the mountain towns. As in the past, the end of a war produced a wave of emigration, not least because past experience had taught that the Ottoman authorities were likely to take revenge on any area which had showed sympathy with the sultan's enemies. After each major conflict huge numbers of Bulgarians emigrated, usually joining departing Russian troops. Precise figures are impossible to give, but after the treaty of Kutchuk Kainardji an estimated 160,000 Bulgarians left and after the wars of 1806 to 1812 the number was in the region of 100,000. After the Russo-Turkish war of 1828–9 there was emigration on a massive scale from eastern Bulgaria south of the Balkans, with some estimates putting the numbers of those who left as high as a quarter of a million. This seems to be a huge figure but many travellers in subsequent years attest to the depopulated state of this area.

The departing Bulgarians settled in what is now Romania, southern Ukraine and Russia. The communities they formed were to play an important part in the later development of Bulgarian culture, none more so than that in Braila, Romania, whose first Bulgarian *émigrés* had been those fleeing after the abortive Tûrnovo rising of 1598. The Bulgarians of Bucharest were also to become powerful and influential in later years, whilst the many thousands who settled further north are still a distinct ethnic group in the republic of Moldova.

The upheavals which beset the Ottoman empire in Europe between the 1770s and the 1820s cut short what had been promising economic growth for the Bulgarians. By the third quarter of the eighteenth century trade was noticeably better than it had been fifty or twenty-five years previously. There were Bulgarian trading concerns with links to Buda, Vienna, Venice, Livorno, Marseilles, Leipzig, Braşov and Odessa, and in most of these cities there were small Bulgarian colonies. In the Vardar valley cotton was being produced for sale in distant markets such as Leipzig, Dresden and Vienna and resident cotton merchants from these and other central European cities were to be found in a number of Balkan towns. Some of this cotton was shipped out through the Mediterranean but most of it went all the way to central Europe by pack horse or was taken thus to Danubian ports such as Vidin or Svishtov. With tobacco, cotton formed the most important export commodity produced in the Bulgarian lands in the eighteenth century, though wax was also exported to western Europe as was some of the rice grown in the Maritsa valley. A commodity with a more limited market appeal was *aba*, a coarse-grained cloth produced by many Bulgarian guilds in towns such as Stara Zagora, Kalofer, Karlovo, Plovdiv, Sliven and others. Another lucrative occupation was animal husbandry. Centres such as Constantinople and Adrianople with their large Muslim populations consumed considerable quantities of meat, particularly mutton, and the Bulgarian sheep raisers who supplied them became wealthy; many inhabitants of Kotel in the Balkan mountains spent their time rearing sheep in the Dobrudja plains and then driving them to market in the cities to the south of the Balkan range. The profits from animal husbandry greatly outstripped those from arable farming, in part because the government exercised a monopoly over the grain trade, buying it in the domestic market at low prices and strenuously forbidding exports. The *kûrdjaliistvo* interrupted but did not destroy their established trade which recovered rapidly as soon as order had been restored. It was upon the wealth thus created that the Bulgarian cultural revival was built.

The *kûrdjaliistvo* had a much more lasting impact on the efficiency of the Ottoman war machine as had become apparent during the war of 1806–12 against Russia. When the war was concluded the Porte could not yet turn its full attention to the reform of the army because first it had to deal with the Serbian rebellion. In doing so it greatly strengthened central authority in the empire. By 1814 the original Serbian leader had been defeated and in the following two years an arrangement was finally made by which a small area around Belgrade was left free to administer its own affairs. The appearance of the Serbian danger, however, had sobered the local *ayans* who had made the *kûrdjaliistvo*, as did the military expedition sent into Vidin to subdue Pasvantoglu's successor. The Bulgarian lands were the first to benefit from this move back towards order and stability because they were those nearest to Constantinople. By 1820 in the Balkans the only warlords outwith the control of the Porte were the Albanian rulers of Janina and Scutari.

Just as operations to subdue these remnants of the *kûrdjaliistvo* were beginning, the Greek revolt broke out in Wallachia and the Peloponnese in 1821. The revolt once more threw the Ottoman empire and the Balkans into turmoil but once again the result was an ultimate strengthening rather than a weakening of central power, even if that power extended to a smaller area, and even before the small Greek kingdom emerged in 1830 the Ottoman empire had embarked upon a thorough-going process of reform.

One cause of the *kûrdjaliistvo* had been the rebelliousness of the janissaries. They had continued to proliferate in the eighteenth century and their discipline seemed to be in inverse proportion to their numbers. By the end of the century they had become a vast force which, like any debased praetorian guard, had become a by-word for intrigue and corruption. They also fiercely resisted any attempt to reform the machinery of the army and government, knowing that any attempt at the restoration of central power and the return to anything approaching honest government must involve an attack upon their powers and their privileges. The war of 1806–12 had shown that the janissaries were also now woefully inadequate and hopelessly outdated as a military force. In June 1826 Sultan Mahmud II, taking advantage of a respite from international pressure on the Greek question, at last seized the janissary nettle. In a swift and bloody operation he liquidated the corps. Thousands were sent to exile in Asia Minor but between 5,000 and 6,000 were slaughtered in Constantinople itself. It was the first step towards the radical reform which the Ottoman empire clearly needed.

THE BACKGROUND TO THE BULGARIAN CULTURAL REVIVAL

The destruction of the janissaries had two results which in the long run greatly affected the Bulgarians. First, to replace the janissaries the sultan and his ministers decided to create a regular army on the

European model. Such an army had to be fed and clothed. And it was primarily to the rearers of sheep and the producers of cloth in the Bulgarian lands that the Porte looked for its sources of supply. The sheep-rearers rapidly grew more wealthy, as did the manufacturers of *aba* and those of *gaitan*, the decorative lace used to adorn uniforms, primarily those of the officers. The large scale purchase of *aba* and *gaitan* began in the late 1820s and in 1848 the Porte concluded a commercial agreement with the *aba* guilds. The need for *aba* was so great that in order to meet it the Ottoman government in the late 1830s built a factory, its first, at Sliven, whilst in the following decade a private mill began operating near Plovdiv.

The second effect of the dissolution of the janissary corps and the setting up of the regular army was to increase pressure for a fundamental reform of the landowning system in the empire. This was still, in theory at least, tied to the need to produce *spahis* for the sultan's forces, a need obviated by the creation of the regular army. The usefulness of the *spahi* as a military factor had been in decline throughout the eighteenth century but the profits to be gained from the land he held had increased, and did so even more rapidly after the foundation of the army had multiplied the returns on sheep-rearing. Thus as the military reasons for a *spahi* holding lands disappeared the economic incentives for him to retain it strengthened. The *spahi* had originally collected a tithe from his tenants in order to furnish troops for the sultan but now that this function had been discontinued it was the state which had to collect the rent from the *spahi* lands. In fact there was no longer any justification for the continuation of the *spahi* system, and during the 1830s it was gradually dismantled. New tenancy agreements were drawn up and though the Ottoman officials generally attempted to carry out this task with fairness and efficiency tensions were sometimes created, especially in the north-west and south-west of the Bulgarian lands where tenancies were particularly complicated. At the same time the judicial powers once exercised by the *spahi* were transferred to state officials, whilst the remaining *spahis* were given a pension and sent into retirement. The *spahis'* pensions were to be funded by a yearly sum paid by each peasant. This occasioned much resentment which, together with the suspicions created by the introduction of the revised tenancy arrangements, added another social factor to the evolution of the Bulgarian national revival. However, agrarian unrest, though it was present, especially in the western regions, was never a dominant feature of the *vûzrazhdane* and in later years the political programmes produced by the nationalists made little or no mention of it.

Whilst the peasantry in the north-west and south-west still encountered difficulties many merchants and manufacturers grew ever more wealthy. Their new prosperity was reflected in the increasingly opulent houses they built. The splendid vernacular architecture of Kotel, Plovdiv, Koprivshtitsa and other towns which the modern tourist can enjoy was almost always the product of the economic revival of the second and third quarters of the nineteenth century.

Wealth was accumulated not merely by individuals. In the successful manufacturing and trading ventures economic activity remained predominantly under the control of the *esnafs* or guilds. By the 1830s they were beginning to have their own disposable surpluses and these they tended to spend on what may be broadly defined as 'public works'. Under the strict rules of the early Ottoman empire Christian villages were not allowed to erect buildings for public use and thus in most communities even the churches were small and insignificant. With greater political and social freedom, and with the necessary funds, guilds in the 1830s and thereafter frequently invested in new church buildings, the old, single-aisle edifice usually being replaced by a much larger, three-aisle structure. Monasteries, whose incomes were often already rising as returns from their lands increased, also benefited from the generosity of guilds, and one of the great symbols of the Bulgarian cultural renaissance was the rebuilding of Rila monastery after a disastrous fire in 1833. In addition to religious foundations, local civic institutions were also beneficiaries of the economic boom. Covered markets replaced the old open-air stalls; fountains were installed, and, most typically, a clock tower was erected in the centre of the community; it gave the time according to the Christian as opposed to the Muslim clock and was therefore a symbol of cultural self-assertion and modernity as well as a material attestation of recent attainments.

THE CULTURAL REVIVAL: EDUCATION, LITERACY
AND LITERATURE

A further outlet for charitable investment was in education, be it in
the form of school buildings or public reading-rooms, in equipment
such as books, or, in later years, in scholarships for gifted children
to study away from home, frequently in Europe; in 1867 the city of
Plovdiv was financing five students in Paris, four in Vienna, seven
in Russia, two in Britain, and forty in Constantinople.

Without the educational movement the Bulgarian national
revival would have been impossible. The cell schools which had
appeared in monasteries and then spread to some villages had not
entirely disappeared but by the 1820s they were widely recognised
as inadequate for a nineteenth-century community. Consciousness
of the need to expand and reshape education came from a variety of
sources. A number of Bulgarians had already received education
abroad, most of them in Russia, but a few had graduated from
Prague and other Slavic centres in central Europe. The French
Revolution and the Napoleonic wars had also brought the concept
of secular education into the Balkans. Some revolutionary literature
had spread to Wallachia, Moldavia and elsewhere, and for a while
the French had even occupied parts of Dalmatia and the Ionian
islands; and the latter after 1815 were to remain under British
trusteeship until 1864. Some adventurous Bulgarians had taken
part in the Greek war of independence and here again they had
come into contact with new, western ideas, all of which depended
on popular education if they were to be spread amongst the Balkan
peoples. After the Greeks achieved independence a number of
Bulgarian students went to schools or universities in Greece; such
experiences only underlined the need for more education for the
Bulgarians.

In 1824, Neofit Bozveli, a monk and a former pupil of Sofroni
Vrachenski, had introduced some Slav liturgical training into the
seminary at Svishtov but for many younger Bulgarians the desire
was now that education in their own language should be secular as
well as religious. However, it was not until a decade later, in 1834
in Gabrovo, that the first lay school teaching in Bulgarian was
established. The Gabrovo school had been set up by Vasil Aprilov

Plate 4.3 National revival buildings: a clock tower in Zlatitsa. Wealth accumulated by merchants was frequently expended on buildings such as these; a clock tower bore national significance in that it relayed time according to the Christian rather than the Muslim system

and taught on the Bell-Lancaster system in which older children taught the younger ones. Thereafter the number of schools increased gradually until 1840, when thirteen had been established, but after 1840 the pace of growth accelerated and by 1850 most Bulgarian communities of any size had a school teaching in the vernacular. In 1840 in Pleven the first school for girls was opened and others followed rapidly. Although most schools could provide no more than primary education there were also a number of specialist schools for older pupils, including a commercial school at Svishtov, pedagogic schools in Prilep and Shtip, and theological schools in Samokov and at the Petropavlovsk monastery near Leskovats. By the liberation in 1878 there were an estimated 2,000 schools in Bulgaria. Almost all of them were financed either by local guilds or by the village council or its urban equivalent.

This pedagogic achievement is all the more remarkable in view of the low level from which the educational movement began. In the 1820s there were no teaching materials. In 1824 in Braşov Petûr Beron had published his *Riben Bukvar* (Fish ABC), so-called because of the motif on its back cover. Like the Greek books on which it was modelled, the *Riben Bukvar* was a compendium of grammatical instruction and general information and it was not ideally suited to classroom use. Others followed, again most of them based on Greek models, but the production of standard teaching manuals was almost impossible when there was no standard orthography or grammar. The early monastic writers had not been consistent even within the confines of a single text, and when the nature of 'correct' Bulgarian grammar was first discussed there were widespread disagreements over such issues as whether the written language should retain the case endings which were disappearing as a feature of spoken Bulgarian, and whether the post-substantive definite article, universally used in the spoken form, should be a feature of the literary language. Venelin argued that the post-substantive article should be jettisoned to make Bulgarian more akin to other Slavonic languages, especially Russian. His arguments were fiercely rejected by later educational activists such as Ivan Bogorov who was ever vigilant against Russian gaining too much influence over his native tongue. In 1844 a grammar published by Bogorov did find widespread acceptance.

Plate 4.4 National revival buildings: the school in Karlovo first built in 1848 with funds provided by the local community. The photograph shows the building after restoration

When, in the 1870s, agreement was finally reached on a standard literary form, one which was based on the Gabrovo dialect with a few west-Bulgarian additions, it was a victory for the Bogorov tendency rather than the small Venelin school. By then elementary literacy was widespread amongst the younger generation of Bulgarians.

In addition to schools the spread of literacy and education was aided by the *chitalishta*. The English translation of this word is usually 'Reading Rooms' but it is inadequate. The German 'Kulturheime' and the cumbersome English 'Community Centres' come nearer to capturing the essence of this particularly Balkan institution. The *chitalishta* provided books and newspapers as well as places in which to read them, but they were also used to stage plays, to conduct meetings, and to present lectures. In many of them adults were taught the rudiments of reading and writing and in later years they were convenient venues for secret conspiratorial gatherings. The first *chitalishta* had been established in Serbia and the first to appear in the Bulgarian lands was that in Svishtov in 1856. They spread rapidly and by 1878 there were 186 of them. Ivan Vazov, Bulgaria's leading nineteenth-century literary figure, described the *chitalishta* as 'Bulgaria's ministry of national education'.

By the time the Svishtov *chitalishte* was established the publication of books, newspapers and journals was expanding rapidly. But such expansion had initially been slow and spasmodic. The first book published in Bulgarian is now generally agreed to be Sofroni Vrachenski's collection of sermons, *Nedelnik* (from the word for Sunday) which appeared in Bucharest in 1806. Between that year and 1834 an average of less than one book per year was published with the largest number in any single year being three. Again, however, the pace of growth intensified with the economic recovery of the 1820s and thereafter, with 9 books being published between 1821 and 1830, 42 between 1831 and 1840, 143 between 1841 and 1850, 291 between 1851 and 1860, and 709 between 1861 and 1870.

Many of these books, particularly in the earlier years, were published outside the Ottoman empire and were mainly teaching manuals and textbooks, but other literature became more common as printing facilities multiplied. The first Bulgarian printing press in the Ottoman empire did not appear until 1840 and then it was in Smyrna (Izmir) in Asia Minor; it was owned by a Greek who had imported Slav type from the United States at the request of the British and Foreign Bible Society. In the same year a Bulgarian press was established in European Turkey; located in Salonika it was again primarily religious in function, mass producing for the first time vernacular Bulgarian bibles and other religious items. The Smyrna press was also used for secular purposes. In 1844 Konstantin Fotinov used it when he began printing *Liuboslovie* (Love of Words). This was the first Bulgarian periodical, though it was to last no more than two years, failing partly because it was written in an archaic form of Bulgarian. The first periodical in Bulgarian to have anything more than an ephemeral existence was *Tsarigradski Vestnik* (Constantinople Gazette) which was edited by Ivan Bogorov and produced in the imperial capital on printing presses acquired by the city's Bulgarian community. It first appeared in 1848 and ran until 1861. Such longevity was exceptional and before the liberation few periodicals or newspapers had anything more than a short existence. Of the ninety such items which appeared between 1844 and 1878 thirty-three lasted for less than a year and only ten survived for over five years. Of those ninety items, fifty-six were newspapers and thirty-four periodicals; thirty-four of the ninety were published in the Ottoman empire and fifty-six by Bulgarian communities in other countries. Of the latter, forty-three (77 per cent) were published in Romania, twenty-one of them in Bucharest and thirteen in Braila.

A significant role in the sponsoring of education and the cultural revival which followed it was played by a number of learned societies. As early as 1823, in Braşov, Vasil Nenovich had founded the Philological Society to promote the use of Bulgarian as a literary medium and to stimulate the publication of books in Bulgarian, but clearly with no agreement on a standard literary form and with no available presses he was destined to disappointment. A much better timed and more successful venture was the Society for Bulgarian Literature founded in Constantinople in 1856; between 1857 and 1862 it published the bi-weekly journal *Bûlgarski Knizhitsi* (Bulgarian Papers), which at the height of its popularity had as many as 600 subscribers. The most important and successful of such societies, however, was the Bulgarian Literary Society founded in Braila in 1869 from which was to emerge the Bulgarian Academy of Sciences.

The spread of education and literacy meant the creation of a new element in Bulgarian society: the intelligentsia. Composed of priests and professional groups, above all teachers, the intelligentsia maintained strong links with the peasantry from which it came. The sturdy alliance of intelligentsia and peasantry was the basis of the successes which the Bulgarian nation was to achieve in the second half of the nineteenth century.

The cultural revival went further than education and the spread of literacy. In the 1840s there was the first attempt to produce a modern Bulgarian literature, especially in poetry, where the early efforts of Dobri Chintulov pointed to the glories that were to follow in subsequent years. By the 1870s Hristo Botev, soon to lose his life in the political struggle, was also writing poetry of real worth. In the

1840s Bulgarian art began to break away from the formalism which had characterised most of it in the previous century or more; new colours and previously neglected folk motifs enlivened even religious art, whilst secular painting at last found a figure of real stature in Zahari Zograf. Folk motifs also enhanced the output of the typically Bulgarian craft of wood-carving. In church music an identifiable Bulgarian form had emerged by the end of the eighteenth century and by the 1840s the first musical ensembles had been formed.

In the Bulgarian lands almost all forms of cultural and artistic activity were transformed in the years 1840 to 1860, but it was in the endeavour to establish a national church that these various forms of educational and cultural activity combined to precipitate the formation of the modern Bulgarian nation.

THE STRUGGLE FOR A SEPARATE BULGARIAN CHURCH

In the early eighteenth century most branches of civil administration in the Ottoman empire were dominated by the Phanariot Greeks. Nowhere was this more true than in the Orthodox church. The growing power and influence of the Greeks which had distressed and enraged Paiisi continued throughout the century. In 1766 the Serbian patriarchate at Peć was dissolved and in the following year the same fate befell the Bulgarian patriarchate in Ohrid. Church appointments at the higher levels had long been a virtual Greek monopoly but in the later eighteenth century there were numerous cases of Greek-speaking priests being nominated even for Bulgarian parishes.

It was not that the presence of Greek clerics or prelates necessarily provoked resentment or tension, and relations between Greek and Bulgarian were not necessarily hostile. Greek bishops mediated successfully between disputing Bulgarian guilds, and if the Greek ecclesiastical authorities were suspicious of teaching in Bulgarian they were equally set against teaching in demotic Greek. Aprilov himself believed that Bulgarian should be taught not in place of but in addition to liturgical Greek, and both he and the first teacher at the Gabrovo school, Neofit Rilski, remained faithful members of the Greek patriarchate.

It is undoubtedly the case that in the first half of the nineteenth century, Paiisi's latent message notwithstanding, many Bulgarians who regarded themselves as cultured or educated preferred to speak Greek, believing this to be the mark of the enlightened person; and given the philhellenic hysteria in western Europe and the United States this was hardly surprising. But Greek also had its advantages in the Balkans as a widespread medium of commerce, and many guilds and trading concerns continued to use it and even keep their records in it into the second half of the nineteenth century. It was not until the 1850s that mounting disagreements over educational and religious issues forced the powerful Plovdiv guild of *aba* makers to split into separate Greek and Bulgarian sections.

The main area of friction between Greek and Bulgarian was the church. Originally this was because the Greek dominated church was also widely corrupt. The practice of selling office and the percolation down of corruption which this had engendered were still very much in evidence at the end of the *kûrdjaliistvo*. In the 1820s many Bulgarian villages were paying to the church twice that which they were required to hand over in state taxes. As early as 1784 a Serb, Gerasim Zelić, had argued the need for Slav rather Greek clerics, but it was not until the 1820s that action was taken in this regard. In 1820 the inhabitants of Vratsa refused to hand over their church taxes on the grounds that the local bishop, Metodi, was incorrigibly corrupt. There were few who would have disputed this contention but neither the Porte nor the patriarchate could tolerate such insubordination and the leaders of the Vratsa protest, most of them local merchants, were sentenced to long terms in exile by the Ottoman authorities. In 1825 a similar protest against the Greek bishop of Skopje was equally unsuccessful.

In the 1830s the nature of this incipient conflict began to change. A growing number of Bulgarian priests were being educated in Russia and their Slav consciousness was greater than those who had remained in the hellenist world of the Orthodox seminaries in the Balkans. When the see of Tûrnovo fell vacant in 1835 there was a concerted move to secure the nomination of a Bulgarian-speaking bishop. The move failed. Although it was supported by the Porte, it was opposed by the patriarchate. In 1839 the former issued the Hatt-i-Sherif, a declaration of intent which promised religious

equality between Muslims and Christians; many Bulgarians chose
to interpret it as also promising equality between themselves and the
Greeks. In the 1840s the Bulgarians' protest became quite clearly
one not against corrupt Greek bishops because they were corrupt,
it was against Greek bishops because they were Greek. In 1841
there was an outburst of social unrest focused on Nish in the north-
west of the Bulgarian lands; the demands produced by the rebels
included one for 'bishops who at least can understand our
language'. By the end of that decade there had been protests
against Greek bishops in Rusé, Ohrid, Seres, Lovech, Sofia,
Samokov, Vidin, Tûrnovo, Leskovats, Svishtov, Vratsa, Tryavna
and Plovdiv.

The patriarchate refused to heed any of these demands, and it was
increasing frustration at the obduracy of the church's rulers that
forced Bulgarian communities into demanding the right to administer their own churches and appoint their own clergy. The movement
was led by Neofit Bozveli and Ilarion Makariopolski, first in
Tûrnovo and then in Constantinople. Initially they made little
progress and both leaders were incarcerated, Neofit eventually
dying in prison, but in 1849 came the first real breakthrough when
the Porte agreed that the Bulgarians should be allowed to build a
church in the Ottoman capital on land donated by Stefan Bogoridi,
a wealthy local Bulgarian who had risen high in the Ottoman civil
service and was a nephew of Sofroni Vrachenski. The church, St
Stephen's, was dedicated the following year and was to become the
focal point of Bulgarian cultural and political activity for the next
two and a half decades. The original church was replaced in 1890
by a building which is still to be seen in the Balat district of
Istanbul, and which remains the cause of intermittent wrangles
between the patriarchate and Bulgarian ecclesiastics.

The church established in 1848 was to be subject to the
patriarchate in matters of dogma and ecclesiastical jurisdiction, and
it was still to be a part of the Orthodox *millet* whose head, the
patriarch, still represented the Orthodox community in its relations
with the Ottoman authorities. The church, however, was to be the
property of the Bulgarian people, was to conduct its services in
Bulgarian, and was be to administered by a twenty-strong
governing council which could appoint priests for the church. This

governing council was the first new and specifically Bulgarian organisation to receive official recognition in the Ottoman empire since 1393.

There were few nationally conscious Bulgarians who did not now believe that the next step should be towards a fully separate Bulgarian church, an idea which was reinforced in 1850 when the Protestants, thanks to strong diplomatic support from Great Britain, had been granted their own *millet*. Much more importantly, in 1850 the patriarchate had finally been forced to recognise the Orthodox church in the Greek kingdom as an autocephalous institution. In 1851 the Bulgarian colony in Bucharest reflected a widespread feeling when it ended a circular letter to other Bulgarian communities with the phrase, 'Without a national church there is no salvation.'

The creation of the Protestant *millet* and the recognition of the church in Greece had shown that hopes for change were not unrealistic, and these hopes were further encouraged by the widespread restructuring of Ottoman social and political institutions which had come about as a result of the dissolution of the *spahi* system. As part of its reforming programme the Porte expected the patriarchate to initiate changes, in particular to increase the influence of the laity within the Orthodox church. In predominantly Bulgarian areas an increase in lay influence could only mean an increase in Bulgarian influence. The patriarchate, however, was not disposed to give way to reformist pressures and would never contemplate a split in the Orthodox community, even more so after its defeat over the church in Greece controversy.

If they were to make any progress towards ecclesiastical independence it seemed the Bulgarians would need foreign sponsorship similar to that which the British had given to the Protestants. For many Bulgarians, especially those educated in Russia, the tsar seemed the obvious source of such backing, not least because Russia had consistently supported the call for the appointment of Bulgarian bishops to Bulgarian sees. Like the patriarch, Russia did not want divisions in Orthodoxy. Her purported right to protect Orthodox Christians (treaty of Kutchuk Kainardji 1774) provided justification for diplomatic intervention in the Ottoman empire. Many Bulgarians were puzzled by the Russian position. To some degree their conundrum about Russia was eased by the latter's defeat in the Crimean war of 1854–6.

The war lessened Russian power and influence and it left the Bulgarians with a choice between pressing ahead on their own or finding an alternative sponsor. The former was always the more popular strategy. And it was one encouraged by the Hatt-i-Humayoun, the Porte's declaration of intent, issued at the conclusion of the war, to further reform the imperial administration.

In 1856 enthusiasts for the Bulgarian church cause decided to act alone, and presented the sultan with a petition asking for a separate church; the petition claimed to represent the 6.5 million Bulgarians living in the empire. In the same year, the Bulgarian communal council in Constantinople circulated a letter to all large Bulgarian communities asking them to send elected delegates to Constantinople to join in pressing for an independent church. These delegates, when they met in the imperial capital, constituted the first remotely representative body in modern Bulgarian history, and included in their number were many who were to achieve prominence in Bulgarian national affairs both before and after the liberation of 1878.

In 1857 the Porte ordered the patriarchate to institute a reform programme. In 1858 the patriarch agreed to call a council which was to include three Bulgarians; it was the first of seven such councils, all of them equally unproductive, to meet between 1858 and 1872. The Bulgarians suffered from a number of disadvantages. Despite the overwhelming popularity of their cause amongst the Bulgarian laity there were small but powerful elements in the Bulgarian clergy who were not prepared to split the Orthodox church; they included the abbot of the Rila monastery and two of the four Bulgarian bishops recently nominated by the patriarchate. Secondly, no official body created by the patriarchate would ever contain anything but an overwhelming Greek majority, and reform through official channels was therefore an illusion. Thirdly, the recognition of this truth strengthened for a while the minority who had always favoured the alternative strategy of seeking new forms of foreign sponsorship.

In 1860 matters came to a head. It was a time of further change in Europe, the Balkans and the Ottoman empire, a time which saw

Plate 4.5 Ilarion Makariopolski

the emergence of a unified Italy, the unification of the Danubian provinces of Wallachia and Moldavia into Romania, and the intervention of the great powers to secure autonomy for the rebellious Ottoman provinces in Syria and Lebanon. In Constantinople 1860 witnessed a virtual declaration of ecclesiastical independence by the Bulgarian church. It happened on Easter Sunday in St Stephen's. According to a pre-arranged plan the congregation interrupted the priest, Bishop Ilarion Makariopolski, at that point in the service where he was to pray for the patriarch. The patriarch's name was omitted and Ilarion prayed directly for the sultan's welfare; this direct prayer was an implicit rejection of the patriarchate which was still legally the body through which all Orthodox Christians were represented to the imperial ruler. In the evening service, for which the customary patriarchal permission had not been secured, the Gospels were read in eleven different languages; Greek was not one of them.

Ilarion's bold move won widespread support amongst the Bulgarian communities; 33 towns petitioned the sultan in support of Ilarion, as did over 700 merchants who had gathered for the annual fair in Uzundjovo. A number of bishops immediately aligned with the Constantinople church, including Gideon of Sofia who, though Greek, dared not offend the feelings of his flock. The events of Easter 1860 undoubtedly emboldened the Bulgarians. Veles broke away from the patriarchate, whilst the towns of Lovech, Samokov, Shumen, Preslav and Vidin all rejected bishops nominated by the patriarchate, even though those bishops were Bulgarian; and in later years many Bulgarian communities refused to pay taxes to the patriarch, and by 1870 almost all the dioceses in Thrace, Macedonia and Bulgaria had committed some act of disobedience towards the patriarch.

The Easter declaration of independence in 1860, despite the widespread support it rapidly gained, did not bring official recognition of a separate Bulgarian church. The Porte did not wish to hasten to a conclusion a dispute which conveniently divided two of its major subject groups; the Russians remained reluctant to see any division in the patriarchate; and the patriarch himself was as adamantly opposed as ever to the loss of his Bulgarian flock, and, of course, the revenue he derived from it. Much more importantly, however, was the impact recognition of the Bulgarian church would have upon other non-Greek Orthodox communities. The Ottoman *millet* system had made cultural identity a consequence of religious affiliation; the Bulgarians wanted to reverse that order and make religious affiliation a consequence of national allegiance. Such a doctrine, if accepted, would fragment the Orthodox church in the Ottoman empire with Romanians, Vlachs and Albanians, as well as Serbs, making similar claims. Understandably, the status of the Bulgarian church now became the central theme in the seemingly endless councils and other discussions held in the higher ranks of the Orthodox church.

Those amongst the Bulgarians who had advocated internal action, the Bulgarian *fara da sè*, had hoped that a bold move such as that Ilarion had made would cut the Gordian knot, force St Petersburg to come off the fence, and free the Bulgarian church from its ties with the patriarchate. That Russia still did not back the call for an independent Bulgarian church inevitably strengthened the confidence of those who all along had believed that the Bulgarians would be better off finding alternative foreign sponsorship. The sponsor they had in mind was the Roman Catholic church; behind the Roman church stood the Habsburg empire and, more significantly, the France of Napoleon III whose taste for foreign adventures and entanglements had not yet been dulled by the Mexican fiasco. The association with Rome would be achieved by joining the Uniate church, which allowed former Orthodox communities to worship in their own language with rites identical to those of the Orthodox church; in return those communities would acknowledge the pope as head of the church.

Uniate propaganda had grown steadily in the 1850s, encouraged in part by Polish refugees in Constantinople and in part by the French and Sardinian successes in the Crimean war, and also by the support of Dragan Tsankov, an influential Bulgarian activist and Ottoman civil servant. In December 1860 a group of Bulgarians in Constantinople signed an act of union with Rome, and nominated as their leader an illiterate octogenarian, Josef Sokolski, who was soon to be personally invested with his new office by Pope Pius IX in Rome. It did not last. Within a few months Sokolski had reneged on his flock, reverting to Orthodoxy and taking ship at dead of night for Odessa. By June 1861 there was no-one in Constantinople who could perform the Bulgarian Uniate services, a situation not remedied until 1863 when Raphael Popov was appointed to the vacancy. He was thirty-five years of age.

The Uniate option was in later decades to be chosen by some Bulgarian communities in Macedonia but after 1861 it was a *non possumus* in Constantinople. The Sokolski fiasco forced the former advocates of Uniatism back to the conclusion that they had to find some form of compromise between the Bulgarians and the patriarchate. After years of hopeless debate a breakthrough came in 1867 when Patriarch Gregory VI offered the Bulgarians an autonomous church within the patriarchate; the church would be headed by an exarch, an ecclesiastical rank between that of archbishop and patriarch. For the first time the patriarch had recognised the Bulgarians' right to a church of their own and the settlement would have found favour with them but for its territorial provisions. The 1867 proposal confined the Bulgarian exarchate to the area north of the Balkans, and it made no mention of where the exarch would have his headquarters. This was an issue of cardinal importance because if the exarch were confined to the area north of the Balkans he and his church would have no influence amongst the Bulgarians of Macedonia and Thrace. The plan was rejected by the Bulgarians. It seemed like a return to square one.

The situation had however changed, primarily because of external developments which alarmed the Porte. There had been signs in the early and mid-1860s of an emergent Bulgarian political movement which was prepared to resort to arms to achieve its goals; the Austro-Prussian war had created instability which could easily spread into the Balkans and Prince Michael Obrenović of Serbia was busy trying to fashion a Balkan alliance in case it did; should the war spread that projected alliance might easily be founded on the territorial ambitions of Serbia, Montenegro and Romania, many of which could be fulfilled only at the cost of the Ottoman empire. Most important of all, however, was the 1866 insurrection in Crete. This fanned Greek territorial aspirations and rapidly led to a serious deterioration in Greek–Ottoman relations. This factor more than any other pushed the Porte towards the

Bulgarians, whilst Russia moved reluctantly in the same direction because of its own worsening position in Athens and its fear that if the Bulgarians were much longer left unsatisfied they would turn again to Uniatism. In February 1870 the sultan issued a *firman*, or declaration of intent, to recognise a separate Bulgarian church headed by an exarch.

The rights of the new Bulgarian church, the exarchate, were not unlimited. Its liturgy still had to mention the patriarch, to whom it had to defer in matters of doctrine, and whose right to procure Holy Oil it had to respect. The territorial division was also of great importance. In 1869 Gavril Krûstevich, a prominent Constantinople Bulgarian who worked in the Ottoman civil service, had submitted a plan for the division of the dioceses between the two churches. According to his scheme the exarchate would take twenty-five of them whilst the rest would remain within the patriarchate. The Bulgarian dioceses were generally to be larger than the patriarchist and were to cover almost all of Macedonia. Though Krûstevich's scheme was used as the basis for the divisions contained in the 1870 *firman* the Bulgarian share had by that time been reduced to fifteen, namely Rusé, Silistra, Shumen, Tûrnovo, Sofia, Vratsa, Lovech, Vidin, Nish, Pirot, Kiustendil, Samokov, Veles, Varna and Plovdiv, although the latter two cities (the Virgin Mary quarter of Plovdiv excepted) were to remain within the patriarchate. Of the remaining fifty-nine dioceses fifty-one were to stay in the patriarchate and eight were to be divided. The 1870 settlement provided that a diocese should be allowed to transfer to the exarchate if two-thirds of its population voted in favour of such a move, but it said nothing on the question of where the exarch was to reside and have his headquarters. The Bulgarians, not for the last time in their modern history, could not rejoice over the territorial terms of a major settlement.

The 1870 declaration was rejected by the patriarch. Impasse had returned and it was to remain until 1872. In that year the patriarch called a patriarchal assembly to condemn the Bulgarians. In response the latter set about choosing an exarch, the choice falling on Bishop Antim of Vidin who was to reside in Constantinople. On 23 May 1872 he celebrated the liturgy in St Stephen's and then read a long proclamation of the independence of the Bulgarian church.

In September the patriarch proclaimed a schism. The exarchate was condemned for the sin of phyletism, that is, maintaining that ecclesiastical jurisdiction is determined not territorially but ethnically; the kernel of the problem was the seat of the exarchate because canon law contained the principle of there being only one prelate in any city.

In the struggle for the establishment of a separate Bulgarian church the modern Bulgarian nation had been created. The process had begun when, in conformity with the then largely unknown injunction of Paiisi, Bulgarians began to know their own nation and to study in their own tongue. They had since then developed a nation-wide educational system, they had produced their own intelligentsia, and they had pitted themselves against the Greek-dominated clerical hierarchy. The exarchate could now represent the interests of the Bulgarian nation in the Ottoman corridors of power; more importantly, it could defend Bulgarian Orthodoxy against the patriarchate and against Uniatism in Macedonia, and sponsor Bulgarian churches and schools in the mixed dioceses and even in some which were still in the patriarchate.

Yet as the cultural revival moved towards its culmination in 1870 there was already a small body of Bulgarian activists for whom the political struggle had already become supreme. For them the goal was not simply the creation of a Bulgarian cultural nation represented in its church. Their aspirations were towards a political nation represented by its own political institutions within its own political borders.

THE STRUGGLE FOR POLITICAL INDEPENDENCE AND THE LIBERATION OF 1878

When Patriarch Gregory VI made his proposals for an autonomous Bulgarian church in 1867 he noted: 'With my own hands I have built a bridge to the political independence of the Bulgarians.' It was a prescient remark but one which would have puzzled his contemporaries, including the Bulgarians amongst them, because the political side of the Bulgarian national movement was little developed.

There had been political action by Bulgarians in the past. A number of Bulgarian volunteers fought with the Serbs between 1804 and 1814, and even more joined with Greeks in their war of independence in the 1820s. In May 1835 there was a small outburst against the Ottoman authorities in the Tûrnovo region but this so-called 'Velchov Rising' was easily suppressed and left little legacy behind it. In the 1840s and 1850s there were outbursts of social unrest in the north-west and south-west of the Bulgarian lands, with serious clashes in Nish in 1841 and around Vidin a decade later, but again the outbursts were contained.

It was not until the 1860s that the first real signs of concerted political action were discernible. In 1862 the Serbs used force to drive the last Ottoman garrison, that in Belgrade, from their country. Taking part in the action was a small Bulgarian Legion led by Georgi Rakovski. Born in Kotel in 1821 Rakovski had attended a local cell school before receiving higher education in Constantinople. By the early 1840s he was already trying to form secret societies first in Athens and then in Braila. For the latter the Romanians sentenced him to death, but he escaped. In the Crimean war he tried to raise a Bulgarian force to assist the Russians but had little success, though during this period he did begin writing and publishing, fields in which he was soon to be prolific. After the Crimean war he wandered through Hungary, Romania and southern Russia before settling for a while in Belgrade. There he continued writing, particularly for the periodical *Dunavski Lebed* (Danubian Swan), and scheming to bring political liberation to the Balkan Christians; his vision was of a Balkan Christian federation. At the same time he formed the Bulgarian Legion which, however, was disbanded by the Serbs after the action against the Ottoman garrison in 1862.

Rakovski then moved to Bucharest where he continued his journalistic activities and also began organising small armed bands, *cheti*, of dedicated revolutionaries. His belief had always been that Ottoman power in the Balkans would be destroyed only by an armed uprising by its Christian subjects; the *cheti* would in the meantime harass Ottoman officials and raise national conscious-ness. In 1867 Rakovski also established a second Bulgarian Legion but it was to have little success, not least because Rakovski himself died that year, struck down by tuberculosis.

A more lasting creation of Rakovski's was the Bulgarian Secret Central Committee (BSCC) founded in 1866. The BSCC made the first sustained attempts to organise and equip *cheti* and early in 1867 two such bands crossed the Danube under the leadership of Panaiot Hitov and Filip Totiu. In 1868 more followed, this time led by Hadji Dimitûr Asenov and Stefan Karadja. They were soon dispersed. The BSCC meanwhile combined political pressure with military action. In 1867 it submitted a petition to the sultan suggesting a Bulgarian–Ottoman compromise on the model of that just reached between the Austrian and Hungarian components of the Habsburg monarchy. It was this combination of attempted military action and political sophistication which alarmed the Porte and made it more anxious to conclude a settlement of the Bulgarian church question.

Rakovski's greatest achievement was to establish the practice of conspiracy for political rather than cultural or ecclesiastical objectives. He left behind some accomplished followers, and leadership of the nascent revolutionary movement passed eventually to three of them: Liuben Karavelov, Vasil Levski and Hristo Botev.

Liuben Karavelov arrived in Bucharest in 1869. Born in 1834 in Koprivshtitsa he was educated there and in Plovdiv before making his way to Russia where he attended lectures in Moscow on history. In 1866 his association with the narodniks or 'populists' brought about his expulsion from Russia; in 1868 he fell foul of the Habsburg authorities who locked him up on suspicion of involvement in the murder of the pro-Austrian Prince Michael Obrenović of Serbia. By this time Karavelov had established himself as one of the foremost Bulgarian men of letters, having published numerous tracts and essays as well as a number of novels. Like Rakovski, Karavelov dreamed of a Balkan republic, and, again following Rakovski, he believed that Ottoman power could only be removed by a revolution of the Balkan Christians, but he dissented from Rakovski's view that the *cheti* would be the means by which that revolution would be brought about. Following the precepts of some Russian narodniks Karavelov argued that before a successful rising the people had to be educated, and this task could only be performed by a small number of trained and dedicated 'apostles'.

Vasil Levski not only shared this view; he acted upon it. Levski was a native of Karlovo in the foothills of the Balkan mountains where he was born in 1837. After initial schooling in his home town he went to Stara Zagora where he received training for the priesthood; in 1858 he entered a monastery. He remained there scarcely two years and after a short period as a teacher went to Belgrade where he joined the Bulgarian Legion and took part in the action of 1862. After the dissolution of the Legion he reverted for a short while to the monastic life, before resuming teaching and then returning to revolutionary activity as the standard bearer in Hitov's *cheta*. At the end of the 1860s he had become one of the most experienced and influential of the small group of Bulgarian political revolutionaries. By now he had also formulated his ideas clearly. He followed Karavelov in urging the need for apostles to prepare the people for their historic task, but he differed from most of his contemporaries when he insisted that it was hopeless to dream of foreign sponsorship or assistance: Bulgaria's liberation could be achieved only by the Bulgarians. Levski became a leading member of the Bulgarian Revolutionary Central Committee when it was established in April 1870, and he spent the next two years primarily occupied in setting up a network of secret organisations in Bulgaria. In 1872 he was arrested together with an accomplice. The latter, in an effort to prove he was a political prisoner, revealed details of the conspiracy in which he and Levski were involved. In February 1873 Levski was hanged in Sofia. He had once written, 'If I succeed, I shall succeed for the whole nation: if I fail, then I alone shall die,' words which are now carved in huge letters on the monument outside the National Cultural Centre (NDK) erected in Sofia in the 1980s.

Hristo Botev was born in Kalofer in 1848, the son of a teacher. He received his basic education at home before winning a scholarship to study in Odessa. He, like Karavelov, became influenced by and associated with the populists, and after a brush with the tsarist police returned to Kalofer in 1867. He taught in a number of schools and was profoundly influenced by the Paris Commune. In 1872 he was in Bucharest where he became involved with the Bulgarian revolutionaries. He never attained the same prominence in the organisational structures as Karavelov or Levski, but he was soon widely known and admired for his writing, above all for his poetry. He was to lose his life in the struggle for liberation in 1876. Of the three most notable heirs of Rakovski only Karavelov, who died in the second half of 1878, lived to see an independent Bulgaria.

The death of Levski was a shattering blow to the revolutionaries in Bucharest. Karavelov and the left-wing Botev could not cooperate and when the Bulgarian Revolutionary Central Committee was reconstructed in 1875 Botev was not a member. A new figure in its inner circles was Georgi Benkovski, a brilliant organiser who had been born in Koprivshtitsa in the early 1840s. Very much under Benkovski's guidance the Bulgarian lands were now divided into four revolutionary districts based on Tûrnovo, Vratsa, Sliven and Plovdiv.

In 1875 the Ottoman empire was facing difficulties in Bosnia where a revolt had broken out over changes in the taxation system. In the following year the disorders spread and were soon to lead to war between the empire and Serbia. To the Bulgarian revolutionary conspirators this seemed too good an opportunity to miss. In April 1876 leaders of all revolutionary districts met in Oborishte in the woods between Pangiurishte and Koprivshtitsa. After three days of discussion it was agreed that a simultaneous rising should be staged in all four districts; it was to begin in May. Owing to a misunderstanding the standard was raised in Koprivshtitsa in April. The April Uprising had begun.

In terms of its immediate achievements the April Uprising can hardly be judged other than a disastrous shambles. In the Sliven district no more than sixty men rallied to the revolutionaries' call, whilst in Tûrnovo there was little or no response except in a few monasteries. In the Vratsa district no-one at all joined the uprising. The major action here was when Botev, having hijacked an Austrian steamer on the Danube, landed with his *cheta* and advanced about 20 kilometres southwards. They were soon surrounded and slaughtered by *bashibazouks*, or Ottoman irregular detachments, many of whose members were Bulgarian Muslims, and who were being used extensively because the main body of the regular army was deployed to meet the Serbs.

If the rising in Sliven, Tûrnovo and Vratsa may be seen as

Plate 4.6 The greatest of Bulgaria's national activists and martyrs, Vasil Levski, born in Karlovo in 1837. This photograph was taken in 1870, three years before his execution in Sofia

Plate 4.7 A contemporary Russian periodical described this as 'The peaceful visit of the *bashibazouks* to a Bulgarian village'

farcical tragedy, in Plovdiv the tragedy was unalloyed. Here Benkovski and his flying column had been active and had persuaded a number of villages to throw in their lot with the revolutionaries. But Benkovski and his men were no match for the local *bashibazouks*. The latter wreaked a terrible vengeance on villages which had joined the rebels, particularly in Bratsigovo, Perushtitsa, and above all Batak, where 5,000 Bulgarian Christians, mostly women and children, were said to have been killed, many of them being herded into the local church and burned alive.

The April Uprising was over. It had not dislodged Ottoman power but it had irreversibly changed the nature of that power in Bulgaria. National consciousness which, in the political sense, had been at a low level was immeasurably raised; the moral power of the Porte, such as it was, had been destroyed. Furthermore, the nature of the Bulgarian question had been transformed. European news-papers had relayed the stories of the massacres in graphic detail and opinion had been outraged. In Russia, Britain and elsewhere there

Plate 4.8   A wooden cannon captured from the Bulgarian
insurgents by the Turks, January 1877

were increasingly loud calls for action to prevent any further
outrages. The Bulgarian question had become a European one.

In December 1876 the ambassadors of the European powers in
Constantinople met to discuss a programme of reforms to be introduced into the Ottoman empire. Agreement on the contents of such
a programme was not difficult to achieve, but it proved impossible
to persuade the sultan to consent to European supervision of its
application. In April 1877 Russia declared war on the Ottoman
empire.

Most observers had expected an easy Russian victory but it did
not come about. The Ottoman forces dug in in Pleven to the north
of the Balkan mountains and could not be dislodged for five
months. An advanced detachment of the Russian army under
General Gurko did manage to take Tûrnovo and then force its way
through the Balkan range only to be repulsed at Stara Zagora by a
large Ottoman force recently returned from the war against Serbia.
Gurko retreated to the Shipka pass where he resisted ferocious
enemy attacks. He was helped by the newly formed Bulgarian
militia, the *opŭlchenie*, whose rudimentary armaments included
cannons fashioned out of cherry-trees. When Pleven finally

Map 4.2 Bulgaria according to the treaties of San Stefano and Berlin

surrendered the Russians could advance with ease. In January 1878, Sofia was taken and in the following month a truce was signed at Adrianople. On 3 March a preliminary peace was signed at San Stefano.

The peace of San Stefano envisaged a vast new Bulgarian state stretching from the Danube in the north to the Rhodopes in the south, and from the Black Sea in the east to the Morava and Vardar valleys in the west; San Stefano Bulgaria included some of the Aegean coast, though not Salonika, and the inland cities of Skopje, Ohrid, Bitolya and Seres. In territorial terms this was as much as any Bulgarian nationalist could have hoped for or even dreamed of.

It was, however, just what the statesmen of Britain and Austria-Hungary had feared. They saw the new Bulgaria as an enormous wedge of potential Russian influence in the Balkans and they demanded that the boundaries be redrawn. The treaty of Berlin of July 1878 satisfied British and Austro-Hungarian demands. San Stefano Bulgaria was dismembered. The Bulgarian principality was to be confined to a small area between the Balkan mountains and the Danube; the region between the Balkan mountains and the Rhodopes, southern Bulgaria, was to form a new autonomous unit of the Ottoman empire to be known as Eastern Rumelia; Macedonia was to return to Ottoman rule with a promise that its administration would be reformed; and the Morava valley in the north-west, including the important towns of Pirot and Vranya, were to go to Serbia.

The Bulgaria of the treaty of Berlin was 37.5 per cent of the size of the San Stefano variant. For every Bulgarian, however, the real Bulgaria remained that of San Stefano. The new Bulgarian state was to enter into life with a ready-made programme for territorial expansion and a burning sense of the injustice meted out to it by the great powers.

The peace of San Stefano and the treaty of Berlin differed little in their provisions for the internal structure of the new state. Bulgaria was to be a principality with a Christian prince who was to be elected by the Bulgarians and confirmed by the powers; he was not to be a member of a major ruling European dynasty. Bulgaria was to remain a vassal state of the sultan whose suzerainty it was required to acknowledge. The principality was to be allowed a militia but it was not to construct fortresses; it was to assume all the international obligations previously entered into by the Ottoman empire in terms of foreign debt payments, railway building, tariffs and the protection of foreign citizens through the so-called Capitulations. Before the prince was elected an assembly was to be convened at Tûrnovo to devise a new constitution for the principality.

Eastern Rumelia was to remain under the direct political and military authority of the sultan, though the latter was not allowed to billet *bashibazouks* in the province, nor was he to quarter passing Ottoman troops on the population. The maintenance of order was to be the responsibility of an Eastern Rumelian gendarmerie whose ethnic composition was to reflect that of the local population and whose officers were to be appointed by the sultan. The senior official in Eastern Rumelia was to be the governor-general who was also to be appointed by the sultan, subject to confirmation by the signatory powers; his period of office was to be five years.

With the signing of the treaty of Berlin, despite its many short-comings from the Bulgarian point of view, the Bulgarian state had been born. Unlike the Bulgarian church it was the creation more of external than internal forces.

5

The consolidation of the Bulgarian state, 1878–1896

THE CONSTITUENT ASSEMBLY AND THE TÛRNOVO CONSTITUTION

The assembly which was to devise Bulgaria's political system met in Tûrnovo in late February 1879. It contained a mixture of elected and nominated deputies, the latter including representatives of the Turkish, Greek and Jewish minorities.

The assembly also contained deputies from Bulgarian lands outside the new principality. This indicated that the great passion over borders had not subsided. Indeed, there had been attempts to rekindle the struggle in Macedonia. Activists in Bulgaria staged a rising in the Kresna-Razlog region of eastern Macedonia, but it was not well coordinated and was suppressed with ease. The territorial question, however, was still the first preoccupation of the delegates when they assembled in the mediaeval capital, and a vocal faction amongst them urged that they disperse and the assembly be disbanded; better, they argued, unity under Ottoman authority than a division of the nation between the free and the enslaved. Others supported this argument with suggestions that Bulgaria should seek a compromise similar to that granted to the Hungarians in 1867. A more moderate view urged that the Tûrnovo assembly be postponed rather than dissolved, and that the breathing space be used to draw up a petition which a delegation should then take around the European capitals. The Russians were embarrassed by all this. They feared that any postponement of the assembly might

Map 5.1 Bulgaria 1878–1912

lead to international complications which, in their enfeebled post-war condition, they could not afford. The Bulgarians were told that it was not in the assembly's power to communicate directly with the governments of the great powers, though there was no reason why private messages should not be sent to the powers' consuls in Tûrnovo.

Such messages were sent after the constituent assembly had debated the issue of national unity. That debate took up the first week of the assembly's deliberation and focused upon a report drawn up by a special commission appointed by the delegates to study the national question. The report favoured the moderate faction which had argued that the disbandment of the assembly would only anger the powers and make matters worse. The week-long debate was intense but the report's recommendations were finally approved. The highpoint of the proceedings had been a speech from Exarch Antim who quoted Jeremiah chapter 31, verses 16 and 17:

Thus saith the Lord; refrain thy voice from weeping and thine eyes from tears; for thy work shall be rewarded, said the Lord; and they shall come again from the land of the enemy. And there is hope in thine end, saith the Lord, thy children shall come again into their own border.

Before the constituent assembly convened Sofia had been chosen as the capital of the new principality. Although small, Sofia had two advantages: it was at the crossroads of the north-east to south-west and north-west to south-east routes across the Balkans, and it offered easy access to the coveted lost lands of Macedonia and the Morava valley.

With the territorial issue decided early in March the constituent assembly began work on defining the principality's political system. The draft constitution was presented by Prince Dondukov-Korsakov, the head of the Russian Provisional Administration which had governed Bulgaria since the war. His draft was amended by a commission elected by the assembly which presented its recommendations early in April. Two tendencies immediately became apparent. Those later to be grouped under the label 'conservative' argued for a system which placed real power in the hands of the small number of wealthy Bulgarians. The peasant masses who made up 90 per cent or more of the population, the conservatives argued, were too immature to be entrusted with real power; after five centuries of Ottoman domination they were too suspicious of the state as an institution and would too easily treat their new one as they had their old. This was anathema to the other group, the 'liberals'. They believed the peasants and the village councils were the repositories of national political wisdom; they rejected outright the paternalism of the conservatives and stressed that the equal distribution of political power throughout the nation was a natural consequence of its basic social homogeneity.

These opposing attitudes were fully developed during the debate on the nature of Bulgaria's parliamentary system. The conservatives wanted a second chamber to reinforce the power of the wealthy minority; a senate, they said, would check the enthusiasms of the lower chamber. The liberals saw no need for a second chamber. It would be needlessly divisive and it would be a dangerous dilution of natural, healthy, peasant democracy.

Although the 230 or so delegates included only 12 from the villages so beloved of the liberals, liberal views enjoyed massive support in the assembly. The second chamber was rejected. The single-chamber parliament (sûbranie) was, however, to have two variants. Copying the example of the Serbian constitution, there was to be an ordinary and a grand national assembly. The ordinary assembly was to meet every year in October, after the harvest had been taken in, it was to sit for two months, and was to be elected for a three-year period. The Grand National Assembly (GNA) was to have twice as many elected deputies together with prominent members of the church, the judiciary and local government. The GNA was to be called to elect regents, choose the head of state, to sanction changes in the state's boundaries, or to change the constitution, a two-thirds majority being necessary in the latter case.

All sane male citizens over twenty-one were allowed to vote for both assemblies, and all literate males over thirty were eligible for election. The obligations of each citizen were to obey the law, to pay taxes, to send all children to school for at least five years, and to send all healthy males to the army for two years.

Executive power was to lie with the prince but was to be exercised via a council of ministers or cabinet chosen from the assembly. The prince could appoint and dismiss ministers; he nominated the chairman of the council of ministers, or prime minister, and he could prorogue the assembly.

An important section of the constitution dealt with the church. The general convention in the Orthodox church is 'One Church, One State', but if that were now applied the exarch would have to leave Constantinople and settle in the principality. Were he to do that he would lose contact with the members of the exarchate in Macedonia, Thrace, the Morava valley and even Eastern Rumelia. This would be an immense blow for the Bulgarian nation, one equal to that inflicted by the tearing up of the San Stefano treaty, because in 1878 members of the exarchate living outside the confines of the principality outnumbered those within it. The Tûrnovo constitution therefore decided that the church in the principality was to be an inseparable part of the Bulgarian exarchate, and that the highest body of the Bulgarian church, the holy synod, was to have its seat in Sofia. The exarch, however, was to remain in Constantinople.

The constitution also decided that the prince must confess the Orthodox faith, only the first prince being exempt from this ruling. That first prince, the assembly decided, was to be Alexander Battenberg, a candidate whom all the great powers found acceptable. Alexander arrived in Bulgaria early in July 1879.

CONSTITUTIONAL CONFLICTS, 1879–1883

Alexander had much to commend him to the Bulgarians. He was young, he was handsome and above all he had served with the tsar's forces in the war of 1877–8. Unfortunately, his paternalist instincts made it almost impossible for him to work with the liberals who dominated Bulgarian politics, and who had now organised themselves into the Liberal Party. The liberals won the first elections held in September 1879 and the second which took place early in 1880 after Alexander had dissolved the first sûbranie. Constitutional issues arising from this contest between the executive and legislature were to dominate Bulgarian politics for the first five years of the new state's existence.

After the second elections Alexander had little choice but to nominate as prime minister, Dragan Tsankov, the erstwhile champion of Uniatism who was now a fierce russophile and leader of the Liberal Party. There was sufficient truce between prince and prime minister to enable the latter to begin the construction of the new state and its apparatus. Tsankov therefore introduced a national currency based on the lev (lion), he regulated the national system of justice, and he took measures to control brigandage which had plagued the mountain areas since liberation. But it was not long before friction arose between him and the prince on constitutional issues. Alexander insisted on using for his title a Bulgarian word to which the liberals took exception, and he greatly offended the majority party by dissolving the city council in Sofia; not even the Ottomans had done such a thing, the liberals declared. On the other hand, the liberals frightened Alexander by bringing forward plans for a citizens' militia which was to compete with if not replace the army.

Tsankov resigned in November 1880 and was replaced by Petko Karavelov, brother of Liuben. The prince's preference would have been for a change of constitution rather than of prime minister, but to this the Russians would not consent, fearing it might excite demands for west European interference in Bulgarian affairs. The Russian veto, however, was withdrawn in March 1881 when Tsar Alexander II was assassinated. His successor, Alexander III, was more reactionary. He raised no objections in May when his name-sake in Bulgaria dismissed the Karavelov government and announced he would convoke a Grand National Assembly to meet in Svishtov later in the year to consider changes to the constitution. The liberals were not unduly perturbed. They believed they had the nation with them, that this would be reflected in the election results, and that they would therefore easily dominate the GNA. Anxiety began to assail them when Alexander published his proposals for constitutional change, for these bore a great resemblance to the conservative ideas expressed at Tûrnovo. Liberal fears intensified when the Russians gave Battenberg's plans their blessing. The Russians also backed the prince in the elections held in July; Russian soldiers were available at the vote to 'help illiterates' and preserve order, though they placed little restraint on the pro-Battenbergist thugs who also congregated around the voting points.

Plate 5.1 Alexander Battenberg, prince of Bulgaria,
1879–1886

Only two electoral districts returned liberal deputies and not all of them reached the assembly. It would have made no difference if they had. The Svishtov GNA which met on 13 July was overwhelmingly conservative in outlook, and in less than two hours it passed all the prince's proposals: a state council was to be introduced, the franchise was to be made indirect, the sûbranie was to be reduced in size, and civil liberties were to be restricted. Prince Alexander had in effect carried out a *coup d'état.*

After the coup many liberals left Bulgaria for exile in Eastern Rumelia, though Tsankov remained hoping to influence Alexander's authoritarianism from within the principality. In fact the authoritarian regime was from the beginning weak and insecure. The fundamental political reality of Bulgaria remained unaltered: the great majority of the politically conscious part of the nation, the intelligentsia, backed the liberals and would not cooperate with the conservatives or the prince. The latter was soon to face another difficulty because when a sûbranie was elected in the autumn of 1882 its conservative majority – the liberals had boycotted the poll – showed a surprising degree of independence. This spirit of independence was to be shown primarily against the Russians.

In the spring of 1882 the prince, desperate to find ministers who would be generally acceptable, had imported two Russian generals, Sobolev and Kaulbars, who were given responsibility for the major share of internal administration. This seemed a sensible move in that the Russians remained widely respected and popular, particularly amongst the liberals. Yet there were dangers in such a policy. Alexander's own relations with the Russians were equivocal at the best of times, the main points of friction being on matters affecting the army. Alexander was determined to strengthen his influence over the ministry of war and the officer corps, yet the ministry was by convention held by a Russian and all officers above the rank of captain in the Bulgarian army were Russians. The appointment of Kaulbars as minister of war did nothing to improve relations in this area.

Whilst the prince and the Russians competed for influence within the army, there were serious disagreements between the Russians and the conservatives over railways. Since 1879 the Russians had been pressing the Bulgarian government to allow them to construct a railway from the Danube in the north-east to Sofia. This would have great strategic importance in any future Russian military operations in the Balkans, but the suggestion was embarrassing for the Bulgarians. The treaty of Berlin obliged Bulgaria to complete that section of the Vienna to Constantinople trunk link which passed through Bulgarian territory. This was an expensive obligation which would more than absorb whatever funds the Bulgarians had for railway construction. The Russians nevertheless urged that the Berlin obligation be placed second to that of the Danube–Sofia line; at the same time they strove hard to secure control of the national bank which the Bulgarians decided to establish. The two issues were obviously connected because Russian control of the bank would ensure funds were made available for the Russian railway project. These arguments the Russians pressed in the state council and the sûbranie but both bodies refused such pressures and in April 1883, with full support from the prince, the sûbranie enacted that the trunk line be built.

The Russians were enraged but there was nothing they could do, not least because the moderate liberals shared conservative attitudes on this issue. The liberals believed that Russia, as the liberating power, had the right to dominate Bulgarian foreign policy, one liberal even arguing that Bulgaria had no need of a foreign ministry because its external affairs should be left in Russia's hands. But the liberals did not expect Russian interference in Bulgaria's internal affairs. After the 1883 decision on the trunk line the conservatives, the moderate liberals and the prince combined to contain Russian pressures. In September Sobolev and Kaulbars left Bulgaria and Tsankov formed a coalition government.

The internal compromise reached in Bulgaria was based on liberal acceptance of the April 1883 railway agreement, and conservative acceptance of a return to the Tûrnovo constitution, together with the acknowledgement that any future constitutional changes could only be brought about by constitutional means. In December 1883 the sûbranie passed a constitutional reform bill which reintroduced much of the 1881 system. The conservatives then left the coalition government, believing they had secured their constitutional objectives. They had not because the December 1883 bill had been passed by very dubious means and it was repealed in the following year before it had been put into effect.

The passing of the December 1883 bill embarrassed the liberals. Their ranks were already divided, particularly between those who had remained in Bulgaria in 1881 and those who had gone into exile, the latter being headed by Petko Karavelov. These divisions were sharpened early in 1884 when Tsankov announced the government had agreed to purchase the British-owned Rusé–Varna railway. Purchase of the line was another obligation laid upon Bulgaria by the treaty of Berlin and no-one could object to the government's decision. They could, however, object to the price. And this the Karavelov wing of the Liberal Party did with some energy. When elections were held in June 1884 they were a contest not between the conservatives and the liberals but between the tsankovist and karavelist wings of the Liberal Party.

The karavelists won and their leader formed the next government. His first act was to repeal the December 1883 constitutional legislation after which he went on to introduce two vitally important bills. The first placed the new Bulgarian National Bank under state ownership. The second nationalised the railways; all existing and future lines in the country were to be the property of the Bulgarian State Railways (BDZh); plans were also drawn up to determine the shape of the future national rail network. By this time the split between the two wings of the Liberal Party had been formalised. The karavelists formed the new Democratic Party, Tsankov's group retaining the title of the Liberal Party.

By the end of 1884 most of the constitutional issues raised in 1879 had been settled. The prince's political wings had been clipped after his too rapid ascent in 1881; the conservatives had become a minor factor in the political equation; and the Russians had been rebuffed by Karavelov's nationalist legislation on the bank and on railways. The decline of the constitutional questions meant that attention could once again focus on the issue which had been at the

Plate 5.2 The sûbranie (parliament) building, Sofia. Its motto means 'Unity is Strength'. The building dates from the 1880s and replaced one destroyed by fire in 1883. The building in the left background is the Aleksander Nevski cathedral, completed just before the first world war; it was built to commemorate the 200,000 Russians who fell in the war of 1877–1878

forefront of discussion before the constitutional debates: that of national unity.

Ever since 1878 there had been a sizeable Macedonian presence in Bulgaria. Some Macedonians were economic migrants, many of them taking part in the construction work which liberation spawned in Sofia and other cities. Others, however, were fugitives or refugees. Most if not all Macedonians in Bulgaria at this period regarded themselves as ethnically Bulgarian and the refugees were a potential political lobby of considerable size. After the end of authoritarian rule they became more active and by 1884 had moved some distance towards forming effective organisations. Movement in this direction was encouraged by the first signs of emergent Serbian propaganda in Macedonia where the exarchist/Bulgarian cause already had to meet strong competition from the patriarchist/ Greek faction. In 1885 two *cheti* crossed from Bulgaria into

Macedonia, one of them equipped with arms taken from a Bulgarian military installation with the obvious connivance of local officials. Both bands were soon rounded up or dispersed by Ottoman forces but alarm signals had been clearly sounded, particularly in Russia. They were heeded by Karavelov. He retained enough of the liberals' original pro-Russian attitudes still to believe that Bulgaria must do nothing in its foreign policy to anger or alienate St Petersburg. And at this period the focus of Russian diplomacy was on central Asia; it was made abundantly clear in Sofia that complications in the Balkans would be most unwelcome as they would make it much more difficult to secure Russian objectives in Asia. Karavelov therefore acted swiftly. In 1885 a number of known Macedonian activists were moved away from the western border areas and settled in central or eastern Bulgaria.

Karavelov's firm line on Macedonia focused attention on Eastern Rumelia. The internal administration of Eastern Rumelia, it had been decided in Berlin, was to be under the control of a governor general but he was to rule through an elected assembly whilst a permanent council of that assembly was to function as a form of cabinet. It had been intended by the Berlin powers that the permanent council would contain representatives of the Turkish and Greek minorities in Rumelia and an elaborate system of proportional representation had been devised for when the regional assembly elected the permanent council from its own membership. These plans were scuppered by one Bulgarian deputy who had a doctorate in mathematics from Prague. He lectured, drilled and rehearsed his colleagues so effectively that when the vote was held all posts in the council were taken by Bulgarians. Though minority rights were safeguarded in Rumelia the election of a purely Bulgarian permanent council meant that the province's political machinery was entirely in Bulgarian hands.

There was an understandable desire to emphasise the Bulgarian nature of the province. To that end the Bulgarian flag and the Bulgarian national anthem were used on every permissible occasion and as many of the province's official institutions as possible were modelled on their equivalents in the principality. Thus the school system in Rumelia was similar to that north of the border; the literary alphabets were the same, and military training was again taken directly from the Bulgarian example.

However, the party system which emerged from the constitutional debates in the principality did not appear in Rumelia where the dominant political elements were small, conservative oligarchies consisting of wealthy merchants and former Ottoman civil servants. Provincial politics, and not least its press, were enlivened by the arrival of the liberal refugees after the coup of 1881 but that coup acted as a hindrance to the development of political links with Bulgaria. Rumelia's economy was more developed than Bulgaria's and its merchants did not want the sort of upheavals which in two years had given the principality seven cabinets and two general elections; even more importantly, serious disturbances or political changes might invoke that clause of the treaty of Berlin which stated that Ottoman troops could be reintroduced into Rumelia if there were a serious threat to its internal stability and if the signatory powers of the Berlin treaty had been informed beforehand. Rumelia could not contemplate union until the principality had returned to an orderly, constitutional life.

Another hindrance to any attempts at union between Bulgaria and Rumelia had been the attitude of the western and central European powers. Initially they had seen Bulgaria as a dependency of Russia and therefore had feared that any expansion of Bulgaria would mean an extension of Russian influence. By 1884 this view was changing. The prince's disagreements with the Russians over the army and above all the decisions on the railway and bank questions had shown Europe that Bulgaria was not a Russian satrapy.

As his reaction to the *cheti* of 1885 showed, Karavelov was not willing to anger the Russians, but there were conspiracies afoot which had no such inhibitions. Early in 1885 a Bulgarian Secret Central Revolutionary Committee (BSCRC) had been established. It advocated extremist methods and had maximalist aims. It wanted to bring about a mass rising of all Bulgarians under foreign rule and to unite them in a single state, to recreate in fact San Stefano Bulgaria. It was a hopelessly ambitious aim and Karavelov's reaction to the 1885 *cheti* showed that the maximalist path would lead nowhere. With Macedonia denied to them the activists of the

BSCRC concentrated instead on what seemed the easiest of their objectives: Rumelia where Bulgarians already dominated the machinery of local administration. The BSCRC became the Committee for Union; it abandoned its call for a mass uprising, deciding instead that the local, Bulgarian-dominated militia should carry out a coup. This would be rapid and could be effected before international diplomacy could be rallied to defend the *status quo*.

The coup was duly carried out on 18 September 1885, although the scheduled date had been a little later. It was enthusiastically welcomed amongst the general Bulgarian population both north and south of the Balkan mountains. Karavelov and Prince Alexander were less sure. Karavelov dithered, caught between his obvious desire to see unification and his reluctance to do anything in foreign policy which would anger the Russians.

Alexander was equally concerned at Russian reactions. He had been informed of the conspiracy and of the date it was due to be carried out. But there had been endless similar rumours over the previous few years and he took this one no more seriously than those which had preceded it; in August he had even assured the Russian minister for foreign affairs that there was no reason to expect any dramatic developments in the Balkans in the foreseeable future. Initially, Alexander also dithered. His mind was made up for him by Stefan Stambolov. Stambolov was born near Tûrnovo in 1854 and had won a scholarship to a seminary in Russia. There, however, he had become involved with the narodniks and had been expelled. He had taken an active part in the 1876 rising and in the attempted Kresna-Razlog revolt in 1878. After liberation he was elected to the sûbranie, although technically he was too young. Despite this he was made chairman or speaker of the assembly in which position he had established a reputation for toughness and efficiency. These qualities he showed again in 1885. He told Alexander that if he did not go to Plovdiv and accept the union he would be totally discredited and might as well return to Germany. Alexander went to Plovdiv. At the same time he ordered the Bulgarian army south to garrison the border with the Ottoman empire in case the sultan should try to move his army into Eastern Rumelia.

Plate 5.3 A group described by the contemporary caption as a Volunteer Detachment of Schoolboys, 1885; the figure second from the left is clearly no schoolboy and could be a teacher. Detachments such as these helped to secure the military victory against Serbia in 1885

THE WAR WITH SERBIA AND THE DEPOSITION
OF ALEXANDER BATTENBERG, 1885–1886

The Union of 1885 created a major diplomatic crisis. The Russians were furious, seeing Alexander's conduct, in the light of his recent assurances, as duplicity. In retaliation the tsar ordered all Russian officers and military advisors to leave Bulgaria; the Bulgarian army was left with no officer above the rank of captain. The dangers for Bulgaria were obvious and were made greater by Greek and Serbian reactions. Both states demanded territorial compensations if Bulgaria were to be allowed to increase in size. The Greeks were contained but the Serbs were not. Prince Milan declared war on Bulgaria on 13 November and moved his troops towards and across Bulgaria's unguarded north-western border. The Bulgarian forces were now required to race from one end of their country to the other; they had no senior officers to organise them, few railways to transport them, and no organised commissariat to feed them or their animals. Despite this the transfer was accomplished mostly on foot and on horseback, Bulgarian troops and Rumelian militiamen being fed *en route* by local inhabitants. In mid-November they faced the Serbs at Slivnitsa on the road to Sofia and in a two-day battle put the Serbs to flight. So complete was the rout that had not Austria-Hungary intervened diplomatically the Bulgarian army would have entered Belgrade.

The battle of Slivnitsa was a remarkable achievement for an untested army shorn of its senior officers. It was equally an achievement of the nation as a whole, and it is worth recalling that the highest incidence of medals for gallantry was amongst Muslim troops. More than any other event the battle of Slivnitsa welded the Bulgarians north and south of the Balkan mountains into one nation.

The diplomatic settlement of the union crisis was effected in the treaty of Bucharest of April 1886. It was a distinct disappointment for the Bulgarians. It stated that the governor-general of Rumelia should henceforth be the prince of Bulgaria, but it recognised no more than the personal union of these two offices, and the governor-general of Rumelia was still required to seek reapproval every five years from the sultan and the powers; nor was any mention made in the text of Prince Alexander. The Russians were leaving the door open for his removal.

Alexander did little to help his own cause. He placed no check on the insensitive treatment of Eastern Rumelia by officials in Sofia. This naturally caused resentment, particularly in Plovdiv which, even in 1885, was a larger and more sophisticated city than Sofia. Even worse, Alexander frittered away the support the war had given him in the army. A large number of the Russian trained officers had always been suspicious of Alexander's German origins and his attempts, most of them futile, to subject the army to German methods of training and organisation. After 1885 Alexander committed the fatal error of promoting only those whom he thought politically reliable, even though this meant discrimination against some of the heroes of the recent war.

The prince could ill afford to alienate so powerful a group. By the spring of 1886 he was being criticised in public meetings for the meagre rewards offered by the treaty of Bucharest and for the deterioration in relations with Russia. In May a new sûbranie was elected in which many of these criticisms were energetically voiced. Even more important in the new assembly was the reappearance of the Rusé–Varna railway question. The recent upheavals had delayed consideration of this issue and in the interim the British shareholders had raised the asking price. When Karavelov, who was still prime minister, announced that he was now willing to pay a sum much higher than that which he had denounced as exorbitant in 1884, there was pandemonium in the assembly.

The Russians watched all this with relish. Their agents had for some months let it be known that they would not be opposed to the removal of the prince. In August 1886 a group of army officers acted and deposed Alexander, who fled across the Danube. Stambolov, however, was not prepared to tolerate such intervention by the military and their Russian backers. He rallied loyal garrisons, seized Sofia, and induced Alexander to return to Bulgaria. He did not stay long. He was not willing to hold office in the face of Russian hostility and he therefore telegraphed to St Petersburg asking for Alexander III's endorsement of his return to Bulgaria. This the tsar refused. He could not forgo the chance to be rid of Battenberg at the latter's own suggestion. The prince had sacrificed himself. On 7 September 1886 he left Bulgaria for the last time. He died in 1893 aged only thirty-six, and was buried in Sofia.

THE REGENCY AND THE ELECTION OF PRINCE FERDINAND, 1886–1887

After Alexander had left Bulgaria the country was governed by a regency of Karavelov, Stambolov and Stambolov's brother-in-law, Mutkurov, who had done much to rally loyal troops in August. A government was formed under Vasil Radoslavov, a young liberal who had no russophile inclinations. The strongest force in the land was Stambolov.

Stambolov's priority was to find a new prince. The first step towards this goal was to call a Grand National Assembly. There were immediately problems with the Russians. The tsar decided to send a special advisor to Bulgaria, appointing General Nikolai Kaulbars, brother of the former minister of war, to the post. Kaulbars demanded the release of those imprisoned for their part in the coup of August, the lifting of the state of siege Stambolov had declared, and the cancelling of the elections for the GNA. The elections could not be valid, Kaulbars insisted, because they were called by the regency which itself had not come to office through due constitutional process. Kaulbars carried his message around the country in a rather shambolic attempt to discredit Stambolov and the regents. There were more sinister threats. In October, Kaulbars talked of Russian warships being sent to Varna to protect Russian subjects, and this was widely but incorrectly seen as opening the way to a military coup which would depose Stambolov. The latter made a number of concessions, releasing most of those imprisoned and lifting the state of siege, but he would not give way over the elections to the GNA which took place in September.

The convening of the GNA did not bring about any immediate improvement. For Kaulbars the fact that the assembly had met was a severe rebuff and in November he left Bulgaria, citing as his justification an alleged insult to a Russian consular official in Plovdiv. Relations between Bulgaria and its liberating power were completely severed and were not to be restored for almost a decade.

If the convocation of the GNA had been a defeat for Kaulbars it was hardly an immediate victory for Stambolov because it made no progress towards the election of another prince; in fact, most delegates would have reappointed Alexander Battenberg had that option been open to them. To make matters worse there was an almost constant threat of subversion by Russia or its supporters. In 1887 a Russian adventurer, Nabokov, made a second incursion into Bulgaria with the hope of raising a revolt; as on the first occasion he had no success and was soon captured, only to be released because, as a Russian subject, he enjoyed protection under the Capitulations. He was to return for a third pathetic attempt at the end of 1887 but this time the Bulgarian forces of law and order made sure that he was killed rather than captured.

In March of the same year a much more serious threat to Bulgarian stability had been discovered. Dissident officers seized the garrison in Silistra and those in Varna and Rusé soon joined them;

Plate 5.4 A contemporary woodcut showing Prince
Alexander's forced abdication in 1886

the rebels also had support in the country's largest military base,
that in Shumen. The plot was suppressed but only with great
brutality. Eight of the leaders were shot and in disaffected regiments
one in twenty of the complement were chosen at random to be
executed by their comrades. Another victim of the Silistra affair was
Karavelov who was clapped in jail without any hard evidence that
he had been involved in the conspiracy.

Stambolov's ruthlessness had understandable causes. He needed
to attract a prince to Bulgaria but this could hardly be done unless
it could be shown that he could guarantee that prince internal order
and security. The GNA had nominated a three-man delegation to
tour Europe in search of a new prince and any sign of internal
instability would make their task much more difficult. Nor had
Stambolov or the delegation been helped by the fact that shortly
before the latter's appointment Karavelov had left the regency,
having come to the conclusion that the crisis could be overcome
only by accepting whatever terms Russia chose to dictate.

It was not until mid-summer of 1887 that Stambolov or the delegation had any reason for celebration. It then became known that Prince Ferdinand of Saxe-Coburg-Gotha was considering taking the Bulgarian throne. His main concern was over the attitude of Russia. Adequate assurances were given on this account, another GNA was convened in July to elect him, and on 26 August he arrived in Bulgaria. The tsar, however, refused to recognise him as the lawfully elected prince and the other powers, not wishing to endanger their relations with Russia over a state as small as Bulgaria, followed suit.

THE *STAMBOLOVSHTINA*,* 1887–1894

Ferdinand was to stay in Bulgaria for thirty-one years. That he survived his first three years there was largely due to the man who had brought him to the country: Stambolov. Ferdinand immediately appointed Stambolov as prime minister, Stambolov having in the meantime formed his own National Liberal Party on which he could rely for support in parliament. But despite the assurances given to Ferdinand, Russian opposition to him continued, and there were strong fears that Russian agents, particularly after the failure of Nabokov's third and fatal incursion, might sponsor conspiracies by Bulgarian politicians in exile. Foremost amongst these was Tsankov who had taken refuge in Constantinople and Russia before moving to Belgrade. His move to the Serbian capital had been made possible by political changes in Serbia which brought a pro-Russian monarch to the throne and gave the Russians, for the first time in years, a secure base in the Balkans. From Belgrade Tsankov could easily intrigue in his homeland.

There was little Stambolov or Ferdinand could do. They expanded the army, nearly doubling its size, in the hope that this would give them more protection and would cauterise discontent amongst the officer corps by enhancing promotion prospects. Ferdinand also made empty and rather foolish boasts about raising Macedonia to a man if the Porte did not reform the administration

---

* In Bulgarian the suffix *shtina* attached to a personal noun means the times, attitudes, atmosphere and events associated with that person.

Plate 5.5 Stefan Stambolov. A young revolutionary in
1876–1878, he served as speaker of the sûbranie in the early
1880s. After the deposition of Alexander Battenberg he
became the strong man of Bulgaria who resisted Russian
intrigues and secured Prince Ferdinand upon the Bulgarian
throne

there in accordance with article 23 of the treaty of Berlin. The first crumb of comfort for Ferdinand and his prime minister came from Britain which at the end of 1888 agreed to lend Bulgaria 46.7 million francs. The loan was to enable the Bulgarians to purchase the Rusé–Varna railway and therefore did not bring real economic benefit to Bulgaria, but it broke the financial ice and other more substantial loans from German and Austrian banks soon followed. At much the same time as agreeing to the loan the British began tariff negotiations with Bulgaria, an agreement being signed in January 1889. In a few months similar agreements were concluded with Germany, Austria, France, Italy, Switzerland and Belgium. Once again the agreements were of little intrinsic economic value to Sofia but a number of European states had dealt with Bulgaria as if it were a fully independent and recognised state.

The turning point for Ferdinand and Stambolov came in 1890. The year began badly. In 1889 another military conspiracy was hatched, this time around the central figure of Major Kosta Panitsa, a talented but flamboyant young officer of Macedonian origin and a hero of the 1885 war. Panitsa had been a close friend of Alexander Battenberg, the prince being godfather to Panitsa's son. Panitsa had no great affection for Stambolov and, as a Battenbergist, none at all for Ferdinand. More importantly, however, Panitsa had by 1889 come to the conclusion that Bulgaria had no hope of advancing its cause in Macedonia as long as it remained estranged from Russia. He therefore resolved to assassinate the prince; the deed was to be done at a court ball on 2 February 1890. Panitsa was far too indiscreet a character to make an effective conspirator. The police were soon informed of the plot, much of their information coming from Panitsa's own valet. The day before the ball all leading conspirators were arrested. Once again retribution was fierce. After due investigation and legal process Panitsa was tied to a tree and shot by a firing squad drawn from Macedonians amongst his own regiment. The government's victory, however, was hedged with anxiety because the investigations into the plot revealed that it had been far more widespread and popular than Stambolov and his associates had originally thought.

Despite this Stambolov used the plot to great effect. In doing so he concentrated on the Macedonian aspects of the conspiracy's origin and strength. If he could do something to advance the Bulgarian cause in Macedonia he would greatly weaken his opponents and greatly bolster his own and Ferdinand's position. He therefore insisted in Constantinople that Ferdinand was in danger from further conspiracies which were likely to use the Macedonian issue as one of their chief recruiting arguments. Should one of those conspiracies succeed, its architects would have to pay off its supporters by demanding concessions in Macedonia. This could only destabilise the Balkans and weaken the Ottoman empire. It would be much better, said Stambolov, if the Porte voluntarily granted concessions to the Bulgarians in Macedonia; this would increase Ferdinand's internal standing and thereby lessen the dangers of an anti-Ottoman faction seizing power in Sofia. The argument worked. In the summer of 1890 it was announced that the Porte intended to issue decrees promising the exarchate the three major Macedonian bishoprics of Skopje, Ohrid and Bitolya. The exarchate was also to be allowed to publish a newspaper in the Ottoman capital, and to establish direct relations with the Bulgarian communities of the Adrianople province.

These were the most important concessions received by the exarchate since 1872 and they greatly increased Stambolov's and Ferdinand's popularity. Since 1885 and the union with Rumelia the Porte had tended to favour the Greek and Serbian churches in Macedonia at the expense of the exarchate with the result that a number of dioceses which had originally voted to join the Bulgarian church were still under patriarchist control and many of their parishes were without priests. Matters had been made worse by a breach between the church in Bulgaria and the government, a breach which led the government in Sofia to suspend the subsidies it had previously given to the exarchate.

Stambolov had never been on good terms with the higher clergy who feared his radicalism; they had good reason to do so because in 1886 he prevented a meeting of the holy synod and adjusted clerical salaries – downwards. By the time Ferdinand arrived in Sofia matters had worsened. Ferdinand made few attempts to underplay his catholicism; his mother, who came with him and exercised great influence over him, made fewer. The Bulgarian clergy refused to pray for him in their services and it was for this that Stambolov suspended the annual payments from the Bulgarian government to the exarchate. The low point in church–state relations came in January 1889 when Stambolov closed a meeting of the holy synod which had produced a series of complaints against the prince. Gendarmes were used to escort the bishops back to their sees.

The concessions of 1890 in Macedonia transformed the situation. The church agreed that prayers for Ferdinand should now be included in the liturgy in Bulgaria, and a synod in November 1890 settled nearly all outstanding issues between church and state; Ferdinand even felt able to invite four leading bishops to his palace, and, equally surprisingly, they accepted. Meanwhile the government had agreed to provide 3 million leva a year for exarchist schools in Macedonia.

Stambolov's victory was consolidated in general elections held later in 1890. A certain amount of influence was used at the polls but Stambolov would have achieved his victory without it. Even the seemingly irreconcilable tsankovists now recognised that the new regime must be accepted; henceforth their criticism was directed not at its existence but at its methods of governing.

These had of necessity been harsh but any hopes that they might be relaxed were dashed by continuing violence on the part of the regime's enemies. In March 1891 the minister of finance was gunned down in mistake for Stambolov and a little under a year later the Bulgarian representative in Constantinople was murdered. Not even the secret police network, greatly expanded after the Panitsa plot, could prevent such outrages.

Stambolov believed that Ferdinand might be safer if he were married and produced an heir; then, even though an assassin might remove the prince, the Russians would not be in a position to nominate his successor. A suitable bride was found in Princess Marie-Louise of Bourbon Parma who, however, would consent to marry Ferdinand only if any children of the union were brought up as Roman Catholics. This would contravene the article of the constitution which demanded that all but the first prince belong to the Orthodox church, an article which according to some commentators Ferdinand had already breached. In February 1893 Stambolov convened a Grand National Assembly and secured the changes in the constitution necessary to satisfy Princess Marie-Louise's conditions, though he did so only at the cost of renewed and serious disagreement with the church hierarchy.

Stambolov had rightly believed that popular enthusiasm for the marriage would outweigh displeasure at the changes in the constitution, and his belief was reinforced by the rejoicing which followed the birth of a son, Boris, nine months after the royal marriage.

By now Stambolov's own position was weakening. He had in effect fulfilled his function: he had brought Ferdinand to Bulgaria and established him on his throne. Despite these successes he was unable to go further and achieve the international recognition for which the prince now craved. That no movement in the Russian position followed the defeat of Panitsa and the granting of the Macedonian bishoprics in 1890 convinced Ferdinand that Stambolov would never secure recognition; this being so Stambolov had to be replaced, and by 1893 the prince was moving towards open conflict with his prime minister. In that year a new opposition group, soon to be known as the Nationalist Party, was formed of dissident liberals, some conservatives, and unionists from southern Bulgaria; they were led by Konstantin Stoilov, a former secretary of Alexander Battenberg. The new opposition exploited the mounting social unrest caused by the decline in world agricultural prices, a danger which the Stambolov regime found difficult to comprehend or contain; the Greek minority was offended by educational laws which forced all Christian, but not Muslim, children to receive their primary education in Bulgarian; and most important of all in 1894, Ferdinand secured the appointment of his own nominee to the war ministry. That nominee was also chief of the general staff and by his appointment Ferdinand secured greater control over the military in Bulgaria than anyone had yet enjoyed.

Shortly after this Stambolov was accused of having an affair with the wife of a ministerial colleague, something which he vehemently denied. It was no use. In May, Stambolov was engineered into a position in which he had to resign. A year later he was brutally murdered in the streets of Sofia.

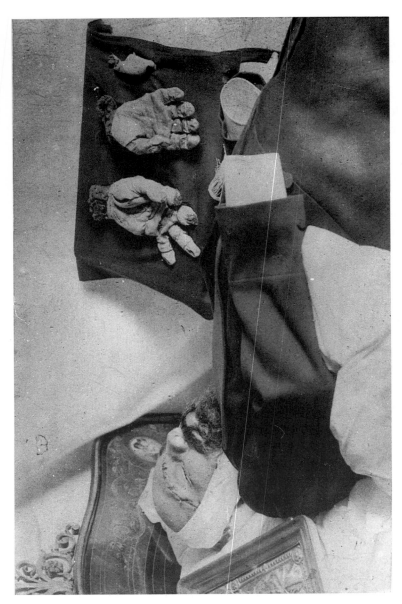

Plate 5.6 Stambolov was brutally attacked in the streets of Sofia in 1895, dying a few days later. His assailants severed his hands

THE RECOGNITION OF PRINCE FERDINAND

The new prime minister was Stoilov. He began his period in office by relaxing some of the strict controls which Stambolov had imposed. Amongst those who benefited from this policy were the Macedonians in Bulgaria who were now able once more to equip bands for operation in the Ottoman empire, much to the displeasure of the Russians. This displeasure Stoilov could ill afford. If it were not his immediate objective, Stoilov had to achieve some progress towards recognition; he had to succeed where Stambolov had failed. Movement towards this goal was made much easier by two external events. First, in Asiatic Turkey a series of massacres of Armenians made some believe that the Ottoman empire had entered its final death throes. Second, Tsar Alexander III died in November 1894. His successor, Nicholas II, was more pliable and both Russian and Bulgarian statesmen realised that the two states must cooperate if they were to maximise their gains from any collapse of the Ottoman empire. In 1895 the first sign of a thaw in Russian attitudes appeared when a sûbranie delegation was given permission to visit Russia to lay a wreath on the grave of Alexander III. From this visit it became clear that in return for the recognition of Ferdinand the Russians would make one major demand: that Prince Boris be received into the Orthodox faith.

This faced the Bulgarian regime with a difficult choice. Conversion would be immensely popular amongst the Bulgarian people as a whole, as would reconciliation with the Russians who had liberated them: how could a Bulgarian government refuse a price which the people were eager to pay for an item which they all wanted to purchase? And, it was pointed out, the king of Romania had recently agreed to the conversion of his son. The difference was that the king of Romania was a Protestant. He did not have the pope to answer to, nor did he have staunchly Catholic families, his own and his wife's, to contend with. Stoilov wisely left the decision to Ferdinand. Ferdinand's was not a conscience frequently troubled but in this case he felt a genuine dilemma, pulled in one direction by his feelings for his mother and his wife and, no doubt, his own immortal soul, and in the other by the obvious political advantages to be gained from accepting Russia's terms. He decided in favour of the latter. He knew that recognition and reconciliation with Russia would bring greater internal cohesion. He knew too that with the situation in the Ottoman empire deteriorating the Macedonian question was bound to become more acute, and should it become critical and his freedom of action be restricted because he had not mended his fences with Russia, he would have failed his adopted nation and would personally be in grave danger of deposition or worse. On 3 February 1896 it was announced that Prince Boris would receive an Orthodox baptism on 14 February; Tsar Nicholas II, though he would not attend in person, would stand as godfather. Two weeks later, on the anniversary of the signing of the peace of San Stefano, the sultan, with Russian backing, recognised Ferdinand as prince of Bulgaria and governor-general of Eastern Rumelia. Within a few days all the great powers, Russia included, had done likewise.

ETHNIC AND SOCIAL CHANGE AFTER
THE LIBERATION

Before the outbreak of the April Uprising about a third of the population of what was to become Bulgaria and Eastern Rumelia were ethnic Turks, almost all of whom were Muslim. The atrocities of 1876 naturally created amongst the Christian Bulgarians an urge to take revenge. This was to some extent gratified during and immediately after the war of 1877–8. A number of Muslims fled during the conflict and there was some destruction of Muslim buildings and cultural centres; a large library of old Turkish books was destroyed when a mosque in Tûrnovo was burned in 1877, and Sofia, which one Russian soldier had described as 'a forest of minarets', lost most of its mosques, seven of them in one night in December 1878 when a thunderstorm masked the noise of the explosions arranged by Russian military engineers. In the country-side a number of Turkish villages were burned and there were many instances of ethnic Turks being driven from land which was coveted by local Bulgarians.

Such events are the depressing feature of wars in the Balkans and elsewhere, but they were not repeated in peacetime Bulgaria. The treaty of Berlin insisted upon freedom of worship for all faiths and outlawed discrimination on the basis of religion. It also guaranteed the property rights of Muslims who chose to reside outside the principality whilst retaining land within it.

After 1878 Bulgaria and Eastern Rumelia abided by the letter of these international laws. But no amount of legislation could prevent Muslim emigration from both areas. There was some cultural pressure on Muslims. A decree of the Russian Provisional Administration, for example, had declared the rice-paddies of the Maritsa valley a health hazard because they were breeding grounds for malaria-carrying mosquitoes. This was no doubt true but Muslims could not help but see the decree as an attempt to make more difficult the growing of their staple food.

More important were laws regulating land tenures and taxation. Regulations affecting land unworked for three years, a period later extended, meant that absentee Turks forfeited their property, whilst in Eastern Rumelia in 1882 the imposition of tax on land owned rather than on the produce it yielded again hit many Muslim landowners; they were accustomed to leave part of their land fallow and if taxes were levied only on produce this had no financial penalty which it obviously did have when a tax based on ownership increased the amount to be paid without any compensating increase in the amount earned. Many of the Muslims left simply because they could not adjust psychologically to living in a Christian state and society. They did not comprehend the way in which women appeared unmasked in public or, even worse, mingled in society at mixed dinner parties, theatrical excursions, balls or picnics. Many Muslims resented the fact that a number of mosques were taken from them. Some of these were reverting to Christian places of worship, but others were given over to secular usage; some became storehouses, one a printing-house, and one even a prison. Even more distasteful to many Muslim families was conscription into a Christian army. Muslim soldiers did not have to wear the cross on their uniforms but they did have to obey Christian officers, observe Christian festivals, and in many cases eat Christian food. In later years exemption from military service for Muslims was made easier but conscription was in force for the first ten years after 1878, a time of maximum disorientation and demoralisation for the Turkish and Muslim population. This makes the loyalty and courage of the Muslims during the war of 1885 all the more remarkable.

Many Muslims, however, had not stayed long enough in Bulgaria to be involved in that war. There was a steady stream of emigration and by 1900 the Turkish element, as measured by mother-tongue, had declined from about 33 per cent in 1875 to 14 per cent of the total population. In absolute terms the Turks were 728,000 in 1880/4 (the figures being for the principality in 1880 and Rumelia in 1884) but only 540,000 in 1900. In the same years the number of Greeks increased from 53,000 to 71,000.

The liberation produced great economic and social as well as ethnic change, and this affected all communities. The majority of the population remained rural and for many villages the departure of Muslims and the relaxation or non-observance of laws forbidding the ploughing up of village communal land or forests meant that there was no land shortage in Bulgaria and an increasing population could be absorbed without any significant increase in agricultural productivity. This perpetuated the small self-sufficient peasant holding which had characterised most of the Bulgarian lands before liberation.

The Bulgarian peasant farmer continued to feed himself and his family but the liberation did bring him nearer the European market and European manners. In the early 1880s most inhabitants of Sofia still had a cow or two grazing on nearby meadows under the care of the cowherd whom most city districts employed; they had all but disappeared by the turn of the century. At liberation the only form of street cleaning in the new capital were the packs of wild dogs which roamed the city and which killed three people in 1882. The dogs were put to the sword in 1884 and by the turn of the century Sofia had modern amenities such as municipal transport and abundant fresh water piped in from the nearby mountains.

Other towns did not fare so well. The traditional textile producing centres along the foothills of the Balkan mountains withered when exposed to greater competition. In Sopot in 1883 women burned bales of imported cloth and attacked the home of the importer. The traditional, workshop-based producers, organised into their old-fashioned and protectionist guilds, could not survive. In 1880 there had been seventy lace-making workshops in and near Gabrovo; in 1900 there were twenty-three, and Gabrovo had survived the post-liberation whirlwind better than most areas.

Cheap, high-quality imports from Europe were one cause for the decline in traditional manufacturing. Another was the loss of traditional purchasers such as the Ottoman army; Samokov had supplied cloth for two army corps and had had a flourishing metal-working industry, but by 1900 it had declined from being a major Balkan city to a small and depressed provincial town. Some traditional industries were crippled because the new political frontiers separated them from sources of raw materials or from established markets. Vidin declined because its natural hinterland was in that part of the north-west of the Bulgarian lands assigned by the treaty of Berlin to Serbia. Kotel, which had grown rich by fattening sheep and goats in the Dobrudja and then driving them to market in Adrianople and Constantinople, now found its grazing grounds cut off by the new Bulgarian–Romanian border, and its markets beyond the Bulgarian–Rumelian and then the Bulgarian–Ottoman frontiers.

Changes in social habits and customs also weakened traditional industries. Many of these new habits were the result of conscription which gave many of the younger generation of peasants their first experience of urban life. And the changes were more pronounced in the Bulgarian than in the Turkish or pomak communities. That leather-making workshops survived in a healthy state only in Sliven and Haskovo was because there were sizable Turkish populations in those areas and they continued to wear the traditional footwear and the broad leather belts which Bulgarians were discarding as old-fashioned. The casting off of the belt damaged the knife-making industry. This was already suffering because it was facing competition from small, cheaper Austrian and German products, because it had been excluded by new tariffs from its established markets in Romania and the Ottoman empire, and because the suppression of brigandage in the 1880s lessened the need to carry a knife for self-protection; now the adoption of western-style belts meant that anyone attempting to carry the old-style large knife would not be able to keep his trousers in a socially acceptable position. The processors and workers of precious metals had relied chiefly on local wealthy Turks for their purchasers; when the latter departed the industry was ruined. The same fate befell the slipper-makers; Christian Bulgarians were not likely to adopt Muslim footwear. Western porcelain became popular and, having the additional advantage of being cheap, soon replaced, in the towns at least, the copper tableware which most Bulgarians had previously used. Beds too became more modish, very much to the cost of the craftshops which for generations had produced the carpets and cushions on which the Bulgarians had until then been content to sleep.

Some manufacturers were able to adapt to changed conditions. Some aped western styles in products such as clothes or furniture, whilst a few even moved over to factory production, importing German or British machinery in order to do so; between 1888 and 1893 seven new textile mills and ten new leather works were opened in Gabrovo, three of them joint stock companies. Another saviour for some depressed areas was to begin producing goods to cater for the new tastes. When, during the war of 1885, a German revisited the Bulgaria he had last seen in 1878 he rejoiced to find that now beer was available; by the mid-1890s there were twenty-nine breweries in the country and commercial distilling was also being developed.

In a country as backward and as poor as Bulgaria industrial advances could not come without government help. Under the early liberal administrations there had been attempts, few of them successful, to make civil servants wear clothes made of local cloth, and the government had drawn up a strategic plan for the development of the railway network. This developed only slowly; in the winter of 1888 Stambolov found that the quickest way to get from Tûrnovo to Plovdiv was to take a ship from Varna to Constantinople. By the mid-1890s the trunk line had been completed, Yambol had been linked to Burgas, and the mines at Pernik joined to Sofia, but there was still no line across the Balkan mountains and the roads remained in a woeful state. Any improvement in either form of transport would require massive investment. There were no internal sources of capital; there was no financial infrastructure and the few wealthy merchant concerns were found in a limited number of urban centres; if any peasant made money he was less likely to invest it in productive concerns than to set himself up as a moneylender because here the largest profits were to be made. And external sources of credit would be almost as meagre as long as Bulgaria remained an international outcast.

6

Ferdinand's personal rule,
1896–1918

Because the early liberal governments had been preoccupied with constitutional issues and Stambolov's first concern always had to be internal security, it was not really until the Stoilov administration came to power that a systematic attempt to develop the Bulgarian economy could be made. Stoilov, who had once declared that he wished to make Bulgaria 'the Belgium of the Balkans', was eager for the task. In 1894 his government passed the encouragement of industry bill. Industries which were included within one of nine defined categories and which had capital of 25,000 leva and at least 20 employees were to receive state encouragement; the chief beneficiaries were mining and metallurgy, textiles and the construction industry. State encouragement was to take the form of free grants of land for factory building together with financial help for the construction of any necessary road or rail links, preferential rates on the state railways for finished products, free use of state or local authority quarries and water power, tax advantages, preference in the awarding of state contracts even if the native products were more expensive than imported ones, and a monopoly in supplying certain items within specified geographic limits. Further acts in 1905 and 1909 both widened the scope of industries eligible for encouragement and lowered the qualifications necessary to receive it.

If home industries were to be stimulated, however, they would need protection from cheap western imports. Any substantial alteration in the Bulgarian tariff regime had been impossible whilst Ferdinand was unrecognised but in 1896 Stoilov was able to raise the general import duty from 8 to 14 per cent; in 1906 it rose to almost 25 per cent. There were a number of exceptions, particularly if the imported items were ones which would help domestic industrial growth, but the only goods allowed in completely duty free were equipment for making silk, coke-fired samovars, and, somewhat mysteriously, church bells.

Stoilov also helped to stimulate commerce. In 1894 the government began work on developing the harbours at Varna and Burgas, work which was completed in 1903 and 1906 respectively. Regulations which had frustrated the development of local banking had already been relaxed by Stambolov in 1893, and in the following year Stoilov hoped further to stimulate local commercial activity by the creation of chambers of commerce. In 1897 commercial law was codified.

Stoilov's efforts to modernise the Bulgarian economy enjoyed some success. In 1894 there were 72 factories with 3,027 workers in encouraged industries, in 1911 there were 345 factories employing 15,886 workers, and between 1904 and 1911 the value of production in this sector trebled. On the other hand, the number of workers per factory changed very little and only just before the first world war did it begin to move ahead of the 1894 figure; this showed the tenacity of the small unit of production. Nor was there any significant change in the structure of industry. Food, drink and textiles completely dominated Bulgarian factory production, and even if this were also the case in all other Balkan countries, it indicated that progress towards a modern industrial economy was quantitative rather than qualitative. Railway building also continued with the total track rising from 220 kilometres in 1880 to 1,566 kilometres in 1900 and 2,109 kilometres in 1912, by which time the basic network as outlined in Karavelov's legislation of 1884 had been completed. Trade too increased and by 1911, with a total value of 384 million leva, it was 60 per cent above the level of the early 1890s. At the same time government expenditure had risen nine-fold from 20 million leva in 1880 to 181 million in 1911. Internal sources could not support such expenditure and the shortfall was covered by foreign loans, the sums borrowed rising by 70 per cent in the decade after 1900. Yet at 149.25 leva Bulgaria's per capita debt was lower than any of its neighbours.

THE ESTABLISHMENT OF FERDINAND'S PERSONAL RULE

The recognition of Prince Ferdinand in 1896 was a turning point in Bulgarian history. The constitutional preoccupations of the first years of statehood and the insecurity caused by non-recognition could now be set aside. Order and stability, it seemed, had been achieved and Bulgaria could now progress to economic restructuring and the pursuit of its foreign policy objectives. But the stability of the late 1890s was apparent rather than real and had been bought at considerable cost.

Between 1879 and 1884 the executive and the legislature had competed for dominance. The executive had made a major advance with the coup of 1881 but had failed to capitalise on its advantages. Alexander Battenberg did not use to the full the powers he had secured for himself, not least because he was restrained by fear of Russian disapproval. In 1883 and 1884 the legislature seemed to recapture the high constitutional ground and with the formation of the Karavelov government the liberals appeared to be in a commanding position. But the liberals had been damaged in the struggle of the previous five years and their weaknesses began to appear at their moment of victory with the split between Karavelov and Tsankov.

In subsequent years the executive rapidly regained the ground it had lost. The events of 1886 had shown that the army had to be kept under control if it were not to become the dominant factor in Bulgarian political life. And it was much easier for the executive than the legislature to exercise this control.

After the departure of Alexander Battenberg only the inveterate russophiles would contest the need to increase executive power. Stambolov did not create but he greatly elaborated on the existing police and informer networks and once boasted that a bee could not cross the coast at Varna without his knowing about it.

Plate 6.1   Ferdinand of Saxe-Coburg-Gotha, prince of
Bulgaria, 1887–1908, King of the Bulgarians, 1908–1918

By the mid-1890s it was established practice for an incoming
government to fill administrative posts with its own supporters.
This trafficking in political office, which was by no means confined
to Bulgaria, was known in Bulgarian as *partisanstvo*. But by the
mid-1890s there were, for the first time, more young men qualified

for civil service posts than there were jobs available for them. This unemployed intelligentsia tended to drift towards opposition groups which promised them jobs when that group was included in government. Parties thus became less and less organisations dedicated to the pursuit of political principles than mechanisms for satisfying the lust for office.

This aspect of *partisanstvo* also encouraged the splintering of parties: if there were ten rather than three opposition parties there were ten rather than three groups offering the prospect of high office. Whereas in the 1880s the liberals had split on constitutional issues and in 1886 Stambolov had formed his National Liberal Party to distinguish himself from the pro-Russian liberal groups, in later years splits in all parties were to occur over trivial issues or over personalities. And the more parties there were the easier it was for the executive to play one off against the others.

The executive had also learned well the art of electoral management which had been practised since liberation. Turnout was generally low in Bulgarian elections and control could easily be exercised at the polling station or in the processing of the results. Elections by the turn of the century were seldom exercises to measure public opinion and to tailor a government's composition to it; they were more often carried out simply to provide a newly appointed cabinet with a dependable majority in the assembly. And by 1900 it was the prince who determined when the composition of a government should be changed and an election held.

Ferdinand had established control over the ministry of war in 1893 and because he had always insisted he should supervise foreign policy he had equal control over the ministry for foreign affairs. When he considered it time to change government he simply had to instruct one or both of these dependent ministers to resign and the incumbent cabinet would be paralysed and forced out of office.

In 1881 Alexander had engineered a coup and given himself powers he failed to use. Ferdinand simply operated the existing system to construct his personal rule. But that rule did not go unchallenged.

SOCIAL CRISIS AND THE EMERGENCE OF THE AGRARIAN MOVEMENT, 1895–1908

After the union of Bulgaria and Eastern Rumelia in 1885 the railways in the latter country remained under the ownership of the Oriental Railway Company (ORC) rather than being incorporated into the BDZh. The main route involved was the Rumelian section of the Vienna–Constantinople trunk line. This became an increasingly irksome factor because the ORC's tariffs were twice as high as those of the BDZh, thus seriously disadvantaging the exporters of southern Rumelia when world agricultural prices were falling disastrously. When the encouragement of industry act was passed the ORC refused to agree to the preferential rates which the BDZh was required to offer encouraged industries; once again southern Bulgarians, this time the industrialists, were greatly discriminated against *vis-à-vis* their northern colleagues. Stoilov was dependent on the votes of southern Bulgarian unionist deputies for his majority in the sŭbranie and he had to act.

He could not, however, nationalise the ORC lines as this was diplomatically too dangerous. Nor could he purchase it. The ORC's chief shareholder was the Deutsche Bank and given the growing interest in Germany in the Berlin to Baghdad railway project there was no prospect of the line being sold. Stoilov had to by-pass the ORC with a parallel line.

The parallel line was a disaster. Work had not been long in progress when it was realised that there would never be enough money to complete it. An attempt to purchase the operating rights on the ORC in Rumelia was frustrated by Germany and the German banks, and by 1899 the government in Sofia had been forced into a humiliating agreement under which it promised to build no line in southern Bulgaria which would compete with the ORC. The latter was also to take over the Yambol–Burgas line, in clear contravention of the December 1884 railway act which had stated that all lines in the principality should be state owned. The ORC's assumption of control over the Yambol–Burgas line showed that the company did not consider southern Bulgaria to be part of the principality; it was another unwelcome reminder of the imperfections of the 1886 treaty of Bucharest and the inadequacies of the personal union which it sanctioned. In return the ORC did promise to grant preferential rates in conformity with the encouragement of industry act.

The embarrassments caused by the parallel line had excited more public anger than any issue except Macedonia. Part of that anger was caused by the fact that the government had been forced to borrow relatively large sums of money on the foreign markets to finance a project which came to nothing. And the loans had to be paid for, despite the fact that the government was already in desperate financial straits. Internal revenues had to be increased. Industry and commerce had recently been marked out as recipients rather than providers of government revenue and therefore the burden was to fall upon the land. In November 1899 the government announced that for the years 1900–4 the land tax, which had been introduced in 1894 as part of Stoilov's modernising programme, would be replaced by a tithe in kind.

This infuriated the peasants. The tax burden on them had almost doubled in the years 1887 to 1897 whilst in the towns, where most of the taxes were spent, the increase had not been as great. Taxation on land had see-sawed between cash and kind and, the peasants suspected with justification, the type levied was that which would yield more revenue for the government; now, just as world wheat prices seemed at last to be moving upwards, the peasant would have less grain to sell. The peasants were in desperate need of cash, many of them having been forced into the hands of the usurer because they could not repay the loans they had taken out to purchase vacant Muslim land. The north-east of the country, with its concentration on grain production, was the most severely hit by the decision to levy the tax in kind, and it was here that the reaction against the new tax regulations was most intense.

There had already been stirrings of new organisations in this area and a number of local activists called a meeting in Pleven in December 1899. From this meeting was to emerge the body which soon became the Bulgarian Agrarian National Union (BANU) which was the most original and important political body to emerge in post-liberation Bulgaria. Its ideology had not been clearly formulated and as yet its leaders would not allow that it was anything more than a pressure group; it was not, said its leaders, a political party and it had no objectives other than to 'raise the intellectual and moral standing of the peasant and to improve agriculture in all its branches'. But it could not be anything but a political phenomenon, and within months Stoilov acknowledged that it was the true representative of the peasant and the strongest political force in the land.

Such a powerful body was bound to come into conflict with the established order. In a series of clashes between agrarian supporters and the police in the spring of 1900 in the Dobrudja villages of Daran Kulak and Trûstenik a number of peasants were killed. A summer of intense agitation followed and when the second congress of the new organisation met in December there was a much sharper political edge to its proceedings.

Stoilov's credibility had been destroyed by the parallel railway fiasco and the agrarian movement. In December 1900 he resigned. In February 1901 one of Bulgaria's few genuinely open elections took place. In the new sûbranie were over twenty agrarians. The established parties still dominated the assembly and a government was formed with Karavelov, the leader of the Democratic Party, as prime minister. His minister for foreign affairs was Stoyan Danev, the leader of the Progressive Liberals (tsankovists) who were the other main party in the new coalition. One of the first acts of the new administration was to abolish the tithe in kind.

Of the twenty-one agrarian deputies elected in 1901 sixteen soon defected to established parties. This strengthened the growing pressure within the movement for a more open commitment to political activity, and in a congress convened in October 1901 this faction had its way; the title of Bulgarian Agrarian National Union was now adopted. In 1908 BANU polled 100,000 votes and took 23 seats, the next largest non-government party having 46,000 votes and 5 seats. The growth in agrarian support had two main causes. At the local level the agrarian movement was becoming increasingly associated with the intelligentsia, primarily teachers, priests and agricultural advisors, and also with the burgeoning cooperative movement which was rescuing the peasant from the clutches of the usurer and therefore gaining great respect in the villages. Second, in 1906 Aleksandûr Stamboliiski was appointed editor of the party newspaper, *Zemedelsko Zname* (Agrarian Standard). He soon became the dominant figure in the movement.

In the party paper Stamboliiski codified agrarian ideas for the first time. The movement's objective was justice for all in a society devoid of extremes and excesses; this applied especially to landed property, and land was to be taken from those who had too much to be given to those who had too little. Stamboliiski believed that human nature had two aspects, the individual and the social, the former requiring private property and the second developing as society became more complex. This rejected the Marxist notion that economic development simplifies social relationships, and Marxism was also rejected when Stamboliiski argued that society was divided not into classes based on the ownership of the means of production, but into estates or occupational categories, the most important of which was the agrarian. There was some anti-urbanism in agrarian ideology, and particular scorn and hostility were directed to those whose labour was unproductive: the bureaucracy, the legal profession, the church hierarchy, the monarchy and the army. Stamboliiski was not overtly republican, that would have invited too much interference from the authorities, but his republicanism was implicit. In foreign affairs he showed little interest in territorial acquisition and looked forward to the solution of Balkan national problems through the creation of a Balkan agrarian federation.

Radical opinion was not confined to the agrarian movement. The Bulgarian Social Democratic Party had been founded in 1892 and in 1894 it won four seats at the general election. In 1897 it secured six seats and in 1901 eight, though five of the latter were immediately disqualified. In 1903 the party split. The extremists, known as 'narrows', rejected cooperation with the established political parties, called for the subjection of the trade unions to party needs, and demanded the confiscation of all private property including that of the peasant. The moderates, or 'broads', were prepared to work with the radical bourgeois parties in the sûbranie, to tolerate some private property, and to open membership of trade unions to all, irrespective of their political affiliations. The party split was replicated in the trade unions and did much to weaken the socialists in the years before the first world war.

The splits in the socialists' ranks meant that they could not take full advantage of the urban discontent which followed the rise in the cost of living in the 1900s. This discontent was registered in a number of strikes, including those by printers and miners in 1905 and by railwaymen in 1906–7, but industrial action secured few positive gains. There was also action on the streets by students. They rioted in 1905 in support of the revolutionaries in Russia, and in January 1907 they joined with striking railwaymen to pelt Ferdinand with snowballs when he opened the new national theatre in Sofia. The university was then closed and all its academic staff sacked.

The most serious outburst of unrest in the 1900s was not social, however, but ethnic. In 1906 the arrival in Bulgaria of Neophytus, the newly appointed patriarchist bishop of Varna, sparked off a series of anti-Greek riots, the worst of them being in Ankhialo (Pomorie). Much of the anger directed at the Greeks had its origins in events in Macedonia.

THE MACEDONIAN CRISIS AND THE DECLARATION OF INDEPENDENCE, 1900–1908

The Macedonian problem was nothing if not complex. By 1900 it was dominated by two factors. The first was the international situation. In 1897, after yet another crisis in Crete, the Ottoman empire and Greece had gone to war, and within a few weeks the Greek army had been smashed in the plains of Thessaly. The war had two main results as far as Macedonia was concerned. The first was that it reversed the opinion which had been gaining ground since the Armenian massacres of 1894 that the Ottoman empire was about to dissolve; a crisis in the Balkans was not, after all, inevitable. The Russians sighed with relief and turned their attention to their internal problems and to the Far East, agreeing with Austria-Hungary that the Balkans should be kept 'on ice'. The second result of the 1897 war was that the Porte now felt that it had little to fear from Greece and, loyal to its traditional practice of dividing its potential opponents, began to favour the patriarchist cause in Macedonia at the expense of the exarchist and Serbian.

The other dominating factor in the Macedonian problem was that two rival Macedonian organisations had appeared. The first had been founded in Macedonia in 1893 and is best known to history by the name it later assumed, the Internal Macedonian Revolutionary Organisation, or IMRO. IMRO's objective was an autonomous Macedonia to be achieved by a mass uprising; some factions in the organisation hoped that an autonomous Macedonia would then become part of a Balkan, socialist federation. The second organisation was the Supreme Committee established in 1894. It also called for an autonomous Macedonia but wanted this to be the prelude to the incorporation of the area into Bulgaria in much the same way that autonomous Rumelia had joined Bulgaria in 1885. The supremacists had no faith in a mass uprising and planned instead to use *cheti* which would produce such disorder that the Porte would have to cede autonomy, probably after intervention by the great powers, much in the way they had after 1876; in 1895 one supremacist band captured the town of Melnik and held it for two days.

The activity of the supremacist bands, which was connived at by Ferdinand and his officials, threatened to melt the ice in the Balkans and therefore angered the Russians. Between 1900 and 1902 the Bulgarian government was in negotiations with St Petersburg for financial help. When Danev, who had become prime minister in January 1902, went to the Russian capital in the following month he was told that such help would be forthcoming only on certain very harsh conditions. The Bulgarians were to put an end to the incursions into Macedonia, and they were to agree to the appointment of a Serb to the critical post of administrator of the Skopje diocese. The Bulgarians had no choice but to accept, even though the latter condition was a huge blow to their cause in northern Macedonia. Danev returned to Sofia and took some measures against the Macedonian activists. They were not enough and in October, on the twenty-fifth anniversary of the battle in the Shipka Pass, the celebrations of which were attended by a number of prominent Russians, a supremacist band crossed into Macedonia and tried to raise a rebellion in Gorna Djumaya, the present-day Blagoevgrad.

Russian and Austro-Hungarian diplomacy now went into action. A reform scheme for Macedonia was drafted and the Russian foreign minister, Count Lamsdorff, appeared in Belgrade and Sofia to demand once more an end to the incursions. This time the Bulgarian government had to bite the bullet. In February 1903 Danev introduced into the sûbranie a bill dissolving all Macedonian organisations and calling for the arrest of their leaders. After two days of intense debate the bill was passed. Shortly thereafter Danev resigned and a new administration was formed by the National Liberal Party, the stambolovists, though the premiership went not to the party leader, Dimitûr Petkov, but to the non-party General Racho Petrov who was a close confidant of Prince Ferdinand.

With the dissolution of the organisations inside Bulgaria the focus of the Macedonian question was entirely on Macedonia itself. In January 1903 the central committee of IMRO, meeting in Salonika, had taken a fateful decision: their long-planned mass uprising would be staged in the coming summer. The central committee had been hustled into this decision. The supremacists had not yet been dissolved and the central committee feared further incursions from their bands would frighten the Ottoman forces into a more advanced state of readiness. The central committee also feared that the reform scheme produced by Austria-Hungary and Russia would be implemented and improve the situation in Macedonia to such an extent that there would be no response to calls for a mass uprising. In April the Ottoman forces were put on their guard by a series of anarchist bomb outrages, and in May IMRO suffered a devastating blow when it lost its most able leader, Gotse Delchev, in a chance encounter with a group of Ottoman soldiers.

Despite these setbacks the rising took place as planned on 15 August, St Elijah's Day, or Ilinden in Slavonic. A few days later, on the Feast of the Transfiguration, Preobrazhenie, a rising was staged in the Adrianople province. The Ilinden–Preobrazhenie rising attracted more support than previous attempts to incite the Christians of Ottoman Europe and administrative centres were established at Krushevo in Macedonia and Strandja in eastern Thrace. But the rebels could not survive without foreign help. And that help could only come from Bulgaria because IMRO was seen as essentially pro-Bulgarian by the Serbs and Greeks. But Bulgaria dared not act alone. To do so would alarm the other Balkan states and would enrage Russia and Austria-Hungary, besides which, after the 1897 war no Balkan state was anxious to face the Ottoman armies alone. The rising therefore proceeded to its inevitable, grim conclusion. The embryonic administrations of Krushevo and Strandja were suppressed, and the rebellion's supporters savagely punished. Many exarchist villages were destroyed, their crops burned, their cattle seized, and their teachers and priests packed off to exile in Asia Minor. Thousands of weary refugees trudged into Bulgaria, some of them going on from there to the New World; those who had remained in Macedonia could often find shelter and sustenance only from patriarchist or Serbian organisations. It was a blow from which the exarchist cause in Macedonia never fully recovered.

The stambolovist government made the best of this dismal situation by the traditional stambolovist means of controlling the Macedonians at home and seeking concessions from the Porte abroad. In a treaty signed in March 1904 the Bulgarians promised to take further steps to control the Macedonian organisations, and the Ottoman government granted an amnesty to most of those arrested after the uprising; the Bulgarians were also to be allowed to appoint commercial agents in important Macedonian towns.

In the same month Petrov's cabinet also concluded an agreement with Serbia. It was basically a military convention aimed at combating any external interference in Macedonia. It was not of lasting importance because the basic problem was not external interference but clashes between Bulgarian, Serbian and Greek supporters inside Macedonia. This was in part because the Austro-Russian reform scheme called for the redrawing of Macedonian administrative boundaries to produce units of greater ethnic homogeneity. The Greek, Bulgarian and Serbian factions interpreted this as an invitation to use ethnic cleansing to create zones of influence.

It was anger at the activity of Greek bands which did much to fuel the anti-Greek outbursts of 1906 in Bulgaria but in other respects the importance of the Macedonian question in Bulgarian politics subsided. Many people were tired of an issue for which they could see no solution. The Macedonian organisations did not help. Within Macedonia they continued to levy taxes on the remaining and impoverished exarchist communities, whilst in exile their leaders fell to unseemly and frequently violent feuding; a series of spectacular assassinations in Sofia in 1906 and 1907 did little to enhance the image of the Macedonian organisations. Meanwhile the stambolovist government argued that the Macedonian issue would be settled either by international diplomacy or, failing that, by armed action. But it would be the armed action of modern states and armies, not of feuding guerilla units, and this being the case, the most appropriate tactic was to wait patiently and prepare assiduously a modern and effective army.

The stambolovists were allowed to wait only until January 1908. The student riots of 1907 had angered Ferdinand and he replaced General Petrov with the stambolovist party leader Petkov, but the latter was assassinated in March. His successor, Petûr Gudev, did little more than fill his own pockets from the public purse. He was replaced in January 1908 in an operation typical of Ferdinand's personal rule. The stambolovist cabinet was destabilised and then replaced by one headed by Aleksandûr Malinov who had become leader of the Democratic Party when Karavelov died in 1903. After the formation of the new government an election was held to manufacture a comfortable sûbranie majority, the Democratic Party having had only two deputies in the outgoing assembly.

Malinov's Democratic Party had no more taste for this way of proceeding than any other of the parties, and one of his government's most notable legislative achievements was to introduce a graduated shift towards proportional representation under which it would be much more difficult to fix electoral returns. For most of its time in office, however, the Malinov government was preoccupied with external affairs, and in particular with the declaration of full independence in October 1908 and its consequences.

The declaration of independence arose from unexpected causes. In July the Young Turks had seized power in Constantinople and announced that they intended to modernise and unify all Ottoman territories; that included, by their book, the provinces of Eastern Rumelia, or southern Bulgaria, and Bosnia-Hercegovina, the latter having been administered by Austria-Hungary since 1878. The first sign of trouble had been when the Bulgarian minister in

Constantinople had been treated not as the representative of a foreign government but as the governor of an Ottoman province. More serious was a strike by ORC workers in Constantinople which spread to the company's lines in southern Bulgaria. The Bulgarians were enraged that at a time of international tension the railways in half the country could be paralysed by a strike in a foreign state. On 19 September, the anniversary of the union of 1885,* the Bulgarians nationalised ORC property in their country. On 5 October Ferdinand declared full independence. The restrictions of vassaldom had not in recent years been great but they had been much resented. Austria-Hungary annexed Bosnia-Hercegovina on 6 October.

The declaration of independence was not universally popular. The Macedonian lobby resented the fact that it had been issued before union with the lost territory had been secured, whilst some thought there were dangers in Ferdinand's being so closely associated with this measure. The most striking expression of such feelings was seen in 1911 when a Grand National Assembly met in Tûrnovo to register the constitutional changes the declaration had made necessary. When Ferdinand opened the GNA Stamboliiski led fifty-odd agrarians out of the hall in protest. It was a symbolic gesture and did not frustrate the GNA's real tasks which were to declare Ferdinand 'King of the Bulgarians', and to enact a constitutional amendment stating that the king and the cabinet should have the right to conclude foreign treaties.

Ferdinand's personal power had been strengthened and secret diplomacy had become possible. It was soon to produce dramatic results.

---

* The union of 1885 took place on 6 September according to the Julian calendar then used by most Orthodox Christian states; in the nineteenth century the Julian calendar was twelve days behind the Gregorian calendar used in western and central Europe. In the twentieth century the Julian calendar was thirteen days behind the Gregorian, the anniversary of 6 September therefore occurring on the 19th rather than the 18th in the western system. Stoilov's modernising impulses had led him to try and switch to the Gregorian calendar for state business, but conservative, religious opposition defeated him. The change was eventually made in 1916.

BALKAN DIPLOMACY AND THE BALKAN WARS, 1908–1913

Shortly before the GNA met in Tûrnovo a new government had been formed under Ivan Geshov who had succeeded Stoilov as leader of the Nationalist Party. Ferdinand was known to loathe Geshov deeply mostly because the Nationalists were amongst the fiercest critics of the prince's personal rule. If the king so mistrusted the Nationalists on internal affairs their elevation to office must mean that the king approved of their views on foreign policy. Geshov's first priority in this area was better relations with Russia, and as Russia had been calling for some time for a Bulgarian–Serbian alliance it was widely believed that Geshov had been appointed to bring that about.

There was reason enough for the two Balkan states to move closer together. Young Turk rule had not brought peace to the peninsula and in particular had angered the Albanians; these former loyal servants of the sultan were now subjected to more central government in the form of taxation, conscription and an attempt to disarm them. They rebelled every summer from 1909 to 1912. This increasing disorder raised two great dangers for the surrounding Balkan states. The first was that the powers might intervene to impose reforms which would work and which they would supervise. The second was that one or more powers might occupy part of the peninsula, and when Italy declared war on Turkey in 1911 over territorial disputes in North Africa this danger became more ominous. In either case the door would be closed on expansion by the Balkan states. But if two or more of those states could form an alliance they would make intervention by any external power more difficult. Russia meanwhile feared Austro-Hungarian rather than Italian encroachment and saw in a Balkan alliance the best barrier against it.

When negotiations between Belgrade and Sofia began, Russian diplomacy was under the illusion that the two states were aiming for a defensive alliance. The Bulgarians and Serbs knew full well that the alliance could only have an offensive purpose. They wanted to seize the Ottoman empire in Europe before there was time for reform or intervention by the powers. The negotiations were not easy. The Bulgarians, obviously hoping for a second Eastern Rumelia, pressed that Macedonia should be given autonomy; the Serbs insisted on partition. To this the Bulgarians eventually agreed but it proved impossible to draw final lines of division and the central area around Skopje was declared the 'contested zone' whose fate would, if necessary, be submitted to the tsar for arbitration.

A treaty on these lines was signed in February 1912. In the spring the situation in Macedonia deteriorated yet further and the Greeks hastily concluded a treaty with the Bulgarians, so hastily in fact that there were no clauses regulating the division of any conquered territory. The Greeks also concluded an alliance with the Serbs. Montenegro was not to be left out and concluded verbal agreements with the other three states.

By the summer of 1912 Macedonia was in chaos. The annual Albanian revolt spilled over into the Vardar valley and reached as far as Skopje, forcing the Young Turk government to resign. The Bulgarians faced mounting pressure at home for action to defend the exarchists in Macedonia, pressure which culminated in a huge, pro-war rally in Sofia on 5 September. Two days later the king and cabinet decided upon war and set about making the final arrangements at home and with their allies. Montenegro declared war on the Ottoman empire on 8 October; the other allies followed suit ten days later.

For the Bulgarian army the main task was to drive back the enemy on the plains of eastern Thrace, although other small forces were sent to join the Serbs in Macedonia, and to race down the Struma valley in the hope of reaching Salonika before the Greeks. In their main campaign the Bulgarians were stunningly successful. By the first week of November the Ottoman forces had been driven back to the Tchataldja lines around their capital.

The king and most politicians wanted to push forward and attempt to take Constantinople; Ferdinand was even said to have ordered a sumptuous uniform for the occasion. The general staff was less enthusiastic; the troops were exhausted and there had been an outbreak of cholera in some units. The civilians prevailed but the soldiers' caution proved justified, and on 17 November the attack was abandoned. Within days an armistice had been signed and all the belligerents had agreed to meet in St James's Palace, London, to

Plate 6.2 Bulgarian and Ottoman representatives meet to discuss the signing of the armistice after the unsuccessful Bulgarian assault on the defensive lines around Constantinople, November 1912. Note the ORC carriage in the background

determine the terms of a peace settlement. The great powers had in the meantime let it be known that an independent Albania must emerge from the wreckage of the Ottoman empire in Europe.

Whilst the discussions in London were in progress fighting broke out again on 3 February 1913 in Thrace when the Bulgarians launched an attack on Adrianople, one of the few fortresses left in Ottoman control. The fighting lasted until the surrender of the garrison on 26 March; during the siege Bulgarian aeroplanes carried out the first aerial bombardment in European history. Despite their success in Adrianople the Bulgarians were faced with a diplomatic problem for which no satisfactory conclusion could be found. The Romanian government had demanded territorial compensation for the gains of its neighbours and, it said, as a reward for its good behaviour during the war. Such compensation could only come from Bulgaria and after an ambassadorial conference in St Petersburg the Bulgarians were forced to concede southern Dobrudja to a line from Silistra to Balchik.

The general settlement of the war came later with the signature of the treaty of London on 30 May 1913. The treaty stated that an Albanian state should be created and its borders defined by an international commission; the rest of the former Ottoman possessions, north of a line from Enos to Midia, were to be divided amongst the allies as they saw fit. This was not going to be easy. The loss of the southern Dobrudja intensified Bulgarian determination to secure its full share of the Macedonian spoils. Sofia pressed for 'proportionality', arguing that as Bulgaria had contributed the major share of the fighting it should receive the largest gains. The Greeks and Serbs invoked the notion of 'balance', stressing that the future peace of the Balkans could only be secured if the victors emerged from the war more or less equal in strength. The core of the problem was the contested zone. When the Bulgarians suggested that the question be submitted to Russia for arbitration the Serbs refused, insisting instead on direct negotiations in which the Greeks must take part. The talks were as futile as the Bulgarians had feared. When they collapsed Geshov gave up and was succeeded as prime minister by Danev.

Geshov was much discouraged by the powerful war lobby then forming in Sofia, a lobby greatly bolstered by the knowledge that a Greek–Serbian alliance had been signed. In the war party were to be found most Macedonian groups, the non-socialist and non-agrarian opposition parties, the general staff, the king and finally Danev who was at last persuaded that nothing acceptable could be expected from Russian arbitration. On 29 June the Bulgarian army attacked its former Serbian and Greek allies.

At first all went well for the Bulgarians but after two weeks of fighting news came that the Romanians were mobilising, shortly after which the Ottoman army crossed the southern frontier and took Adrianople. The northern borders were undefended which meant there was nothing to stop the Romanians entering Sofia and the Bulgarians therefore sued for peace. In the treaties of Bucharest (10 August) and Constantinople (13 October) they lost much of the territory recently acquired. They retained only Pirin Macedonia to a point half way down the Struma valley and a strip of Thrace which included the Aegean port of Dedeagach.

The second Balkan war had caused more casualties than the first;

Map 6.1 Territorial changes after the Balkan wars

it had witnessed horrific crimes against civilians; and it had produced a second partition of San Stefano Bulgaria. It was in every respect a disaster for Bulgaria. The loss of the southern Dobrudja, confirmed in the treaty of Bucharest, deprived Bulgaria of its most advanced agricultural areas and the chief source of its grain exports; the territories acquired were by contrast backward and expensive – even Dedeagach was useless because the railway to it wound in and out of Ottoman territory. If full advantage were to be taken of this new territory on the Aegean coast a new line to, and harbour facilities at Porto Lagos would have to be constructed. Furthermore, the new masters of Macedonia were not the Ottomans whose *millet* system allowed the exarchists cultural autonomy, but aggressive, assertive nationalist states which would impose their own culture on all Macedonians.

During the disastrous second war Danev had resigned on 17 July to be succeeded by a coalition of liberal factions under the premiership of Vasil Radoslavov. In November Radoslavov went to the polls but, in a legacy left by the Malinov administration, was forced to conduct the elections under proportional representation. He did not secure a dependable majority and therefore called another election in April 1914. This time he allowed the new territories to vote, but he did not permit the opposition parties to campaign there. The new territories had little political experience and fell easy prey to Radoslavov's electoral managers. He secured his desired majority.

BULGARIA AND THE FIRST WORLD WAR

The most pressing task facing the Radoslavov government after the elections of April 1914 was to find money to pay for the recent wars and to develop the newly acquired territory. In July 1914 a loan of 500 million gold leva was granted by a consortium of German banks. As war clouds gathered in Europe a loan of this size inevitably had international significance, and many believed that it was Radoslavov's pro-Austrian and pro-German attitudes that had led to the German loan. There was some substance to these allegations. The French had also been approached but they had insisted that if they lent the money Bulgaria must follow a policy favourable to the western powers. Ferdinand and Radoslavov refused such conditions and when war broke out in Europe declared 'strict and loyal neutrality' and introduced a state of emergency.

In a Bulgaria exhausted by the recent wars neutrality was popular but the loan was not. This was in part because its conditions, many believed, amounted to a virtual contradiction of neutrality. The Bulgarians were required to earmark a series of state revenues to service the debt; they were obliged to grant the contract for the construction of a railway to Porto Lagos to a German consortium; and the Germans were to take over the running of the state mines in Pernik and Bobov Dol. There were rowdy scenes in the sûbranie when the issue was debated, at one point Radoslavov waved a revolver above his head, and few of the neutral witnesses present believed the government when it claimed the loan had been approved by a show of hands.

The loan did not, however, commit Ferdinand to the German cause, and both sides to the European conflict courted him. Bulgaria, despite its war-weariness, still had a large and well-equipped army, and it commanded a strategic position in the Balkans; through it the allies could reach Serbia, whilst it was also the vital link between the central powers and the Ottoman empire which had joined them in October; and from Bulgaria Constantinople and the Straits could be controlled. Ferdinand and Radoslavov listened to suitors from both sides but made no commitment until the late summer of 1915, mobilising and declaring 'armed neutrality' on 21 September and joining in the central powers renewed offensive against Serbia on 11 October.

Two factors determined this fateful decision. The central powers could offer more, and by the summer of 1915 it seemed they would win. What the Germans could offer was all of Macedonia and much of Thrace; they even persuaded the Porte to allow Bulgaria full control of the railway line to Dedeagach. The allies, on the other hand, would talk only of Thrace up to the Enos-Midia line, whilst for them what Bulgaria could be allowed in Macedonia would depend on how much the Serbs were prepared to relinquish. And the Serbian leader, Nikola Pašić, said he would not concede one square inch. The Russians backed the Serbs. In early 1915 Russian and allied intransigence on Macedonia was increased by military success; the Russians took the vital fortress of Przemyśl, the allies established themselves in Gallipoli whence they could reach Constantinople, and in May the Italians joined the war on their side. Two months later the position had been reversed. The Italian intervention had had little impact, other than to make the Serbs, who feared Italian designs on Dalmatia, more determined to hold on to Macedonia; allied troops were pinned on the murderous beaches of Gallipoli; and the Russians had lost Przemyśl and huge swathes of territory in Russian Poland together with its important industries. Furthermore, allied diplomacy in Bulgaria had been less adept than that of the central powers. The allies tended to court opposition politicians whereas the Germans paid much more attention to Ferdinand and his immediate advisors. Given the nature of Ferdinand's personal rule, his control over foreign affairs, and the state of emergency which limited the opposition's freedom of manoeuvre, the central powers were backing the stronger horse.

The opposition parties did not welcome mobilisation. They all declared themselves 'resolute partisans of peace' and all of them, with the exception of the narrows, joined together in a United Bloc to demand that the sŭbranie be allowed to debate and decide upon the issue of war or peace. Radoslavov refused such a debate. Ferdinand, however, did agree to receive a delegation consisting of leaders of the opposition. The meeting ended in a furious row between the king and Stamboliiski and when the latter published details of this he was thrust into gaol. No parliamentary debate on the war took place until December. By then the opposition parties had decided to rally to the cause of the nation and all of them, again with the exception of the narrows, voted in favour of war credits.

For the Bulgarian forces the first world war was for the most part not a war of rapid movement. Serbian Macedonia had been occupied in 1915 and in 1916 they advanced into Greek territory as far as Fort Rupel, and later in the year, following a Greek attack, took Drama, Seres and Kavalla; in the same year Bitolya was lost after a ferocious battle on mount Kaimakchalan. Also in 1916 Romania entered the war on the allied side only to suffer huge defeats; the Bulgarians, accompanied by Ottoman units, took the southern Dobrudja and later moved across the Danube into Romania proper. Thereafter the military fronts, especially in the

Plate 6.3 Bulgarian soldiers on Belassitsa mountain during the first world war, just over a thousand years after their predecessors were defeated and blinded by the Byzantine emperor, Basil the Bulgar Slayer

south and south-west, remained more or less stable until the late summer of 1918.

Despite general rejoicing at the reacquisition of Macedonia problems soon began to appear on the home front. In Macedonia itself the military became more and more concerned at the nature of the civilian administration. Too many free-booters and incompetents had been given office in the new territories. By August 1916 the military were seriously concerned lest maladministration destabilise the area immediately behind the front line, and they attempted to seize control of the Macedonian administration. They failed and the problems intensified.

These problems were not confined to the new lands. Almost from the beginning of the war there were difficulties with supplies. By 1916 there were shortages even of bread. The deterioration in supplies was reflected in the inflation rate. Taking the cost of living in 1914 as a base of 100, by the end of 1916 it stood at 200, and by July 1918 it was 847. And these were official figures which took no

Map 6.2 The southern Balkan front during the first world war

cognisance of the black market where prices were even higher and which was often the only source of supply. By the late summer of 1918 these difficulties were so severe that they entirely undermined civilian and military morale, and were a major factor in Bulgaria's collapse in September.

The roots of the supply problem were varied. In 1915 mobilisation had had some impact on the distribution if not the gathering of the harvest, and far too much of that harvest had been requisitioned for the army. As the war went on future sowing and harvesting were hit by the mobilisation both of men and of draught animals, the latter being needed in huge numbers to transport supplies to the army in Macedonia where the terrain was mountainous, the roads primitive and railways almost non-existent. There was also competition between civilian and military procurement agencies. The evil of corruption was omnipresent; and the requisitioning agencies became increasingly unpopular as their personnel took commodities such as sugar and salt which they had no right to take but which they could sell at high prices on the black market. An aggravating factor was the presence of German and Austrian troops in Bulgaria. They were better paid than the Bulgarians and they bought increasing quantities of food to send home, frequently exceeding the quotas officially allowed them. In this they were much aided by the fact that the Germans controlled both the railway and the telephone systems, and that after December 1915 German and Austrian currency was legal tender in Bulgaria. Official German and Austrian procurement agencies were equally rapacious, often having no consideration for local requirements or for the long-term needs for fodder and seeds; in 1917 three-quarters of the immensely fertile arable area of the Dobrudja was reported to be untilled because so much of the previous year's harvest had been taken that there was no seed. Nor was the problem of supplying civilian and military markets helped by changes in administrative responsibility. In March 1915 the public welfare act had given the government the right to control the price of deficit goods in time of war. In 1916, as the situation worsened, a central committee for economic and social welfare was established, again under civilian control. It had hardly had time to organise itself when, in April 1917, most of its powers were transferred to the newly established directorate for economic and social welfare which was under military domination. The military body was no more successful than the civilian.

Inevitably there was reaction, particularly in the occupied areas where deprivations were at their worst. The Morava valley saw a series of outbursts against Bulgarian occupation, even in villages which were purely Bulgarian. Protest was encouraged by events in Russia. In March 1917 Stamboliiski, writing from his prison cell, declared that the fall of tsardom would allow the USA to enter the war on the allied side and that the central powers were therefore doomed. By the summer soldiers on the front opposite the Russians in Romania were forming 'soviets' and 500 troops, many of them agrarian supporters, had been gaoled for political agitation. The Russian Revolution also produced the call for a peace 'without annexations or indemnities', calls which were echoed in March 1917 by the leader of the Radical Democratic Party in Bulgaria, Tsanov, who publicly questioned the right of Bulgarian troops to occupy parts of Romania which had no Bulgarians amongst their population. By the end of the year public pressure was much stronger, and the narrow leader Dimitûr Blagoev could attract over 10,000 to a rally in Sofia to call for an end to the war and to the political system which had made it possible. Early in 1918 there was a mounting tide of social unrest with protests in Gabrovo and riots in Stanimaka and Samokov, whilst in May a woman was killed in Sliven while taking part in one of the many meetings called throughout the country in what came to be known as the 'women's revolt'.

As the internal situation deteriorated Radoslavov was faced with unexpected and unusual difficulties on the diplomatic front. In May 1918 the treaty of Bucharest regulated the northern Dobrudja. The Bulgarians had confidently expected that they would be given responsibility for this area but they were to be disappointed as it was placed under joint German, Austrian and Bulgarian administration. Radoslavov remarked that his country had been treated more like a defeated enemy than a victorious ally, and on 20 June 1918 he resigned.

Malinov, the leader of the Democratic Party, now formed a government. He had hoped to include Stamboliiski in it but the latter would accept office only if the war were ended, and to this

Ferdinand would not consent. Malinov did manage to wrestle sole control of the northern Dobrudja from his allies, but it was a hollow victory. Bulgaria's capacity to continue fighting was exhausted; to use a figure of speech almost too literal for comfort, the Bulgarians had no more stomach for war.

The people, particularly those in the towns, were on the verge of starvation, and some in Macedonia had gone beyond it with deaths from malnutrition being reported in Ohrid and other centres. Soldiers, who at the front were already suffering shortages of food, ammunition and clothing, came home on leave or to help in the harvest and found that their loved ones were in no better and perhaps even a worse condition. Their morale collapsed and when the French and British launched an offensive on 15 September resistance broke. Within a week Franco-British troops had entered Bulgaria. The government sued for peace and on 29 September 1918 signed an armistice in Salonika.

On the day allied troops entered the country Stamboliiski was released from prison. It was hoped that he would contain a military revolt centred on Radomir between Sofia and the advancing allies. There was no need for him to do so. When the armistice was signed the soldiers gained their principal demand – peace – and the revolt fizzled out. For the second time in half a decade Ferdinand's personal regime, it was alleged, had led the nation to humiliating defeat. He abdicated and left the country on 3 October 1918. He was succeeded by his son, Boris III.

7

Bulgaria, 1918–1944

THE PEACE SETTLEMENT OF 1919

The peace treaty with Bulgaria was signed at Neuilly-sur-Seine on 27 November 1919. Bulgaria was required to relinquish all lands it had occupied during the recent conflict and it was also deprived of three small pockets on its western border, despite the fact that the vast majority of the local population was Bulgarian. Bulgaria also lost those parts of Thrace it had gained in the Balkan wars, although this loss was tempered somewhat by article 48 of the treaty which guaranteed Bulgaria 'economic access' to the Aegean; however, there was no indication of how that access was to be achieved. In peacetime it never was. The Neuilly settlement ruled that the Bulgarian army was to have a maximum effective strength of 20,000 men, all of whom were to be volunteers. Reparations were to be paid both in kind and in money. Deliveries of coal, livestock and railway equipment were to be made to the governments of Greece, Yugoslavia and Romania, whilst Bulgaria was required to pay 2,250 million gold francs to the allies over a period of thirty-seven years. It was a preposterous sum and was soon recognised as such. In 1923 it was reduced to 550 million to be paid over sixty years, and in 1932 it was scrapped altogether.

Compared to Hungary, Germany and Austria the territorial provisions of the peace settlement were not harsh for Bulgaria. It lost just under 9,000 square kilometres of territory and 90,000 more Bulgarians now found themselves under foreign rule. The total number of Bulgarians living outside the national state was in the region of 1 million or about 16 per cent of all Bulgarians. Another and indirect result of the peace settlement did, however, much affect Bulgaria. The reversion of Macedonia to Serbian and Greek rule produced yet another wave of refugees. Many of these lived in appalling conditions on the south-western borders of Bulgaria, their upkeep placing a substantial burden on the Bulgarian exchequer.

AGRARIAN RULE, 1919–1923

The domestic factors which played a major role in Bulgarian politics during the inter-war years were the agrarians, the communists, the old sûbranie parties, the Macedonian organisations, the army and the throne.

Immediately after the war the two dominant factors were the agrarians and the communists. At the end of hostilities an interim cabinet was formed under Teodor Teodorov of the People's Liberal Party. Its actions were closely observed by representatives of the allies who had troops stationed in Bulgaria. Its main duty was to preserve order until elections could be held in August 1919.

Those elections registered massive popular anger with the system which had taken Bulgaria into the war and approval of those parties which had opposed it. The agrarians took 31 per cent of the vote; the narrows, who had become the Bulgarian Communist Party (BCP) in May 1919, 18 per cent; and the democrats, the most left-wing of the old parties, 10 per cent. Stamboliiski formed a coalition with the democrats but his initial instinct had been to work with the communists; they, however, spurned him. They did not intend to form a coalition with anyone; they wanted and believed they could seize unadulterated power. The agrarians had the same ambition and an equal self-confidence.

The communists and the agrarians were in fact competing for the vacancy created by the collapse of the old parties. Open confrontation was to come at the turn of the year. The communists were full of confidence. As living standards in the towns continued to plummet their support increased, particularly in the trade unions and, on 24 December they joined with the social democrats, the

Map 7.1 Bulgaria's borders after the first and second world wars

Legend:

Territory transferred to Bulgaria from the Ottoman empire in October 1915 but ceded to Greece under the treaty of Neuilly-sur-Seine, November 1919

Territory lost by Bulgaria under the treaty of Neuilly-sur-Seine, November 1919

The southern Dobrudja, regained by Bulgaria in September 1940 and retained after the second world war

Bulgarian borders according to the treaty of Paris, 1947

**Map labels:**

BLACK SEA

ROMANIA

YUGOSLAVIA

TURKEY

GREECE

Aegean Sea

Danube

Danube

Maritsa

Struma

Varna

Burgas

Plovdiv

Sofia

Tsaribrod

Petrich

Strumitsa

Dedeagach

N

100 miles
50
0

160 kilometres
80
0

former broads, to stage a day of protest in Sofia. It was the first time the two socialist factions had cooperated since the split of 1903, and that cooperation continued when the transport and telegraph workers went on strike. Two days later a general strike was called. Stamboliiski reacted toughly. Strike leaders were arrested, their families' ration cards were withdrawn, and some were evicted from their homes. To enforce these measures Stamboliiski used the army, allied troops, the police and the Orange Guard. The latter, armed with clubs, had been set up recently by BANU to counteract the semi-armed groups established by the social democrats and the communists. On 5 January the general strike was called off, although some transport workers and the miners in Pernik continued the struggle for another six weeks.

Having defeated the communists on the streets Stamboliiski called a general election for 28 March 1920 to register popular endorsement of his victory. It produced a not entirely comforting result. One in three of the electorate voted for BANU but another one in five voted for the BCP. BANU returned 110 deputies and the BCP 51. Stamboliiski was just nine seats short of an absolute majority and therefore annulled the returns of thirteen deputies, nine of whom were communists and who were now replaced by agrarians. Stamboliiski had secured his absolute majority in a fashion worthy of the old sûbranie parties he so despised.

The agrarians were now in a position to implement their ideology and, in the words of the great Anglo-Irish journalist and friend of Bulgaria, James Bourchier, to transfer power 'from the political coteries of the towns, the office seekers and the parasites of the court, to the honest hard-working tillers of the soil, the bone and sinew of Bulgaria'. The agrarians' programme, which had not been drawn up until 1918, wanted to create a society in which all held enough but none too much land, and which was dominated by clean, modernised villages with paved streets, clean water, proper sanitation, good schools, adequate libraries and cinemas. The peasant proprietor was to be helped by the cooperatives which would provide credit, store crops and find markets; the cooperatives would fit the square peg of peasant proprietorship into the round hole of commercialised, capitalised agriculture.

Despite his parliamentary majority there were limitations on

Stamboliiski's freedom of action. Reparations complicated matters not only because revenue had to be diverted to meet payments, but also because the government was forced to requisition draught animals for delivery to Bulgaria's neighbours. This impaired productivity and created yet another opportunity for corruption. Meanwhile, the allies remained suspicious of so radical a government, and in September 1921 they intervened to insist upon the dissolution of a government grain purchasing consortium which had restricted merchants' sphere of operations, to say nothing of their profits.

The grain consortium had been intended to restrict such profits and was part of BANU's offensive against those whom it considered parasites. Lawyers were even more in the firing line. They were denied the right to sit in parliament or on local councils, and were barred from major public office. The agrarians also established new lower courts to deal with issues such as boundary disputes, and in these courts peasants were to plead their own cases before judges elected by the local populace. The agrarians also greatly limited the king's power to make appointments, and they required banks to help fund credit cooperatives. BANU's main objective, however, was to redistribute land.

In June 1920 a bill was passed to establish a state land fund. Into this would go excess property. All Bulgarians were allowed 4 hectares of inalienable land but absentee owners were to lose anything above that amount. For those working their land the maximum holding was to be 30 hectares in arable areas and a little more in forest regions; there was to be an extra 5 hectares for the fifth and every subsequent member of a family. For those who lost land there was to be compensation in the form of government bonds, with payment being on a sliding scale which reduced the amount per hectare as the number of hectares increased. In April 1921 a second act was passed clamping down on the corruption which had allowed some owners to escape the first bill. The 1921 act also stated that monastic lands were now to be included within the act's provisions, and it made it easier for dwarf-holders and the few landless peasants to purchase more land. The agrarians had hoped to redistribute over a quarter of a million hectares but they were to be disappointed. The process of redistribution was slow and

Plate 7.1 The old and the new in the Bulgarian peasantry;
Aleksandûr Stamboliiski with his father

still open to corruption but most important of all there were very few individuals who owned large estates, and institutional owners were more difficult to tackle. By June 1923 only 82,000 hectares had changed hands, and in 1926 only 1 per cent of all the land held in the country had been acquired as a result of redistribution. On the other hand, after the fall of the agrarian government almost all of their land legislation, including the principle of maximum holdings, remained in force. This did not apply, however, to the extension of the maximum property regulations to urban areas and the ruling that all families should have only two rooms and a kitchen, with extra rooms for larger families. This legislation was repealed as was that placing limitations on office space.

Another major item of BANU legislation which survived the fall of the regime was the compulsory labour service introduced in June 1920. This required all males between twenty and forty to perform a total of eight months labour, whilst unmarried females between sixteen and thirty were to perform four months. The labour service was usually carried out on public works such as road or school building, and until October 1921 it was impossible to purchase exemption. The compulsory labour service no doubt benefited the nation but it aroused suspicion amongst the allies not least because it was organised along military lines, used military terms for its officials, and originally had a former general as its director.

The BANU government carried out many other reforms. A progressive income tax was introduced. Dwarf-holders who received land were required to consolidate separate strips into one holding before they were allowed to purchase more land from the state land fund. Secondary schooling was made compulsory, its vocational content was increased, and a massive school-building programme produced over 1,100 new schools. At the same time the teaching profession was purged of communists.

In foreign policy Stamboliiski sustained his pre-war lack of interest in territorial expansion. This pleased the victorious allies, as did the fact that he kept well away from Lenin's revolutionary regime. After Stamboliiski had toured European capitals in 1920 Bulgaria became the first defeated state to be admitted to the League of Nations.

Also pleasing to the allies was the agrarian leader's desire for good relations with his western neighbour. The main problem was that posed by the Macedonian organisations. These had become fragmented but one of them, that led from October 1923 by Ivan Mihailov, had established a virtual state within the state at Petrich where the Bulgarian, Greek and Yugoslav borders met. From here the mihailovists launched raids into Greek or Yugoslav Macedonia. There was little Stamboliiski could do to contain these irreconcilables but he did attempt to purge the frontier police of Macedonian sympathisers. In November 1922, when he was at last allowed to visit Belgrade, he used the Yugoslav capital as the venue for a vehement denunciation of the Macedonian extremists, and in March 1923 he signed the Nish convention by which Bulgaria and Yugoslavia agreed to cooperate in the struggle against those extremists; in the following month the Bulgarian government banned all organisations suspected of terrorist activities, suppressed their newspapers, and confined their leaders to internment camps.

Naturally the Macedonians were greatly angered by these measures. Nor were they the only ones dissatisfied with agrarian rule. All sections of the nation suffered from the corruption which, though always a feature of Bulgarian life, reached enormous proportions under the agrarians, especially amongst the petty officials appointed by BANU to administrative posts in the villages. But it was in the urban areas that resentment was most bitterly felt.

The working class could not escape the effects of inflation which by 1923 had reduced the leva to a seventh of its 1919 value; and the tough action taken against the strikers of 1919–20 and other measures to limit communist activities increased resentment. For the more wealthy townspeople the regulations limiting personal and business accommodation were intensely hated. Amongst professionals the lawyers had clear reasons for dissatisfaction but they were not the only ones to bear grudges or harbour fears. Doctors were alarmed by agrarian talk of forcing many of them to work in remote villages. Teachers resented action taken against the communists in their ranks and even more so the rule that all teachers had to be periodically reelected; academics so resented governmental interference with the autonomy of the university that in 1922 they went on strike; even the Academy of Sciences was angry, not least because of the minister of education's obsessive and eventually unfulfilled desire to reform the alphabet. The church, too, had a number of causes for complaint. The religious content of the school curriculum had been reduced, church property had been subjected to the land redistribution acts, and the holy synod had been moved to Rila, its Sofia headquarters being turned into an agronomy institute. The professional civil servants meanwhile were disturbed by the propensity of the government to by-pass official, state channels in favour of BANU party organisations which were becoming a by-word for corruption. The Orange Guard, for example, were taking over some of the functions of the police; local BANU organisations, the *druzhbi*, rather than local government officials were told to draw up the fine details of the land reform scheme; and the *druzhbi* rather than the village or urban district councils were given the major role in the periodic reelection of teachers.

An extremely important element of the discontented in the towns were the former army officers who had been decommissioned as a result of the treaty of Neuilly. They had lost status as well as their careers and their livelihood. They knew that there had been little Stamboliiski could do to ameliorate the terms of the treaty but they greatly resented his apparently dismissive attitude towards the military profession, and even more so the fact that he did not even maintain the army at the permitted level of 20,000 men. Nor did they like the increasing use of the Orange Guard for state rather than purely party purposes. In 1922 a number of discontented officers formed the Military League. There was another military force in Bulgaria in the early 1920s. Over 30,000 refugees from the Russian civil war under the command of General Wrangel had entered the country and they brought with them a quantity of heavy weaponry. In May 1922 Stamboliiski dissolved their organisation; amongst the population at large this was a welcome measure but Stamboliiski had created yet another group with cause for resentment.

The old political parties were also fearful and angry. They had established an electoral alliance, the Constitutional Bloc, and some leaders had formed a smaller, closer-knit organisation, the National Alliance. They feared Stamboliiski intended to establish a republic and a one-party state, their fears being greatly fuelled late in 1922 by the forcible disruption of the National Alliance's plans for a series of rallies culminating in a march on Sofia; Mussolini had 'marched' on Rome that October. Their fears increased when Stamboliiski abolished proportional representation and called an election in April 1923. BANU romped home with 212 deputies to the BCP's 16 and the Constitutional Bloc's 15.

After the election a conspiracy was formed consisting of some mihailovists from Petrich, the National Alliance, the Military League and even some social democrats. The conspirators informed the king of their intentions and, calculating correctly that the communists would remain inert, acted in the early hours of 9 June 1923. The agrarian regime was dismantled in hours, though it was not until 14 June that Stamboliiski was found and brutally tortured to death by his Macedonian captors. A new government was formed under the premiership of Aleksandûr Tsankov, an academic economist.

The Bulgarian communists had stood idly by in June 1923 but for so doing they were severely criticised by Moscow and told to redeem their honour. This led to an abortive communist uprising in September 1923. The Tsankov government had no difficulty in suppressing it and used it as an excuse to impose further restrictions on individual rights and political liberties.

Within less than four months the two most radical factors in the Bulgarian political arena had been immobilised. In effect the left had been dealt a seemingly crippling blow.

THE RULE OF THE DEMOCRATIC ALLIANCE, 1923–1931

After seizing power Tsankov fashioned a new grouping, the Democratic Alliance, to provide him with reliable support in the sûbranie. The Democratic Alliance was a coalition of the National Alliance, the Military League, the mihailovists, and a motley collection of factions from the Democratic and Nationalist Parties.

Initially Tsankov's rule was firm but tinged with attempts at consensus. A defence of the realm act was passed in November 1923 which once again banned terrorism and gave the government powers which it used to influence the elections held that month. The act was also used in April 1924 to ban the BCP, confiscate its property, and dissolve its trade union; using the same legislation the eight BCP deputies elected in November 1923 were deprived of their seats in March 1925. Yet at the same time the government repealed very little of agrarian legislation and continued with the programme of land reform enacted by Stamboliiski.

Any pretence at conciliation ended in 1925. On 16 April a bomb planted by the communists exploded in the roof of Sofia's Sveta Nedelya cathedral during a state funeral due to be attended by the king and the entire political establishment. Amazingly no prominent figure was amongst the 120 or so fatalities. The bomb unleashed a ferocious reaction. Martial law was declared and thousands of left-wing activists were detained. Many of the detainees disappeared and there were rumours that some of them had been fed into the furnaces of the Sofia police headquarters. The fate of others was all too clear: they were executed in public.

Violence was not a communist or a government monopoly. In the early 1920s there had been further divisions in the ranks of IMRO with one faction calling for cooperation with the communists. This led to more feuding and consequent assassinations in Sofia and elsewhere. The mihailovists meanwhile retained their hold on the Petrich enclave and continued their guerilla activities in Serbia and Greece. After one raid in October 1925 the Greek army moved into southern Bulgaria; that it withdrew without further complications was one of the League of Nations' more notable successes.

Despite this help from the League of Nations the internal excesses which Tsankov had allowed were making Bulgaria into a pariah state. The king had already suggested to leading army officers that changes had to be made, but as yet his political standing was weak and his words went unheeded. International bankers were more effective. By 1925 Bulgaria was in desperate need of a loan. In an astute move it asked for one to help finance welfare schemes for the thousands of Macedonian refugees most of whom were still living in abject poverty. The refugees, the government argued, were a fertile recruiting ground for communist or Macedonian extremists, and could only be kept immune from such viruses by an injection of welfare spending, particularly if that spending were directed towards providing them with land of their own. The League of

Plate 7.2 Sveta Nedelya cathedral, Sofia, after its bombing by the communists on 16 April 1925

Nations was persuaded but in London, where the bulk of the cash would be raised, there were doubts. It was made clear that a government headed by Tsankov would never be in receipt of such a loan. In January 1926 therefore he resigned and was succeeded by Andrei Lyapchev, the leader of the Democratic Party and himself a Macedonian. The loan was then granted and over 650 village communes used the funds received from it to provide land for Macedonian refugees.

Lyapchev relaxed many of the restrictions imposed by Tsankov. Trade unions were allowed to function again and in 1927 the communists reformed under the title of Bulgarian Workers' Party (BWP) and had soon established attendant trade union and youth organisations. The Macedonians were also allowed to continue their often murderous activities.

By 1926 the tsankovist terror was over, the Bulgarian left had been eliminated, and the right had not, outside the ranks of the mihailovists, produced any significant movement. The moderate centre was therefore in control. It did not acquit itself well. The Lyapchev government had no great legislative programme and it fell into a form of aimless drift. This applied to the political scene as a whole. The agrarians, deprived of power and of the leader who had dominated them, splintered to such a degree that it was later said they had fragmented not into wings but into feathers. Even the communists, renowned for their cohesion and discipline, showed signs of division. On the right a group around the journal *Lûch* (ray) called for cooperation with other parties, a view strongly opposed by the 'left sectarians' who seized control of the party in 1929. The old sûbranie parties split even more. In 1926 there were nineteen identifiable factions within the assembly; by 1934 there were twenty-nine. Lyapchev took one step to counter drift in this sector. He introduced an Italian-style bonus system whereby the faction securing most of the votes in an election was awarded an automatic majority in the sûbranie. This system was in place in time for the 1927 elections which the Democratic Alliance won, albeit with a reduced majority.

By the end of the decade and in the early 1930s there were increasing calls for radical action. One such call came from Zveno (link), an organisation founded in 1930 with a small membership associated with a newspaper of that name. The zvenari were of the intelligentsia and were avowedly élitist. They were also étatist, advocating increased power for a centralised and rationalised administration. They were authoritarian and saw in the political parties the origin of most of the ills besetting the country, believing that the present system encouraged politicians to put party before country. In foreign affairs they wanted better relations with Yugoslavia and were therefore hostile to the Macedonian organisations. They had powerful support from a number of republican-minded army officers and members of the Military League.

The hour of the zvenari had not yet come. When general elections were held in June 1931 the electorate was preoccupied with the intensifying economic crisis triggered by the world depression. It was an open election for which PR was reintroduced. Victory went to the People's Bloc which took 47 per cent of the vote and 150 seats as opposed to 31 per cent and 78 seats for the Democratic Alliance. The latter was now a broken force and it fell apart, Tsankov shearing away to form his own, avowedly fascist National Social Movement.

The People's Bloc consisted of factions from the Nationalist, Radical and National Liberal Parties, together with one group of agrarians, the first time that any BANU faction had been back in office since the coup of 1923. The prime minister of the new government was the leader of the Democratic Party, Aleksandûr Malinov, but in October ill-health forced him to make way for his party colleague, Nikola Mushanov.

Any hopes entertained by the peasantry that the return to government of BANU, albeit only one faction of the party, would bring about an improvement in the peasants' lot were soon dashed. In part this was because the government had to weather the worst part of the great depression. In the five years from 1929 to 1934 peasant incomes fell by 50 per cent, urban unemployment soared, and for those lucky enough still to be in work real wages fell by almost a third. The government took a number of steps to cope with the crisis. Debt obligations were reduced by 40 per cent and the repayment periods extended; Hranoiznos, a government grain purchasing agency, was introduced in 1930, and encouragement was given to crop diversification, particularly into higher-price export commodities such as fruit and vegetables. But setting these efforts aside, the People's Bloc ministers did little to endear themselves to popular opinion. Whilst the peasants were experiencing almost unparalleled hardships, the ministers, the agrarians no less than the others, were engaged in a grotesque exercise of self-enrichment accompanied by the most unseemly squabbles over the spoils of office. It was against this background that the communists secured notable successes in the local elections of November 1931 and took control of Sofia city council in February 1932. The government waited a year before dissolving the council. Another beneficiary of the depression was Tsankov's National Social Movement which began to find an increasing number of adherents, particularly amongst the young of the towns and cities.

Bulgaria also faced difficulties abroad. A series of Balkan conferences in the early 1930s had failed to secure significant moves towards unity in the peninsula because Bulgaria could never accept that existing borders were permanent, a condition upon which the other states insisted if Bulgaria were to be included in any agreement. For this reason Bulgaria was not included when the Balkan entente was signed in Athens in February 1934. The combination of Turkey, Greece, Yugoslavia and Romania had an ominous similarity to the hostile coalition of the second Balkan war. Foreign relations were further complicated by the mihailovists who became even more extreme in their utterances. In June 1933 Mihailov himself called for an attack on the Yugoslav embassy in Sofia which he called a 'nest of vipers'. In the following month a convention in London included in its definition of an aggressive state the support of or failure to suppress any subversive groups operating on that state's territory. Under this description Bulgaria could easily be branded an aggressive state and because of its isolation would then be in an extremely vulnerable position.

By the spring of 1934 external and internal tensions were rising. Tsankov had called a large rally for 21 May and confidently expected an audience of over 50,000; the rally was to coincide with a private visit to Bulgaria of Hermann Göring. There seemed no-one able or willing to curb the Macedonians or restrain the fascists. The agrarian left was too divided, the communists would be suppressed, the old parties were enfeebled, Zveno talked much but did little; only the army and the king were left.

On 19 May 1934 the army stepped into the breach. Taking advantage of yet another dispute amongst ministers as to who should have which cabinet office, pro-Zveno officers with strong connections to the Military League seized power. The coup was orchestrated by Colonel Damyan Velchev, but he chose not to become prime minister, this position being taken by his co-conspirator, Colonel Kimon Georgiev.

THE RULE OF THE *DEVETNAITSETI*, MAY 1934–JANUARY 1935

The *devetnaitseti* (the '19thers'), as Velchev's group became known, ruled for only a short period but with considerable vigour and much in conformity with the ideas of Zveno.

They suspended civil rights and set up the directorate for social renewal which was given great influence over the press and other publications, over the arts, and in the organisation of youth activities; its objective was 'to direct the cultural and intellectual life of the nation towards unity and renewal'. One way in which unity was to be fostered was by changing Turkish topographical names to Bulgarian ones, and more such name changes took place under the *devetnaitseti* than at any other point in pre-war Bulgaria. Party political divisions were to disappear and the parties themselves were dissolved. So too were most existing trade unions, and in those that remained all officials had to be approved by the central government authorities. Plans to establish one large union, the Bulgarian Workers' Union, were drawn up and were implemented by the successor government. Although the Bulgarian Workers' Union was technically a voluntary organisation by 1936, 120,000 out of a total of 145,000 industrial workers had joined it. Membership was not by occupational category but by estate; the *devetnaitseti*, copying the Italian fascists, had divided society into seven estates: workers, peasants, craftsmen, merchants, intelligentsia, civil servants and members of the free professions. The estates were also to provide the basis for the election of three-quarters of the members of the new sûbranie, the existing one having been dissolved.

Rationalisation and centralisation, much championed by Zveno, were also very much a feature of the *devetnaitseti's* programme. In the central administration the number of ministries was decreased, as was the number of civil servants. Nearly a third of the latter lost their jobs, many of them being replaced by others of a more dependable political disposition. The banks were also rationalised and centralised in a series of reforms which included the amalgamation of nineteen commercial banks into the Bulgarian Credit Bank, one purpose of this reform being to establish greater central control over provincial banks.

Central control over local government was increased to a degree unparalleled since the liberation of 1878. The 16 existing regions were reformed into 7 provinces and the 2,600 village communes made into 837 units. Elected mayors were replaced by centrally appointed figures all of whom had to have either a legal training or a civil service rank equal to that of officer status in the army. The new local councils were to be half appointed and half elected, with the franchise for the latter being based on the seven social estates.

Since the fall of Stamboliiski Bulgarian foreign policy makers had tended to regard Italy as the great power most likely to provide the patronage a small state such as Bulgaria needed. The *devetnaitseti* wished to break away from this association. In July 1934 they recognised the Soviet Union, but their main hope was for an understanding with Yugoslavia. This would relax Balkan tensions and would make it easier to improve relations with Britain and France. The main obstacle to better relations with Belgrade was, of course, the mihailovist enclave in Petrich. The *devetnaitseti* took resolute action. They moved in the army. In what proved to be a surprisingly easy and immensely popular operation the mihailovists were dispersed. They did not disappear but they were no longer the formidable force they had been since the early 1920s. Furthermore, the feuding between various Macedonian factions which had taken over 800 lives in the decade before 1934 greatly subsided.

The *devetnaitseti* had proved effective conspirators and energetic rulers, but they were not expert politicians. There were divisions within Zveno on the advisability of creating a mass party organisation to sustain the government, one faction fearing that to do so would give new life to the party system. More importantly, there had been no decision as to what to do about the king, an issue on which both Zveno and the Military League were divided. Velchev was generally acknowledged to be in the republican camp and when rumours began to circulate that he was about to promulgate a new constitution it was assumed that this would greatly reduce royal powers.

Velchev and Georgiev, being preoccupied with the government's full programme of reforms, did not have time to guard their political backs. They were therefore relatively easy prey to a plot by their royalist opponents who in January 1935 manoeuvred them out of office and made General Pencho Zlatev prime minister. By April of the same year the royalists had removed Zlatev and installed a civilian, Andrei Toshev, in the prime ministerial chair.

THE PERSONAL RULE OF KING BORIS, 1934–1941

The king had been angered by the officers' intervention in the political arena in 1934 and he was determined that they should not dominate the country. But if he were to establish his own supremacy he had to find a means to build bridges with the nation and he had to secure himself against further action by the military.

When appointing Toshev in April 1935 Boris had issued a declaration promising to return the country to an 'orderly and peaceful life'. He also stated that there was to be no turning back and although the directorate for social renewal was to be abolished most of the reforms introduced since May 1934 were to remain. Toshev's task was now to contain the military, to work out a new constitution, and to construct a new popular movement. He made no progress on any of these fronts, and he resigned in November after it was discovered that Velchev had slipped back into the country with the intention, it was presumed, of conspiring against the king. Toshev's successor was Georgi Kioseivanov, a diplomat very much open to influence from his royal master.

The Velchev conspiracy made the containment of the military easier. Velchev himself was tried and sentenced to death in February 1936, his life being spared by that royal prerogative which he had wanted to abolish. The following month Boris used the revelations of the Velchev trial to justify his dissolution of the Military League. Immediately afterwards he toured the country's most important garrisons in an attempt to bolster his image amongst the officer corps.

In the declaration of 1935 Boris had promised a return to constitutional government but under a new constitution which would correspond to 'the present complications and to the requirements of the times'. Amongst these complications were, it was believed, a potential threat from the left. The communists had been encouraged in 1931 and 1932 by their successes in local elections, and then in 1933 when their leader in exile, Georgi Dimitrov, had made a fool of Göring in the Reichstag Fire trial in Leipzig. In 1935 the Comintern had switched its strategy to the Popular Front making the communists more ready to cooperate with other parties. In 1936 there were enthusiastic celebrations of May Day, and the communists boasted that they had cells in every garrison in the country. Credibility was given to this chilling statement when army officers in Plovdiv showed support for the traditionally communist tobacco workers who had gone on strike. Meanwhile, after the January 1936 elections in Greece the small communist group held the balance of power in parliament. Nor had the fear of the right entirely disappeared. Tsankov's National Social Movement had not been classified as a political party and had therefore survived the ban on such bodies. At its 1936 congress it changed its statutes to make it more of a fascist organisation, and its public support seemed to grow with every fresh triumph Hitler recorded. The Nazis, like most Bulgarians, wanted to revise the peace settlement of 1919.

The old parties, though proscribed, continued to lead a shadowy existence and in May 1936 a number of them formed the 'Petorka', or group of five, to demand a return to the Tûrnovo constitution. Later, this regrouped as the People's Constitutional Bloc which included some members of the Democratic Party, a radical agrarian faction and the communists.

By the beginning of 1936, sensing these and other dangers, Boris was in no hurry to rush into constitutional reform. He did not want to return to the old system and did not feel he could work with the older generation of politicians. He decided that there should be a slow return to 'a tidy and disciplined democracy imbued with the idea of social solidarity', that the constitution should be amended gradually, and that any changes introduced should be tested in local elections before a new sûbranie, due in 1937, was convened. Local elections were accordingly held in January 1937 after a number of changes had been decreed. Before voting all electors were to sign a statement attesting that they were not communists; voting was to be spread over three Sundays to enable the police to concentrate units where they were thought most needed; married women and widows were able to vote for the first time, if they wished, though voting for males was to be compulsory; and rural voters were required to have primary and the urban electorate secondary education. The local elections went off to the government's satisfaction but it was not until March 1938 that a general election was held. Before then further changes had reduced the size of the sûbranie to 160 deputies

Plate 7.3 Boris III, King of the Bulgarians, 1918–1943 with Princess Maria Louise, Crown Prince Simeon and Queen Giovanna

and proportional representation had been abandoned in favour of carefully constructed single-member constituencies. Despite these measures the People's Constitutional Bloc still managed to win over sixty seats, though five communists and six agrarians were soon expelled from the assembly. That assembly, however, was never entirely pliable and at the end of 1939 Kioseivanov dissolved it, holding fresh elections spread over December 1939 and January 1940. Before the poll yet more restrictions were imposed on the opposition, particularly with regard to their freedom of movement during the short campaign, and the government vote rose accordingly. But having secured this majority Kioseivanov was sacked and replaced by Bogdan Filov.

Filov was an avowed pro-German and his appointment reflected the fact that in Bulgaria, as elsewhere in Europe, the overriding political problems were now in foreign rather than domestic affairs.

After the fall of Stamboliiski the strategy of Bulgarian foreign policy had been to redress Neuilly through 'peaceful revisionism' via the League of Nations with Italy as its patron within that body, the first objective being the implementation of article 48 giving Bulgaria economic access to the Aegean. The relationship to Italy was symbolised by the marriage of Boris to an Italian princess in 1930, but in other respects reliance on Italy had not produced results. In the early 1930s Italy began to move away from Bulgaria whilst the League of Nations declined in effectiveness, particularly after the Nazis took power in Germany. By then Bulgarian policy-makers were looking towards Yugoslavia as a means of avoiding isolation but with little hope of real success as long as the Macedonian enclave in Petrich continued to operate. That problem had been resolved by the *devetnaitseti* and Boris and his advisors were anxious to maintain the momentum towards better relations with their western neighbour. In 1936, as a gesture of goodwill to Belgrade, Kioseivanov banned all demonstrations calling for the dismantling of the treaty of Neuilly, and in January 1937 Bulgaria received its reward when a pact of friendship with Yugoslavia was signed. This was of little more than symbolic significance but it did procure Yugoslav diplomatic backing and in July 1938 the Salonika agreements allowed Greece to remilitarise Thrace and Bulgaria to disregard the arms limitation clauses of the treaty of

Neuilly, which in fact the Sofia government had been doing for some time.

By 1938 all European diplomacy was dominated by the German resurgence. The Munich settlement in September and the Vienna award which followed it in November, by virtually destroying Czechoslovakia, ruined the little entente upon which Czechoslovakia, Yugoslavia and Romania had relied for their security; both Yugoslavia and Romania now became more conciliatory towards Bulgaria. But Munich had another effect. After the Vienna award Bulgaria was the only power defeated in 1918 not to have received back some of its lost territory. It was a point frequently made by the more vociferous of Bulgarian nationalists and especially by those amongst them who championed a pro-German foreign policy.

Boris would not listen to them, fearing that Germany might plunge Europe once more into war. Boris believed Bulgaria's best interests were served by peace or, failing that, neutrality without commitment to any great power; he once despairingly remarked, 'My army is pro-German, my wife is Italian, my people are pro-Russian. I alone am pro-Bulgarian.'

When war did come in September 1939 he immediately declared Bulgaria's neutrality. And for months he remained deaf even to the most alluring of siren calls. In October 1939 the Soviets approached him with the suggestion of a Soviet–Bulgarian mutual assistance pact and Soviet support for Bulgarian claims in the Dobrudja, but Boris refused. He did so again, this time to the Balkan entente powers when they offered Bulgaria membership in February 1940, Boris calculating that this would commit Bulgaria too much to the allied side.

Yet the pro-Axis pressures were mounting, not least because the Nazi–Soviet pact of August 1939 meant that friendship with Germany would not mean offending Russia and therefore disturbing the majority of peasants who still revered the liberating power of 1877–8. Early in 1940 Bulgaria concluded a commercial treaty with Moscow which allowed the import of Soviet books, newspapers and films, and in August of the same year the first visit for many years of a Soviet football team occasioned widespread popular pleasure.

In September 1940 Nazi–Soviet cooperation brought the Bulgarians their first territorial revision. After the Nazi conquest of Scandinavia and France Stalin demanded compensation in the east. This was made at the expense of Romania which was so weakened that it also lost northern Transylvania to Hungary and, in the treaty of Craiova signed on 7 September 1940, was forced to return the southern Dobrudja to Bulgaria.

Whilst these benefits were being reaped a number of internal changes appeared to bring Bulgaria closer to Germany, on which it was already heavily reliant for manufactured goods, including armaments. A youth organisation, Brannik (Defender) was established to instil discipline and patriotic sentiments; one of Bulgaria's very few outspoken anti-semites, Petûr Gabrovski, was made minister of the interior in February 1940; and in the summer the masonic lodges, to which most Bulgarian politicians belonged, were dissolved. In October the defence of the nation act consolidated these measures and others which had been taken against the communists. It also extended anti-semitic legislation enacted earlier in the year. At the same time steps were taken to increase Bulgaria's war-readiness. In May the compulsory labour service was placed under military control; a directorate of civilian mobilisation was set up which had the right to regulate manufacturing in time of war; and, again in the event of war, the ministry of agriculture was given much greater powers to requisition food and control prices.

Bulgaria had been placed on a potential war footing, but it was not yet known if it would go to war and, if so, on which side. After the fall of France and the treaty of Craiova, however, pressure from Germany, Italy and the Soviet Union outweighed that from the west. In October Mussolini offered Boris access to the Aegean if Bulgaria would join in the forthcoming Italian assault on Greece. Boris refused. In the following month another offer of a mutual assistance pact came from Moscow. This time the deal was for Bulgaria to take Thrace and the USSR the Dardanelles; the Soviets were also to have use of Bulgarian naval bases on the Black Sea. Boris knew that the Soviets had used different language in Berlin when talking of this deal, nominating Bulgaria as 'a Soviet security zone'. The Baltic states had been described in those terms shortly before they were incorporated into Stalin's empire a few months earlier.

The situation changed early in December when for the first time Hitler had a pressing reason for direct help from Bulgaria. Mussolini's attack on Greece had not prospered and Hitler, fearing an allied landing in the Peloponnese, had decided to occupy Greece, whence he could also harry British supply lines through the Mediterranean. His troops would need the right of passage through Bulgaria. On 8 December 1940 some forty German staff officers arrived in Sofia for secret discussions. Thereafter an increasing number of German tourists entered Bulgaria; they were all male, they all had short hair and shiny boots, and it was not the tourist season. The Americans made a last effort to persuade Boris that in the long run Britain, with the moral and material backing of the USA, was bound to win the war, but it was to no avail. In February Bulgaria consented to the construction of a pontoon bridge across the Danube and on 2 March agreed to allow German forces to cross Bulgaria *en route* to Greece. The day before Filov had travelled to Vienna to sign the agreement by which Bulgaria became a member of the German-Italian-Japanese tripartite pact.

Bulgaria was in effect now a member of the German alliance and the British minister left Sofia. Not until after the attack on Pearl Harbor, however, did Bulgaria declare what it chose to describe as 'symbolic' war on Britain and the United States. Immediately after the sûbranie ratified this declaration the king disappeared. He was found hours later deep in prayer in a remote and dark corner of Sofia's Aleksandûr Nevski cathedral.

BULGARIA AND THE SECOND WORLD WAR, 1941–1944

The Germans attacked Yugoslavia and Greece in April 1941. By the end of that month the Balkans had been partitioned between the Axis powers, and Bulgaria's share was the western territories lost in 1918, western Thrace including the islands of Samothrace and Thassos, and Serbian Macedonia except for an undefined strip in the west under Italian rule. The Germans retained control of Salonika and Bulgaria was not given full ownership of its new territory lest it pocket its gains and leave the Axis. The Bulgarians, however, saw this as the reunification of their nation, and if liking for the Germans was far from universal, British attempts to incite the Bulgarians to revolt against them met with no response whatever.

In Thrace the Bulgarian occupation produced terrible savagery. In September 1941 the local Greek population staged a rising and committed atrocities against Bulgarians; the latter took fearsome revenge in an effort, some believe, to drive the Greeks out of the region. There was no such confrontation in Macedonia. Here the Bulgarians were initially warmly received as they were a welcome relief to the centralising and serbianising policies of the Yugoslav government; a Bulgarian archimandrite officiated at the 1941 Easter service in Skopje cathedral and Bulgarian nationalists everywhere rejoiced that 'unified Bulgaria' had been recreated. The Bulgarians set about building schools and in Skopje opened Macedonia's first institute of higher learning, the King Boris University. The Bulgarian church did all it could to restore or introduce exarchist organisations, and all former exarchist priests were urged to forsake retirement and work in Macedonia or Thrace. Church leaders in Sofia hoped that now national unity had at last been achieved a patriarch might be elected for the Bulgarian church; all Bulgarian communities, acting through their church, would take part in the election of a patriarch who would remain as a symbol of national unity regardless of what political or territorial changes might come about. The king, however, feared an elected patriarch might be a potential rival and he and Filov therefore filibustered and the holy synod did not receive permission for the election of a patriarch, nor were bishops chosen for the sees of Macedonia and Thrace. This caused some frustration in the newly acquired lands which also felt resentment at the alleged insensitivity of Sofia-appointed administrators. By 1944 there was evidence of growing resentment at the over-centralisation practised by the Bulgarian authorities.

After the occupation of Thrace and Macedonia the dominant issue for Bulgaria's leaders, and in particular for King Boris, was not the nature of Bulgarian rule in the new territories but the degree to which Bulgaria would retain its freedom of action. This applied both to foreign and domestic affairs.

In foreign affairs the critical question was what Germany would require of Bulgaria in the military sphere. Boris was anxious that the Bulgarian army should not be deployed outside the Balkans, and this feeling was immeasurably strengthened when the Germans launched their attack upon the Soviet Union in June 1941. Boris argued that his army was not modern enough for a *Blitzkrieg*, and the peasant conscripts would not fight well far from home, particularly if they were pitted against their beloved Russians. Much better, said Boris, to keep the men in the Balkans where they could help deter a Turkish invasion or a Soviet descent on the Black Sea coast. The Germans did not object and even agreed to supply the modern equipment which the Bulgarians insisted was necessary even for these limited tasks.

The German failure to take Moscow at the end of 1941 and the beginnings of partisan activity in occupied Yugoslavia changed the picture. The Wehrmacht had to call upon troops from the Balkans to reinforce the eastern front and pressed the Bulgarians to help garrison parts of German-occupied Yugoslavia. To this Boris agreed and a new Bulgarian army corps of three divisions was formed and placed under German command. The new Bulgarian army guarded railways, mines, ammunition dumps and other strategic installations, and was later to take part in operations against the growing partisan movement; Bulgarian troops had not been deployed outside the Balkans but they had been used outside areas under Bulgarian political control in support of a non-Bulgarian civil authority. It was a qualitative change in Bulgaria's involvement in Germany's war.

This was not the end of German pressure for Bulgaria to extend its duties. In May 1943 Hitler asked the Bulgarians to take over an area in north-eastern Serbia to release more German troops for duty on the eastern front. He also wanted the Bulgarians to take over most of Greek Macedonia. Boris declined to accept all of the latter on the grounds that for Bulgaria to take Salonika would be too much of a provocation to the Turks and the Italians, but he agreed to help garrison Serbia on the grounds that the German troops so released might prevent a Soviet landing in Bulgaria, an eventuality which would bring about what Boris and Filov feared most: full Bulgarian involvement in the German–Soviet war. As a result of the

Map 7.2 Bulgaria and the second world war

The southern Dobrudja, ceded to Bulgaria, September 1940

Occupied by Bulgaria, April 1941

Occupied by Bulgaria, July 1943

Annexed to Italian-held Albania

Occupied by Germany

Frontiers in 1938

ROMANIA

YUGOSLAVIA

ALBANIA

GREECE

TURKEY

BLACK SEA

Sea of Marmora

Aegean Sea

Adriatic Sea

Danube

Morava

Vardar

Sofia

Skopje

Seres

Drama

Xantia

Kavalla

Salonika

Thasos

Samothrace

N

0   50   100 miles
0   80   160 kilometres

May meeting Bulgarian soldiers assumed guard duties along the Belgrade–Salonika railway and replaced the Germans in northern Serbia and along much of the Aegean coast of Thrace. In August Hitler asked for two more divisions for northern Serbia to which Boris agreed.

Boris had succeeded in avoiding any commitment in the east beyond voluntary contributions to the *Winterhilfe* fund and the provision of one Red Cross train. He had refused to allow the recruitment even of a volunteer legion for duty on the eastern front and when the Germans asked for permission to use fifteen Bulgarian pilots trained in Germany Boris agreed only on condition that they served in North Africa, and even this permission was soon revoked. Boris was no doubt sincere in arguing that his forces were not equipped, materially or emotionally, for service in the Russian war, but there was another reason for this policy. He feared a victorious general might return and, with German connivance, depose him. Right-wing groups which had the sympathy of German officials in Sofia had been very active in the spring of 1942, and in May, Boris said he had heard from Berlin that Gestapo sources favoured a government led by General Lukov because the king was anti-German and the present administration was dominated by masons who were protecting the Jews. In September Boris refused General Lukov permission to travel to Berlin.

There was fear of the left as well as the right. The attack on the Soviet Union mobilised the communists in Bulgaria and exiled comrades were landed in an attempt to help them. The government clamped down hard, and in the next three years over 11,000 people were detained as suspected communists, 6,000 of them being sent to internment camps and the remainder to labour battalions. On 5 April 1942 communist conspiracies were unearthed in the 1st and 6th regiments of the Bulgarian army. Swift action was again taken against the conspirators and on 6 April it was decided to close the Soviet commercial mission in Varna.

There was, of course, no disagreement between the Bulgarians and the Germans on the need to contain any communist threat. Where German and Bulgarian views and jurisdiction did clash in domestic Bulgarian affairs was over the Jewish question. In October 1941 the German minister in Sofia, Beckerle, had begun pressing for more restrictions on the Bulgarian Jews. Further measures were introduced early in 1942 with a 20 per cent levy on Jewish property, the enforcement of the wearing of the yellow star, the compulsory sale of Jewish businesses with the proceeds being deposited in blocked accounts, and the disbandment of almost all Jewish organisations. Yet so unpopular were these measures amongst the general population that the press was forbidden to report them immediately but had to let out the information gradually. After yet more pressure from Beckerle the sûbranie agreed in August 1942 to pass a bill depriving Jews in the occupied territories of their Bulgarian citizenship; it was a decision which was to cost most of those Jews their lives.

After the Wannsee conference and the decision to implement the final solution Nazi pressure intensified. A deputy of Eichmann's arrived in Sofia as assistant police attaché in the German mission with the brief to implement the next stage of the final solution. True to the agreement of the previous summer the Bulgarians did not impede the deportation in March 1943 of the Jews in the occupied lands. In the following months there was much less cooperation over the Jews with Bulgarian citizenship living in Bulgaria proper, at least 6,000 of whom the Nazis had wished to deport in the first wave of transports. When this became public knowledge in Bulgaria there was a spontaneous outburst of anger in the press, in the Orthodox church, and in the sûbranie; all these protests had the wholehearted support of the king. Boris was no doubt aware that the Americans had warned that any Bulgarians who persecuted Jews would be punished after the war, but there is also no doubt that he, like the vast majority of Bulgarians, was revolted by the proposed deportations. The deportations never took place and Bulgaria's 50,000 Jews survived the war.

The German minister in Sofia acknowledged in August 1943 that the Nazis would not persuade the Bulgarians to deport their Jews. At the end of that month the Jewish question faded into the background even for such a dedicated Nazi as Beckerle. On 15 August King Boris had returned exhausted and greatly depressed from a visit to Hitler. Sources close to the king indicate that there had been a terrible row when Hitler demanded a Bulgarian commitment to the eastern front, but no confirmation of this demand can be found

Plate 7.4 Jews detained in Bulgaria, 1943–1944; they were incarcerated in labour camps in the provinces, but thanks to the intervention of the Bulgarian political establishment escaped deportation to the death camps

in German documents. Whatever the cause of his dejection Boris hoped to dispel it by climbing Bulgaria's highest peak, Musala. He returned in a worse state and rapidly declined. On 28 August he died, aged forty-nine. Mystery has surrounded his death ever since but there is no firm proof that it was due to foul play.

On the day before Boris's death a perceptive senior official in the German ministry in Sofia had noted: 'In the eyes of the Bulgarian people the king is less a monarch than a leader. He is a symbol of national unity and his disappearance could . . . lead both to an internal crisis and to external realignments.'

Boris's successor, King Simeon II, was a minor and therefore a regency was formed, though without the constitutionally proper Grand National Assembly to confirm it. The dominant figure in it was Filov, the other members being Boris's brother, Prince Kiril, and a soldier, General Mihov. Filov chose the pliant Dobri Bozhilov as prime minister.

In the summer of 1943 the war was at a critical juncture for Bulgaria as for other powers. In the west Italy was facing collapse and was soon to surrender, whilst in the east the relaxation of German pressure on the Caucasus gave Turkey greater freedom of manoeuvre and made it more likely that it would join the allies. Towards the end of the year the war was brought to Bulgaria itself in the form of allied bombers. There had been some light raids on Sofia and other towns earlier in the war but in November the capital experienced its first heavy bombardment; on 9 January 1944 there was an even larger raid and in March Sofia was subjected to a series of incendiary attacks, culminating in a huge onslaught on 30 March. The raids had been intended to produce social chaos and push Bulgaria towards changing sides. At least in the first objective they were successful; after the January raid many Sofiotes fled in terror and the government had to order civil servants back to their posts.

By this time Bulgaria's urban population was facing privation similar in kind if not in intensity to that endured during the first world war, and for much the same reasons. Food shortages were causing inflation and a flourishing black market where in early 1944 goods were nine times their pre-war price. The shortages were caused by over-enthusiastic requisitioning, by German soldiers sending home more than they should have done, by peasants refusing to hand over to the official procurement agencies produce which they knew would command a much higher price on the black market, by widespread corruption, and by the general dislocation of the distribution system.

The growing plight of the cities together with a general war weariness encouraged the opposition forces. Of these there were two: the legal opposition, consisting of small groups of moderates and rightists from the old parties; and the Fatherland Front (FF). The FF had first been formed in 1941 but had made little progress because few parties were willing to cooperate with the communists who were demanding control of the organisation. In the summer of 1942 a second FF emerged, consisting of communists, zvenari, a social democrat faction and the left agrarians under Nikola Petkov,

Plate 7.5 King Boris's funeral, Sofia, September 1943

son of the premier assassinated in 1907. The new FF broadcast regularly to Bulgaria from the Soviet-controlled Hristo Botev radio station. As relayed in these broadcasts the FF programme called for absolute neutrality on the part of Bulgaria, the withdrawal of Bulgarian troops from operations against the partisans in Yugoslavia, the removal of the army from royal control, a ban on the export of food to Germany, the guarantee of a decent standard of living for all Bulgarians, the full restoration of civil liberties and a ban on all fascist organisations. In 1943 a new central committee was established which included Petkov, Kimon Georgiev, a communist and two social democrats. The loyal opposition, however, was still not ready to work with the FF. The democrats refused to work with the communists, and the non-petkovist agrarians could not cooperate with Georgiev and his associates who had been involved in the coup of 1923. Another weakness of the FF was that, despite its own propaganda, it had little in the way of military muscle, the partisan movement in Bulgaria not assuming any significance until well into the summer of 1944.

Within the political establishment the feeling that Germany had lost the war and that Bulgaria should therefore seek an accommodation with the western allies had been current since before Boris's death; indeed, Boris himself had shared that view. After his death approaches were made to the Americans in October 1943 but their terms were too harsh: unconditional surrender, the evacuation of all occupied territory and an allied occupation. The allied raids on Sofia strengthened the desire to escape from the war. In February and March 1944 further approaches were made to the western allies but their terms were unchanged. Filov and Bozhilov continued to believe that the nation would not tolerate the loss of Macedonia and Thrace and that, in any case, there was no possibility of unconditional surrender with German troops still in the country. Bulgaria, said Bozhilov, would join the allies when the allies joined Bulgaria by landing in the Balkans. That illusion was finally dispelled on 6 June 1944 when the allies landed not in the Balkans but in Normandy.

By then Bulgaria had come under increasing pressure from the Soviets. They had refused a Bulgarian request to intercede with the allies for a cessation of the air bombardment, and instead launched a diplomatic offensive in Sofia. Notes from Moscow arrived in the Bulgarian capital on 1 March, 17 April, 26 April and 18 May, insisting that Bulgarian territory cease being used by anti-Soviet forces. The Bulgarians were prepared to make some concessions over the construction of naval vessels in Varna and they also decided to turn down a German request that German troops be withdrawn westwards via the Bulgarian railway system. In April there were further concessions to the Soviets when Sofia accepted in principle their demands that Soviet consulates be opened in Burgas and Rusé. The consulates were the subject of the next Soviet note, that of 18 May, and this time Moscow threatened the breaking of diplomatic ties if the consulates were not opened.

Soviet pressure, backed as it was by the rapid advance of the Red Army through Ukraine, raised the ultimate nightmare of the Bulgarian administration: involvement in the Russo-German war. What the Soviet pressure amounted to was that if Bulgaria did not break with Germany she would suffer Soviet occupation. But if she obeyed the Soviets and broke with Germany she would suffer German occupation; the experience of Hungary in March 1944 proved that beyond reasonable doubt.

Seeing these dangers Bozhilov resigned on 1 June 1944 to be

replaced by Ivan Bagryanov, who had been educated in Germany and had served with the German army in the first world war, but who was generally regarded as pro-western. He was anxious to secure an armistice with Britain and the USA and to placate the Soviets before relations with them deteriorated any further. In the meantime a direct break with Germany could not be risked. Beckerle was informed on 18 June that Bulgaria would fulfil all its obligations under the tripartite pact but in order to avoid complications with the Russians the Germans should remove their troops from Varna. The Germans, suggested Sofia, could surely not wish another front to be opened in the Balkans by the Soviets, or by the Turks who were now pouring armour into Turkish Thrace. This was an argument which struck home and on 13 July the Germans signified their willingness to remove their steamers and hydroplanes from Varna to make it easier for Bulgaria to pursue 'a policy of peace, friendship and loyalty *vis-à-vis* the Soviet Union'.

As an indication of his good will to the allies on 17 August Bagryanov declared strict neutrality, granted an amnesty to all political prisoners, repudiated the policies of his predecessors, and repealed all anti-Jewish legislation. It was too late. On 20 August the Red Army crossed into Romania and three days later King Michael locked Marshal Antonescu in a safe containing the royal stamp collection and changed sides. At a stroke the Russians were on the lower Danube and astride Bulgaria's northern frontier.

The pressures from the Soviets were now overwhelming and the Bulgarian government had to bend to them. On 25 August Sofia demanded the evacuation of all German troops and the following day the Bulgarian armies were ordered to disarm German forces arriving from the Dobrudja; there was little resistance and by 7 September over 14,000 German personnel had been interned in Bulgaria. The Soviets were not to be placated. On 30 August the Kremlin announced that it would no longer respect Bulgarian neutrality. Bagryanov was defeated and resigned to make way for Konstantin Muraviev, an agrarian.

Muraviev knew that he had to make the final concession to Moscow. On 5 September, therefore, whilst German troops in Bulgaria were still being disarmed, the Bulgarian cabinet decided to break off diplomatic relations with Berlin, though the war minister

Plate 7.6 Sofia welcomes the Red Army in September 1944;
the slogan in the lower picture reads, 'Eternal Glory to the
Red Army'

successfully argued for a delay of seventy-two hours to enable him to bring Bulgarian forces back from the occupied areas. At around 15.00 hours on 7 September the last German vehicles crossed the border and three hours later Bulgaria declared war on Germany with effect from 18.00 hours on 8 September. But by then the Soviet Union had declared war on Bulgaria which for a few chaotic hours was therefore at war with all the major belligerents of the second world war except Japan.

On the same day, 8 September, Soviet troops crossed the Danube and entered Bulgaria to a wildly enthusiastic welcome. Their arrival greatly encouraged the FF, whose partisan units had grown considerably in the chaotic summer months, as had their support amongst the population as a whole, particularly the intelligentsia. On 4 September a series of strikes had been staged to put pressure on Muraviev to break with Germany, and when he did so on the following day there were massive desertions from the army to the partisans. But, contrary to the post-1944 communist school of history, the action which brought the FF to power on 9 September was not carried out by partisans but by units of the army loyal to the war minister Marinov. He it was who, with those practised coupsters Georgiev and Velchev, arranged for the door of the war ministry to be unlocked so that the rebels could take this key point in the city. With no resistance the Muraviev government was deposed within a few hours and a new administration formed by the FF. The new cabinet, which was led by Kimon Georgiev, consisted of five zvenari, four agrarians, three social democrats and four communists. The communists held the key ministries of the interior and justice.

In October, after Marshal Tito had withdrawn his prohibition on Bulgarian troops entering Yugoslav territory, Bulgaria continued fighting, this time on the allied side. Its army joined with Marshal Tolbukhin's Third Ukrainian Front and fought with that army through Hungary and into Austria; 32,000 Bulgarians died in this campaign.

8

Bulgaria under communist rule, 1944–1989

Although the communists dominated the Fatherland Front government from the start, a monolithic, one-party system was not
imposed until the end of 1947.

In their rise to power the communists, still operating as the
Bulgarian Workers' Party (BWP), were helped by a number of
factors. They were, initially at least, extremely popular, especially
amongst the influential urban intelligentsia; that their membership
grew from 15,000 in October 1944 to 250,000 a year later was not
entirely due to careerism and opportunism on the part of the new
members. Their close association with Russia also helped them; the
traditional russophilia of the majority of the Bulgarians could not
but be intensified in the months immediately after the expulsion of
the Germans, months during which the full horrors of Nazi rule in
Europe first became known. The fact that the war was to continue
for eight months after September 1944 also helped the communists
because the western allies had little time to spare for Bulgaria;
the Soviets were given the permanent chairmanship of the Allied
Control Commission (ACC) which was to oversee internal
Bulgarian affairs until the conclusion of a peace treaty. And until
then the Red Army was to remain in Bulgaria, another factor which
certainly did not militate against the communists.

The communists had a sharp nose for political power. One of
their first acts was to place political commissars alongside serving

officers in the armies fighting with Tolbukhin. Some officers were considered too politically unreliable and 800 of them, including 42 generals, were removed. In December 1944, Colonel Ivan Kinov, a Bulgarian who had served in the Red Army, was made chief of the general staff. Whilst most of the existing trained army was engaged against the enemy, the former partisans formed the backbone of a new force, the People's Guard, which was kept in Bulgaria. It was entirely dominated by the communists.

The government controlled the radio and the distribution of newsprint, whilst the ACC, in effect the Soviets, had the right to sanction the import of foreign films and printed material; thus the FF had a virtual strangle-hold over the media, but should a fail-safe be needed opposition newspapers could always be muzzled by the communist-dominated unions in the printing and distributing sectors.

The local FF committees were equally under the communist thumb. These sprang up immediately after 9 September and by November there were 7,000 of them. They conducted an implacable war against local representatives of the old order, policemen, teachers, and priests being prominent amongst them. Some of these were simply murdered; others went before the new people's courts to be sentenced to death or to long periods in labour camps. So energetically did some local committees conduct this campaign that they had to be restrained by the central BWP leadership in Sofia. The workers' councils, established in all industrial concerns, were another new feature of the Bulgarian social landscape and were also totally under communist domination. They had the power to scrutinise company accounts and were to report to the local FF committees who had had dealings with the Germans, the Italians or the Bulgarian 'fascists'.

At the central government level the communists' control of the ministry of the interior enabled them to establish an entirely new police force, the people's militia, as well as a covert political police to which the Soviets attached advisors, as they did to all central government bodies. At the same time the people's courts were controlled by the ministry of justice, which was also in communist hands. The new courts were required to punish 'collaborators and war criminals', but as Bulgaria had not been occupied by a foreign power and had not been engaged on the eastern front there were few Bulgarians who fell into either category. Yet per capita more Bulgarians were accused of these crimes than any other East European nation. For the communists the problem was that the local intelligentsia and political establishment had not been decimated by the Gestapo or its local equivalent, and therefore the potential pool of opposition was greater than in other states; the Bulgarian intelligentsia and political classes were paying now for their relatively easy war.

A major payment was made in February 1945. A month before, the police had arrested the former regents, royal advisors, all members of the last sûbranie, and all who had served in government since 1941. Most were found guilty and the prosecutor demanded death for fifty of them. Twice that number were taken out and executed in batches of twenty the night the verdicts were pronounced. The old right and centre of Bulgarian politics had been eliminated.

The left, however, was still an active force. Though still divided the agrarians remained powerful. The faction which had joined the FF was led by G. M. Dimitrov, known as 'Gemeto' to distinguish him from the communist leader of the same name. Gemeto, however, did not join the government and was soon being attacked as a spy working for the British, for whom he had acted as an advisor during the war. In April he fled to avoid arrest. His place was taken by Nikola Petkov who was a member of the cabinet. Petkov had long been a staunch opponent of association with Germany, had an impeccable war record, and had great oratorical and parliamentary skills. By 1945 he had become anxious at the actions of the local FF committees which he wanted freed from communist domination to ensure a return to full political liberties.

The agrarians were the major obstacle on the communists' road to power. The bulk of the peasantry, who still formed over four-fifths of the population, had always remained loyal to BANU despite the splits and the discreditable behaviour of its ministers between 1931 and 1934. After 9 September 1944 the peasants' allegiance to BANU was increased by their growing revulsion at communist brutality and by their suspicions of communist intentions with regard to collectivisation of the land. The communists were in a difficult position. They could not, as they had done in Hungary, Poland, Czechoslovakia, Romania and eastern Germany, win over the peasants by offering them confiscated aristocratic or *émigré* land; there were no aristocrats or *émigrés* and the peasants had enough land anyway. All the communists could do was launch a frontal assault on agrarian institutions and personalities.

In May 1945 communist intrigues forced another split in the agrarian party and the ministry of justice conveniently declared that all the party's property, including its newspaper and bank accounts, belonged to the anti-Petkov, pro-communist faction. Petkov resigned from the cabinet on 2 August, his group now becoming the Bulgarian Agrarian National Union – Nikola Petkov (BANU–NP). The communists engineered a similar split in the Social Democratic Party whose anti-communist group was led by Kosta Lulchev.

After splitting the agrarians the communists demanded a general election, but they wanted all parties within the FF to appear on a single list. Petkov, with the backing of the western powers, declared this to be anti-democratic. He succeeded in having the elections postponed until 18 November but when he failed to get his own way on the issue of the single list he told his supporters to boycott the poll. He believed the communists were losing support at home, which they were, and that the western powers were exercising more influence over the Soviets, which, in the long run, they were not. However, in the short term there was encouragement for Petkov; the USA refused to acknowledge the legitimacy of the new government which was headed by the BWP leader Georgi Dimitrov who had returned from the USSR on 7 November 1945, and at a meeting of the powers in Moscow the west persuaded the Kremlin to agree that two oppositionists should be included in the Bulgarian cabinet; but the matter went no further than that because Petkov and Lulchev insisted that the communists relinquish control of the ministries of the interior and of justice, dissolve the sûbranie and hold free elections; the communists, with full Soviet backing, refused all three demands.

In 1946 the battle ground of Bulgarian politics widened. A concocted trial of a journalist was said to have disclosed another military conspiracy. This resulted first in a fresh purge of the army which removed over 2,000 officers from the active list, and secondly in a bill in July which passed control of the military from the ministry of war to the cabinet as a whole. As the minister of war was Velchev the move was clearly intended to diminish the already declining influence of the zvenari. Shortly afterwards two votes were announced: a referendum on the monarchy was to be held in September, and in the following month elections for a Grand National Assembly were to take place.

Both votes were meant to send signals to the Paris peace conference which in August began discussion of the Bulgarian peace treaty. The referendum on the monarchy resulted in the declaration of a republic, the simple, or simplistic message for the peacemakers supposedly being that Bulgaria had rid itself of the dynasty which had twice taken it to war on Germany's side. The convocation of a GNA was intended to show the negotiators in Paris that Bulgaria was keen to create a new form of government which could be relied upon to behave in a mature and cooperative manner. These gestures made little impact upon the basically anti-Bulgarian disposition of the allies. Bulgaria, despite the sacrifices made in the campaigns in Hungary and Austria after September 1944, was not recognised as a co-belligerent, and the loss of all territories occupied during the war was confirmed. The southern Dobrudja, however, was retained.

The Paris debates indicated declining western interest in Bulgaria and the opposition therefore combined resources to run on a single ticket in the elections to the GNA on 27 October. The opposition won 101 seats to the FF's 364; and of the latter deputies the communists were given the absurdly high number of 277. This was naked ambition and a violent distortion of any notion that the allocation of seats to the communists should represent their share of FF supporters or of their share of votes cast for the FF list.

The battle was now moving to its final phase both at home and abroad. At home the communists were clearly losing ground. The holy synod rejected a plan put forward by the FF for the democratisation of the church and even the old leftist party of the pre-9 September era, the democrats, enjoyed something of a resurgence. This was mainly because what remained of Bulgaria's bourgeoisie was being pushed into oblivion. From September 1944 there had been restrictions on profits, and the property of alleged collaborators, war criminals and speculators had been confiscated. Regulations on living space, grudgingly accepted at first in view of the post-bombing housing shortage, limited the size of households, and thereby decreased the already much diminished quality of life; many of the intelligentsia, for example, were forced to dispose of their personal libraries. In 1946 new tax laws required all arrears from 1942 to be paid off in a very short time, but the heaviest blow came with currency and banking reform in March 1947. The new currency was issued at rates which disadvantaged those with savings, in addition to which private accounts above a certain level were blocked and a once-and-for-all tax was levied on all savings. And this during one of Europe's worst ever winters.

Even the workers in the towns were showing signs of discontent. Unemployment was high and the winter affected them even more because food and fuel were especially short in urban areas. There were frequent strikes and many workers left the towns to cultivate their own or their relations' plots. The communists felt an increasing need to act before matters became any worse.

The same message came from abroad. In February 1947 the peace treaty had been signed and within ninety days of its final ratification the Red Army would be leaving Bulgaria. In March the Truman doctrine was promulgated threatening to resist further communist encroachment.

Meanwhile, in the GNA Petkov was castigating communist incompetence and arrogance, and lampooning these alleged friends of the people who were spending far more on the police and prisons than the so-called fascists had during the war. He demanded the restoration of the Tûrnovo constitution together with the return of full civil liberties. The communists decided to act. In June Petkov was arrested in the sûbranie and in August was subjected to a grotesque trial in which the defence was denied the rights to legal representation or to present evidence; this, it was decided would be 'of no use or importance'. Petkov was sentenced to death and hanged, being denied even the last rites and a Christian burial, despite the fact that he was one of Bulgaria's few genuinely religious public figures.

The death of Petkov broke the opposition. In October the founding meeting of cominform enjoined all European communist parties in government to intensify the drive towards socialism. The BWP needed little encouragement. It rapidly mopped up what remained of political opposition and in December 1947 pushed through the GNA the 'Dimitrov constitution', so-called even though it had been drafted in the USSR.

The Dimitrov constitution declared Bulgaria a 'people's republic'. It was a typical Soviet-style system in which all freedoms were promised but where in reality power lay not with the official state organs but with those of the communist party. The means of production were to pass into public ownership and the higher ranks of the judiciary were to be subjected to parliamentary control; this in effect was communist control because local party organisations, acting through the local FF committees, had to sanction all parliamentary candidates. Within a few months all the parties within the FF had come to acknowledge the leading role of the communist party and accept that Marxism-Leninism was the ruling ideology. Untypically, however, rather than fuse all the elements of the coalition into one communist dominated party, in Bulgaria there were to be two distinct parties in the ruling coalition. Because of the respect the peasants had for the agrarian tradition, that faction of BANU which had cooperated with the communists was to remain a separate party and was to join in a coalition government with them; it was to remain their coalition partner until 1990. The coalitionist agrarians, however, had little real power because they were represented only in state and not in communist party organisations.

In its fifth congress in December 1948 the BWP reverted to its former name, the Bulgarian Communist Party (BCP). Together with the other ruling parties in Eastern Europe the BCP adopted as its guiding, organisational principle that of 'democratic centralism'. This meant in effect that the chain of command was always vertical, from the centre down; there were to be no horizontal links because the centre could not tolerate the possibility of local conspiracies against it. The supreme body of the party was its congress which convened usually every five years; the congress elected the central committee which met in plenum at irregular intervals, and which could make important policy decisions. Those decisions, however, were usually to implement those already taken by the party's most

Plate 8.1 Nikola Petkov on trial, August 1947

powerful organism, the politburo, whose dozen or so members were chosen by the central committee.

Party control was exercised through a number of mechanisms. In all factories and other places of work and in government units at every level the local party cell, 'the primary party organisation', played a vital role in the running of the economic enterprise or government unit. Each primary party organisation kept two lists; one, the *nomenklatura* list, contained those posts in its area of responsibility which were important enough to be taken only by trustworthy individuals; the second, the cadre list, contained the names of trustworthy individuals; information on all individuals was kept up to date by the informers each primary party organisation recruited. The *nomenklatura* system ensured that anyone who wanted access to a decent job would keep his or her political nose clean; this was the base of the party's social power. For those within the party who carefully towed the party line there was the promise of rewarding jobs together with privileges such as access to better shops, holiday resorts, hospitals, schools and other facilities.

Soon after December 1947 the trade unions, the youth organisations, the Soviet friendship societies, professional bodies and women's groups were all brought under communist control, this control being exercised by the Fatherland Front.

Once its monolithic system was established the BCP hastened to the construction of a socialist economy and a society based on the Soviet model. The nationalisation of industry was quickly and easily accomplished, foreign trade was soon made a government monopoly, and Bulgaria was rapidly integrated into the system of alliances and agreements, economic and political, which Stalin's Soviet Union was building in Eastern Europe. In 1947 an emergency two-year plan for the economy had been introduced, but in 1949 the first five-year plan came into operation designed to shift the emphasis of the Bulgarian economy from the agricultural to the heavy industrial sector. In its plans for the collectivisation of the land, however, the BCP met with opposition. Historians do not yet know the full extent of this opposition but it seems that it was at its most obdurate in north-west Bulgaria where armed clashes are known to have taken place, but protest was by no means confined to that area and all over the country peasants committed acts of defiance such as burning their crops or killing their cattle rather than let them be taken into a collective farm. The resistance, however, had been critically weakened in February 1948 when farm machinery had to be handed over to the new machine tractor stations. By 1951 resistance had virtually ceased.

Even the setting up of the monolithic system did not mean the end of political persecution. The Orthodox church was amongst a number of organisations to be brought into line. The Exarch Stefan was packed off to a monastery and his clergy required to choose between joining the new Union of Bulgarian Priests or being sent to a labour camp. In February 1949 a new law on church organisation confirmed the subjugation of church to state. In 1951 the exarchate was raised to a patriarchate, further weakening the already tenuous links between the Bulgarian church and Istanbul. The non-Orthodox churches suffered a worse fate because their links with the non-communist world could not be dissolved, and links with the outside world were something which communist regimes greatly feared in these early days of the cold war. In 1949 the Sofia government had refused to allow the pope's newly appointed delegate to Bulgaria to take up his place and in the same year fifteen Protestant pastors had been put on trial, convicted and sentenced to long terms of imprisonment.

One of the organisations which was most heavily purged in the early years of communist rule was the communist party itself. In March 1949 a popular leading communist, Traicho Kostov, was sacked from his government posts and made director of the national library. In December he was put on trial and sentenced to death. His execution was the prelude to a savage purge in which at least 100,000 party members were expelled, many of them being sent to labour camps. Greater numbers from the civil service, the armed forces and all sections of society were purged at the same time. The purges were an East European phenomenon provoked by Stalin's paranoia. For justification of the purges the Soviet leader used the alleged danger of national communism as exemplified by Tito, whom he had expelled from the cominform in the summer of 1948. But there were deeper reasons for the purges. The great social transformation caused by collectivisation and industrialisation would inevitably cause discontent which, equally inevitably, would seek some political vehicle for its expression. In Eastern Europe all political vehicles but one, the communist party, had been immobilised. The purges were therefore meant to warn the communist parties themselves not to have any dealings with the social discontent which their own policies were creating. There were also specifically Bulgarian factors in the Kostov case. In part the succession to the BCP leadership was at stake. Dimitrov had died in July 1949 and his nominated successor, Vasil Kolarov, was ill. Kostov was a natural candidate but his pro-Soviet credentials were not good because he had criticised Soviet economic policies in the post-war years.

Also, in Bulgaria the Yugoslav dimension of the purges was especially large. Immediately after the war the BCP had agreed that those parts of Pirin Macedonia within Bulgaria should be ceded to Yugoslav Macedonia when a Balkan federation was established. In the meantime teachers were imported into Pirin to teach the locals how to read and write in the new Macedonian language recently defined by scholars in Yugoslav Macedonia. In Bulgaria this was an intensely unpopular policy and was abandoned the minute Tito and his Yugoslavia were ostracised. Kostov was not properly pro-Soviet so he could be accused of pro-Yugoslavism; and thus the BCP could try to shift onto Kostov some of the opprobrium for its Pirin policy. Also, the Kostov trial coincided almost exactly with the first elections under the Dimitrov constitution; it was a timely call for obedience to the official party line.

After the Kostov trial Vûlko Chervenkov, who had succeeded Dimitrov as head of the party and prime minister, was secure. Bulgaria's 'little Stalin' could continue the task of constructing socialism with a Soviet face. Every aspect of national life seemed to be refashioned on the Soviet model: education, culture, the economy, architecture and the military. To keep the Bulgarians on the correct line there were ever more Soviet advisors attached to every arm of government.

True to Stalinist practice the purges also continued. Accusations that a Bulgarian translator at the US embassy had spied for the United States were used as the excuse for another round of repression against those who had any connection with the non-socialist world and especially America; the USA broke off diplomatic relations in protest. A victim of this purge was the Roman Catholic bishop of Nevrokop who was tried together with twenty-seven other priests and twelve members of the laity. On the other hand, Chervenkov did permit the emigration of almost all Bulgaria's surviving Jews, despite the fact that the Soviet Union had entered an extreme anti-Israeli phase. Chervenkov also encouraged the emigration of Turks. In fact he terrified Ankara in January 1950 by announcing that a quarter of a million Turks would be allowed to leave. After a good deal of negotiation the Turks admitted 162,000 before closing the border in 1952. Most of the *émigrés* came from the Dobrudja, the richest arable area of Bulgaria and the one Chervenkov wanted to collectivise fastest; the Turks were in fact displaced persons forced from their homes not by military events but by the social and economic changes brought about by the application of Stalinist dogma.

DESTALINISATION AND THE RISE OF TODOR ZHIVKOV, 1953–1965

Chervenkov sailed on in seemingly untroubled waters until 3 March 1953 when Stalin died. There was also a wave of industrial unrest in Eastern Europe, Bulgaria being one of the first countries to experience it when strikes broke out amongst the tobacco workers in Plovdiv. Within a few months Stalin's successors in the Kremlin had called for a 'new course' in Eastern Europe.

The regime in Sofia soon adapted itself to the revised Soviet attitude. Bulgaria's new course was seen in improved relations with Greece, talk of repairing the breach with the USA, and the restoration of diplomatic relations with Yugoslavia. At home it was announced that more investment would be allocated to the consumer sector and to agriculture. More dramatically, the terror was relaxed. Police activity was reduced and thousands of detainees were released from prison and the labour camps. Other aspects of the new course included a decline in Soviet influence. Most advisors returned home and the joint-stock companies which had given the Soviets great influence in certain sectors of the Bulgarian economy were disbanded. In March 1954 at the BCP's sixth congress Chervenkov announced that he would no longer hold the offices of prime minister and general secretary of the party, deciding to relinquish the latter. His successor was a young, efficient, but self-effacing apparatchik named Todor Zhivkov.

The introduction of the new course was only the beginning of a series of events which were to convulse the USSR and Eastern Europe between 1953 and 1956. In 1955 Khrushchev began the rehabilitation of Tito; given that Chervenkov's eminence was a result of his defeat of Kostov on the grounds of the latter's Titoism, this seriously undermined Chervenkov's legitimacy. When Khrushchev, speaking to the twentieth congress of the Communist Party of the Soviet Union in February 1956, criticised Stalin's mistakes he pulled another plank from Chervenkov's political platform. At the April plenum of the BCP central committee Chervenkov's cult of personality was denounced and he resigned. The new prime minister was Anton Yugov.

During the upheavals of 1956, which were to end with the Hungarian anti-Soviet revolution, Zhivkov remained steadfastly loyal to Khrushchev. The relaxations of 1956 had produced in Bulgaria a notable cultural thaw but after Hungary there was an equal and opposite reaction with the purge of the so-called 'anti-party group' in 1957 which was both a copy of events in Moscow and an assurance to the Soviet comrades that the Bulgarian party was in full control of events. The crack-down of 1957 enhanced Yugov's political stature. He was seen as the strong man of the party, a reputation he had earned between 1944 and 1949 when he had been minister of the interior. He had dropped out of favour after the Kostov trial but was back in the saddle as deputy prime minister in time to deal with the Plovdiv strikers in 1953. By 1957 he and Zhivkov were obvious contenders and probable competitors for supremacy within the party and therefore the country.

The late 1950s were dominated by economic policy. In 1958 Bulgaria announced it was the first state after the Soviet Union to have completed the collectivisation of agriculture. In the same year a drastic reform of the collective farms reduced their number from 3,450 to 932. Other reforms in the same year required all bureaucrats, both party and state, to work for a set number of days in a factory or on a farm to make sure they did not lose touch with the proletariat. In 1960 Zhivkov produced a fantastic, or phantasmagoric plan for economic expansion. The figures were absurd and were reduced in 1961 before being abandoned in 1963 after inflicting considerable damage on the economy, particularly on agriculture. These 'Zhivkov Theses' of 1960 were sometimes referred to as Bulgaria's 'Great Leap Forward' but they were copied from Khrushchev not from Mao.

Both Yugov and Chervenkov were critical of the Zhivkov Theses. But Chervenkov himself was finally discredited in 1961 when Khrushchev launched his second and much more vitriolic attack upon Stalin and Stalinism. Chervenkov, after being denounced for not having learnt the lessons of 1956 and the April plenum, disappeared from public life.

Chervenkov's elimination intensified the duel between Zhivkov and Yugov. Zhivkov's strength was his backing from Moscow, and his position was bolstered in May 1962 when his patron, Khrushchev, paid a week-long visit to Bulgaria, touring the country with his *protégé* in the fashion of a Russian general of old. Zhivkov's weakness was the fast deteriorating agricultural situation which was producing shortages so severe that grain had to be imported from North America. Yugov capitalised on this, as he did on Khrushchev's mishandling of relations with China and his disastrous adventure in Cuba.

The final battle was due to be fought in the eighth congress of the BCP which had originally been scheduled for August 1962 but which was postponed until November because of the agricultural crisis. Shortly before the congress convened a plenum of the central committee met. Half way through its proceedings Zhivkov flew to Moscow; when he returned a few days later he announced that Yugov had been removed from the politburo and relieved of his post as prime minister. Yugov retired into obscurity, to emerge as an old man in 1984 to receive the award of 'hero of socialist labour'.

Zhivkov's victory had clearly been engineered and confirmed by the Kremlin and henceforth Zhivkov was to be a byword for slavish obedience to the Moscow line. He did not rely on the Soviets alone, however. Soon after Yugov's ouster he brought his own supporters into the politburo and into other critical party posts at national and local level. By 1964 he was strong enough to survive the fall of his patron in Moscow and in the following year he defeated a military conspiracy aimed at lessening Bulgaria's subservience to the Soviet Union. Zhivkov was to remain virtually unchallenged for twenty years.

THE *ZHIVKOVSHTINA*, 1965–1981

In 1965 the Bulgarian leadership introduced a series of reforms which were to bring in greater economic accountability and, under the new system of 'planning from below', were to allow local enterprises and their managers greater responsibility. The upheavals in Czechoslovakia three years later stopped the reform programme dead in its tracks. Not only did the party return to economic orthodoxy, it actually tightened political controls. The Fatherland Front took into its fold seemingly innocuous organisations such as the temperance society and the slavic committee and a call went out to make sure that all committees in urban residences and all those dealing with the supply of water, food and other necessities were firmly within the party's grasp. Inside the party itself there was to be 'iron discipline'.

Much of this renewed centralisation and ideological conformity were reflected in two important innovations in 1971: a new constitution and a new party programme.

The 1971 constitution declared Bulgaria to be a socialist state headed by its working class. The leading role of the BCP was recognised, as was Bulgaria's membership of the socialist community. A new body was established, the state council, which was to have legislative and executive powers, and whose chairperson was to be head of state. That person was Zhivkov. The state council was also to exercise certain supervisory functions over the administration, functions which in most other East European states were the responsibility of party organs. The new party programme announced that the guiding principles of the BCP were still those laid down in the 'April Line' of 1956, but now that socialism had been built a new strategy was needed to guide the party and the nation through the process of constructing mature socialism in 'a unified socialist society'. In the long term this process would involve the homogenisation of Bulgaria; the emphasis at this stage was on the amalgamation of urban and rural life, and of physical and mental labour, but for those who chose to exploit it the idea of a unified socialist society could also have ethnic connotations. The move towards mature socialism would mean the transition from extensive to intensive growth, a transition which was to be facilitated by the scientific-technological revolution which alone could bring the required increase in productivity and therefore wealth. Though the 1971 party programme was to be greatly modified in the mid-1980s, the 1971 constitution remained in force until after the collapse of the communist system.

The changes of 1971 did not greatly alter Zhivkov's regime. Its main feature remained an almost total obedience to the Soviet Union, especially in foreign policy; in September 1973 Zhivkov remarked that Bulgaria and the Soviet Union would 'act as single body, breathing with the same lungs and nourished by the same bloodstream'. On issues such as the Vietnam war, the third world, the Middle East, and Latin America there was not a hair's breadth of difference between Sofia and Moscow. So far did Zhivkov's devotion to the Soviet Union go that we now know that on two occasions he proposed that Bulgaria should be incorporated into the USSR. Khrushchev turned him down because he thought Zhivkov saw in such a union easy access to higher living standards; Brezhnev rejected the offer because he knew it to be impracticable in diplomatic terms.

Whilst he always followed the Soviet line in foreign affairs Zhivkov did develop more links with the west. In October 1966 he paid his first visit to the non-communist world when he was received in Paris by General de Gaulle, whose anti-American virtues were considered compensation enough for the vice of his conservatism. In December 1973 full diplomatic relations were established with the Federal Republic of Germany with whom Bulgaria had already developed considerable trading links. In June 1975 Zhivkov visited the Vatican and was received by Pope Paul VI. Later in the year the Bulgarian government sanctioned the nomination of Uniate bishops in Bulgaria and allowed a party of Bulgarian Catholics to make a pilgrimage to Rome; by 1979, for the first time since the 1940s, no Catholic see in Bulgaria was without a bishop.

Increasing links were also established with the third world. African students had been receiving university education in Bulgaria since the early 1960s, though life there was not always to their taste as demonstrations in April 1965 had proved. In the late 1960s and 1970s many trained Bulgarians went in the opposite direction to work as doctors, teachers, engineers, etc.; by 1981 there were over 2,000 Bulgarian doctors working in Libya alone. In the 1970s and 1980s well-heeled, dollar-earning Bulgarians enjoying leave at home were a familiar feature of the country's somewhat exiguous fleshpots.

At home the vast majority of the population were content or apathetic. Despite occasional rumblings of discontent there was no prospect of dissidence on the Polish scale; Bulgaria had no independent church to act as an alternative focus of loyalty, and when confronted with a political system which he disliked the Bulgarian tended to respond with apathy and withdrawal rather than with opposition and confrontation; the bogomil legacy lasted long. Zhivkov did not utter the world dissidence in public until 1977, and some years later when an acrostic reading 'Down With Todor Zhivkov' appeared in a literary journal he laughed it off, declaring that the regime would not be brought to its knees by a couple of poets.

Another, and more important reason for the relative stability of Bulgaria during the 1960s and 1970s was that for most of the population life was gradually becoming better. The political terror of the late 1940s and 1950s had given way to a reactive policing against the few who spoke out or caused the regime embarrassment. In December 1972 a central committee plenum had promised that in the new phase of economic and social development more attention would be paid to providing consumer goods and social facilities such as education and housing. Progress was always to be slow in these sectors, and there were periodic downturns, but anyone who had visited Bulgaria in the late 1960s and then returned in the late 1970s would have had no doubt that conditions had in general improved.

One reason for this gradual improvement was that Bulgaria benefited from Comecon schemes for economic specialisation introduced in the early 1960s. Under a 1965 agreement with the USSR Bulgaria was to assemble cars and lorries manufactured in the Soviet Union; Bulgaria also began to specialise in ship-building and in the production of railway rolling stock and fork-lift trucks; by 1975 one-third of its industrial output was for the transport sector. By then Bulgaria was beginning to produce magnetic discs and

Plate 8.2 Typical communist propaganda: party boss Todor Zhivkov with a group of children at the First Congress on Public Education, Sofia 1980

other computer parts for the East European market. Agreements such as these tied Bulgaria to the East European and even more to the Soviet customer, but on the other hand they provided Bulgaria with easy markets for its low-quality manufactured goods and they also allowed Bulgaria to import oil from the Soviet Union at low prices. In later years a good deal of this oil was sold on the open market for a profit in hard currency.

In the early and mid-1970s food production was stimulated by another major reorganisation of the agricultural sector. In 1969 in the Vratsa area seven collective farms employing some 40,000 workers and covering 38,700 hectares were grouped into a loose federation or Agro-Industrial Complex (AIC). In 1970 the experiment was endorsed by a central committee plenum and applied nationally. The AICs employed at least 6,000 workers and were between 20,000 and 30,000 hectares in extent. They were intended to capitalise on the advantages of the local soil and climate by concentrating on two or three crops and one or two brands of livestock. In their early years the AICs gave encouraging returns and were another reason why most Bulgarians in the 1970s felt they had little reason to complain about their lot.

The placidity of the domestic political scene did not mean that Zhivkov was indifferent to potential opposition. One literary man who learned that to his cost was Georgi Markov, poisoned with a pellet shot from an umbrella on Waterloo Bridge, London, in September 1977. Markov had revealed too many details of the life style of Bulgaria's political élite; two weeks later a similar but this time unsuccessful attempt was made on the life of Vladimir Kostov in Paris, his sin being that he had exposed the workings of the Bulgarian secret police and the extent to which it, and much of the Bulgarian establishment, was subordinated to the Soviet Union.

Nor did Zhivkov tolerate any potential challenge to his leadership in the upper echelons of the party. Throughout his rule he conducted a game of musical chairs, moving ministers or senior party officials sideways if they seemed to be building up too strong a power base. Such changes seldom involved loss of office but occasionally more firm action was taken. In May 1977 Boris Velchev was removed from the politburo and extensive changes were made in a number of provincial party organisations. At the same time party membership cards were called in for examination; this was the standard method of carrying out a purge and in this one some 38,500 members were expelled from the party. This was the largest 'cleansing' of the party which took place whilst Zhivkov was in power, though there were further sackings of leading figures, particularly in the mid-1980s.

Like other Balkan communist regimes that in Bulgaria was not devoid of a nationalist tinge. This was useful because as ideological commitment declined the party needed greater legitimacy at home, particularly after the post-1968 tightening of the reigns. There were, it seemed in the late 1960s, two easy roads to enhanced legitimacy: consumerism and a greater assertion of national identity. The Bulgarian economy was not yet developed enough to offer consumerism, but there were also problems with the second course. Because Bulgarian policy was so closely aligned with that of the Soviet Union national assertion was difficult in foreign affairs. The answer was more national, Bulgarian self-assertion at home; 1968 saw the end of all but one newspaper and one journal for the Turkish reader; gypsy textbooks could henceforth be published in Bulgarian only; and Sofia's gypsy theatre, which had flourished in the postwar years, became a thing of the past.

After the 1971 party programme had called for the creation of a unified socialist nation the assimilationist pressures on the gypsies and on other minorities increased. In the early 1970s pomaks who had become Turkified were required to adopt Slav names, and those who did not were punished; in 1974 500 of the 1,300 inmates of the notorious Belene labour camp were pomaks who had resisted pressure to change their names. The Turks were not yet put under such pressure but increased emigration was encouraged. In 1968 Bulgaria and Turkey signed an agreement allowing for the reunification in Turkey of families separated by the exodus of the early 1950s. In the ten years during which the agreement remained in force some 130,000 Turks left Bulgaria.

The Macedonian question was also one where nationalist heart strings could be tweaked. After the break with Tito in 1948 the expression of Macedonian identity became more and more difficult. By the early 1960s severe penalties were being imposed on anyone who attempted such expression in public, and even though the 1963 edition of the shorter Bulgarian encyclopaedia still carried an article on the Macedonian language the 1965 census, which measured ethnicity by mother tongue, did not recognise Macedonian as an ethnic category. Any action on the Macedonian question inside Bulgaria inevitably affected and was affected by relations with Yugoslavia. If the Soviet Union's relations with Belgrade were bad the Bulgarians did not hesitate to take the offensive on Macedonia. In 1969, for example, the party circulated to its members a pamphlet claiming that two-thirds of the population of Yugoslav Macedonia were ethnic Bulgarians, an assertion to which Skopje naturally took great exception. Other disputes, most of them of an academic nature, were to break out periodically but Zhivkov never lost control of them and there was never any likelihood under his rule that the Macedonian dispute would cause real international complications.

The most interesting and unusual aspect of Bulgarian nationalism in the 1970s focuses not so much on Zhivkov as on his daughter, Liudmila Zhivkova. Born in 1942 she was of the generation which had grown up under socialism, albeit in its most privileged circles. That privilege had been responsible for her being able to spend an academic year in Oxford and in 1971 helped her to the post of deputy chairperson of the committee for art and culture. She became its head in 1975 and in the following year took over responsibility for radio, television and the press. In 1980 she was given charge of the politburo commission on science, culture and art. With the help of established scholars she published a number of books and in private she began to show an increasing and wholly un-Marxist interest in mysticism. In the small world of the Sofia intelligentsia such private interests soon became public knowledge.

The intelligentsia were fascinated by the discussion of non-materialist ideas and they could not help but be gratified by the stress which Zhivkova placed on Bulgaria's long cultural traditions and the individuality and separateness of those traditions. In 1981 she orchestrated a huge celebration of the 1,300th anniversary of the founding of the first Bulgarian state. This was no doubt an exaggerated and an extremely expensive affair but it was part of the process of emphasising that Bulgaria's history and culture were unique and that therefore Bulgarians were culturally different from other peoples. And of course this was immediately interpreted in private as meaning different from the Russians. The 1981 celebrations highlighted the fact that the Bulgarians had had an organised state long before the Russians. Later the Bulgarians were to mark their conversion to Christianity where, once again, the Bulgarians preceded the Russians. But by then Zhivkova was dead. She died in July 1981 aged only thirty-nine. There were immediately rumours that the Russians had murdered her, but there is no

Plate 8.3 A critical cartoon of Liudmila Zhivkova as patron
of the arts. Those in line are mostly caricatures of leading
Bulgarian academics and men of letters

evidence to cast doubt on the official cause of death, cerebral
haemorrhage, perhaps induced by the effects of a serious motor
accident a few years before. Zhivkova's nationalism had been
cultural not ethnic and was a call to celebrate Bulgarian achievements not to discriminate against indigenous minorities; even if she
lived a privileged and extremely self-indulgent life, Zhivkova was
probably more mourned at her death than any public figure since
King Boris.

THE DECLINE AND FALL OF TODOR ZHIVKOV, 1981–1989

The death of Liudmila Zhivkova was a symbolic turning point
after which hope seemed to turn increasingly to despair amongst
Bulgaria's ruling élite, no matter what contortions of organisation
and policy it imposed.

In the first place, the gloss of Zhivkova's cultural self-
congratulation was tarnished by a series of international scandals.
These had begun with the Markov and Kostov affairs in 1977 but
they showed no signs of ending. There were accusations that

Bulgaria was involved in the production of counterfeit whisky; that the state trading agency, Kintex, was enmeshed in a complex operation which smuggled drugs into the west and used the money so gained to send arms to subversive groups in countries such as Turkey which the communists wished to destabilise; in 1981 came the accusation that Bulgarian secret service agents had been implicated in the attempted assassination of Pope John Paul II in Rome; and in July 1982 the United States branded Bulgaria as a country engaged in 'state-sponsored' terrorism. Since the fall of the communists Bulgaria has acknowledged its guilt in the Markov affair but continues strenuously to deny any implication in the attempt on the pope's life.

By 1981 a more general problem was becoming clear in Bulgaria as it was in other East European states. The transfer from extensive to intensive economic growth was not being accomplished as easily or as rapidly as planned. The scientific-technological revolution in which so much hope had been placed proved disappointing, not least because planned economies could not keep pace with the increasingly rapid changes in computer sciences and fibre optics. The import of western technology, upon which some reliance had been placed, became more difficult partly because of the trading restrictions President Reagan imposed, but much more so because the oil-price hikes of the mid-1970s had made western goods so much more expensive. At the same time efforts to expand trade with central and western Europe were doomed to frustration because all that Bulgaria could offer in the way of high-quality exports were agricultural goods, the very ones which the EEC was determined to exclude. Bulgaria did find some alternative markets in Scandinavia, North America and the Far East but it was becoming more difficult to meet foreign debt obligations; much more difficult, indeed, than the fabricated figures published in the 1980s indicated. By 1981 growth rates were slowing and expectations becoming correspondingly more sober; the eighth five-year plan introduced in that year anticipated an increase in national income of 20 per cent as opposed to the 45 per cent of the seventh plan in 1976.

The regime's answer was the New Economic Mechanism (NEM) outlined in a plenum of March 1979 and applied to the entire economy by 1982. The purpose of the NEM was to raise productivity, to improve the quality of Bulgarian goods and services, and thereby secure the exports needed to eliminate existing trading deficits and hard currency debts. To achieve this the NEM was to provide 'a new approach to the management of the economy in the scientific-technological revolution'. The new approach was based on five principles. First, decentralisation was to mean greater freedom for all enterprises which would now receive from the central planning agencies not detailed production quotas but general guidelines. Second, democracy was to be implemented by the election of brigade leaders and other officials in a new system of 'mobilisation from below'. Third, competition was to be extended and would determine investment allowances as well as wages. Fourth, market forces were to be allowed into the economy with enterprises being left to find their own resources and outlets for their products. And fifth, self-sufficiency was to be applied to all plants which could no longer automatically count on government subsidies.

These were grandiose schemes but they had little real impact. The quality of production showed no sign of improvement. In 1983 Zhivkov gave a lecture, which was broadcast live on radio and television, in which he savagely denounced the quality of Bulgarian goods, even alleging that foreign products assembled under licence had been 'bulgarised' by sloppy workmanship and poor labour discipline. In March 1984 a special party conference met to discuss the problem. It produced yet more exhortations and suggestions for industrial reorganisation but once again these had little effect.

The NEM, the attempt to improve quality, and the efforts to increase the supply of consumer goods to the home market, faced a number of obstacles. In the first place the need to tackle the foreign debt had to take priority over other needs if future imports of technology were to be assured and export markets secured. This meant that foreign currency had to be diverted to debt payments rather than to importing foreign consumer goods or the machinery to manufacture them at home. It also meant that much of the best of domestic production had to be diverted into the export trade. The Bulgarians did not have to suffer the privations Ceausescu's manic determination to overcome Romania's foreign debt inflicted on his country, but the Bulgarian home buyer was denied enjoyment of the best his country had to offer, not least in wine. It made life in Bulgaria grey and uniform just at a time when foreign travel was becoming easier and when more western films, TV programmes and videos were being seen, thus making an increasing number of Bulgarians more conscious of that greyness.

Energy was another problem facing the Bulgarian economy. The country has little in the way of indigenous fossil fuels and is forced therefore to rely heavily on imports. In the 1980s the Soviets, facing economic problems of their own, were forcing up their prices and in the second half of the decade were to switch to world prices. Bulgaria had developed a nuclear power capability at Kozlodui on the Danube and was constructing a second facility further down the river at Belene. But construction work at the latter and repairs at the former were way behind schedule by the mid-1980s, and as Kozlodui produced in the region of 30 per cent of the nation's electricity, not having it at full capacity was an extra economic burden. So too were the severe droughts of 1984 and 1985 which reduced hydro-electric power generation.

The most important obstacle in the path of economic advance, however, was that Bulgaria's managerial cadres were not trained for operating in a system which called for self-reliance, responsibility and the making of decisions on purely economic grounds. Managers were reluctant to buy western machines if similar Soviet ones were available because they feared they might be suspected of political disloyalty; plant managers who had for decades been used to having their production routines settled for them by central organisations often did not know how to find their own raw materials or their own markets; and producers accustomed to sacrifice everything to achieving plan totals were deaf to calls to improve the quality of their goods, particularly if that meant reducing the quantity of production. By the mid-1980s the NEM was seen not to be working. For the first time in twenty years there was no perceptible improvement in living standards, nor any expectation of one. This was a quiet but profoundly important shift in public attitudes.

From 1985 economic difficulties combined with two other factors to wreck the Zhivkov regime. Those two factors were the attempted assimilation of Bulgaria's ethnic Turks and the advent of Gorbachev.

The decision to enforce the assimilation of the Turks, beginning with the requirement that they should take Bulgarian or Slav names, was taken in the highest echelons of the party late in 1984. In the 1940s when the southern Dobrudja had been reincorporated into Bulgaria place names had been changed but it had been considered too draconian to change personal ones. The experience with the pomaks in the 1970s suggested that the more extreme step was possible. But it was soon to be apparent that it was not easy. In 1985 Bulgarian Turks were told to choose from a list of Slav names that which they wished to adopt; and if they delayed or refused one was chosen for them. In many cases they resisted and troops had to be called in, with even tanks and the élitist paratroop red beret units being deployed. It was the largest military operation undertaken by the Bulgarian army since the end of the second world war. Nor was the new policy confined to making Turks change their names. Turkish newspapers were closed and radio broadcasts in Turkish ceased; it was even declared unlawful to speak Turkish in public. The official government line was that the Turkish speakers were not in fact Turks but the descendants of Bulgarians who had been forcibly converted to Islam and turkified after the Ottoman conquest. The new 'regenerative process' would allow these lost Bulgarians to return to the bosom of their mother nation.

The attack was not merely against the Turks. The taking of an Islamic name is an integral part of the maturation of a Muslim and the new prohibition on taking Islamic names was a continuation of a quiet assault begun some years previously on Islam itself. The washing of the dead had already been prohibited as a danger to public health; circumcision had been outlawed; and for years it had been all but impossible to make the pilgrimage to Mecca or the other holy places, whilst inside Bulgaria itself many treasures of Islamic architecture had been destroyed.

The regenerative process produced a world-wide storm of protest. Bulgaria was condemned by the United Nations, the Islamic Conference Organisation, the European Court of Justice and other international organisations. Given the weight of such disapproval, and the small apparent internal gains, it is difficult to understand why such a policy was adopted. It has been suggested that there was a belief that Islam was fundamentally conservative and could never coexist with the modern mentality demanded by the scientific-technological revolution. But if this were so, why attack the Turkish language as well as Islam?

It is also possible that the regime was frightened of the long-term demographic trends which were apparent by the mid-1980s. By then the Turks formed approximately 10 per cent of the population but differential birth rates meant that this proportion would grow rapidly. This could easily create difficulties in a conscript army, or if Turks in any one area demanded autonomy. That could be the prelude to an Eastern Rumelia in reverse, and if such a notion seemed fanciful those who feared it pointed to the example of northern Cyprus. These dangers would be decreased if the difference between Bulgarian and Turk were made to disappear. This argument is strengthened by the fact that a census was to be held in December 1985.

A more likely explanation is the simple one that the regime believed that beating the nationalist drum would increase popular support or at least mask some of the economic difficulties which were being encountered. The lack of progress on the economic front and the bad image of Bulgaria abroad had depressed the population to some degree. What later became known as 'civil society' was spreading in the form of martial arts clubs, wild-life protection associations and other groups which were operating outside the control of local party officials and often outside the law. More sinister was the reappearance of terrorism. On one day in 1984 bombs exploded in Plovdiv railway station and at Varna airport; on that day Zhivkov was to visit both cities, and shortly after the explosions leaflets appeared in the street proclaiming, 'Forty Years, Forty Bombs'.

If the regenerative process were meant to produce political stability in Bulgaria it failed miserably and it greatly reduced Bulgaria's standing in the world, even in Moscow. And it was in Moscow that the second great change of 1985 took place. When Mikhail Gorbachev became first secretary of the Communist Party of the Soviet Union Todor Zhivkov was seventy-four years of age and was the longest serving communist leader in Eastern Europe. In

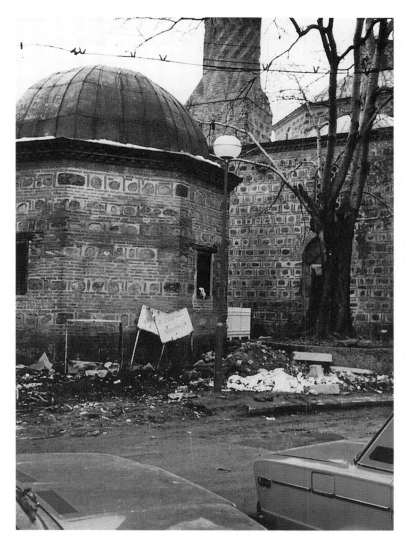

Plate 8.4 The Imaret Mosque, Plovdiv, also known as the Sehabüddin Pasha Mosque, built in 1444; during the 'regenerative process' the grounds of the mosque were turned into a rubbish tip; this photograph was taken in 1987

Map 8.1 Bulgaria in the 1980s

1981 the central committee of the BCP had an average age of 57.5 years, and only 27 per cent of its members were under 50. The contrast between the new broom in the Kremlin and Zhivkov, to whom still clung the odour of Brezhnevite corruption and stagnation, was enormous. When Zhivkov paid his first visit to Gorbachev's Moscow he was kept waiting till the second day before meeting the Soviet leader, an unprecedented snub. What Zhivkov found hard to realise in subsequent years was that the Kremlin, so long the ultimate bastion of his power, had now become indifferent to his fate; Gorbachev was content to leave each East European party and state to conduct its own affairs.

In 1985 the Bulgarian party's main preoccupation was with the economy. Party plena in February 1985 and in January 1986 heralded more changes. The move was being made, said the propagandists, from bureaucratic to economic planning. In December 1986 another plenum, called to draw up the ninth five-year plan, having faced uncomfortable facts about the recent performance of the economy, moved the engine of reform into a higher gear, emphasising now the idea of self-management.

These events were but the overture to the restructuring which was put on stage at the plenum of 28–29 July 1987. Zhivkov admitted to the many failings of socialism and launched a massive attack on the middle bureaucracy; this was now to be made self-managing and was to be much more accountable to popular feeling. So great was the reordering of party priorities that the 'July concept' was to replace the 'April Line' of 1956 as its guiding principle. In August 1987 the sûbranie enacted a raft of reforms meant to give legislative substance to the ideas expressed in the July plenum. A number of ministries were abolished, local government was extensively reformed, and a commission was established to consider constitutional changes. In economic terms the welter of reforms in the 1980s brought little beyond massively destructive dislocation in economic administration, but Zhivkov did try to put the reforms to some political purpose.

In his speech to the July plenum the Bulgarian leader had admitted that the party had reached a turning point at which, he said, it should remember Levski's words: 'Either we shall live up to our times, or they will destroy us.' One danger which faced

Zhivkov himself was that since the advent of Gorbachev, Moscow, previously the fount of all wisdom for the BCP leadership, had become the centre of dangerously subversive ideas. With one channel of Bulgarian TV relaying Soviet programmes, those subversive ideas were available to all. Zhivkov responded by arguing that the purpose of glasnost in the USSR was to expose the need for perestroika in the economy, but since Bulgaria had already introduced economic perestroika it had no need for glasnost.

This convinced few outside the party or even within it. And the ranks of the unconvinced and discontented were growing rapidly in number. The ethnic Turks were still angry at the regenerative process but they had no established intelligentsia of their own to orchestrate their campaign. The Bulgarian intelligentsia, however, was becoming more and more active. It also found a means by which it could form positive links with the mass of the population: environmental degradation. The Chernobyl disaster of April 1986 had given rise to ugly rumours of contaminated food being placed on the open market for public use whilst the party élite enjoyed safe products imported at great cost from outside the affected zone. The authorities were prepared to acknowledge a problem in Rusé where poisoning from a chemical plant across in the Danube in Romania was having devastating effects. The party allowed an exhibition in which one item was a plain notice showing the local incidence of lung disease which had risen from 969 per 100,000 in 1975 to 17,386 per 100,000 in 1985. Throughout 1988 there was constant agitation on this and on other issues, and despite hamfisted efforts by the police to silence poets or philosophers, oppositionists even began to form groups. By the spring of 1989 these included: The Discussion Club for the Support of Perestroika and Glasnost; the Independent Association for Human Rights in Bulgaria; Ecoglasnost; an independent trade union, Podkrepa (support); and the Committee for the Defence of Religious Rights.

Zhivkov's regime was facing unprecedented challenges and these were made much more serious by the continuing legacy of the regenerative process which was to dominate the fateful spring and summer of 1989 in Bulgaria. By the late spring the oppressed Turkish minority had found its champions amongst the Bulgarian intelligentsia. In late May, shortly before the Paris meeting of the

CSCE, a number of leading Turks began a hunger strike. Within days there was a confrontation and when Zhivkov on 28 May called a meeting of the politburo on a Sunday it was clear that the leadership was seriously concerned. They had every reason to be. The Turkish areas of the north-east were in a state of virtual revolt. Zhivkov's response was to go on TV and announce that if they really preferred capitalist Turkey to socialist Bulgaria the ethnic Turks were free to leave. Zhivkov seems to have believed that this would call the Turks' bluff and that few would emigrate. He was wrong. By August, when the despairing authorities in Turkey itself closed their borders, some 344,000 ethnic Turks had left Bulgaria.

Emigration on such a massive scale clearly created difficulties with the Turkish republic. President Bush promised backing to Ankara but Moscow informed Sofia that it did not wish to become involved in Bulgaria's national question. Zhivkov was isolated internationally.

He was virtually isolated at home too. Within the party leadership, Petûr Mladenov, a member of the politburo and minister for foreign affairs, was more aware than anyone how damaging the regenerative process had been to Bulgaria's standing abroad. He it was who led the cabal against Zhivkov. By the end of October the two were in bitter conflict and Mladenov's hand was much strengthened when on 26 October, in full view of foreign journalists, police manhandled demonstrators during an ecological protest. It was a most convenient occurrence for Mladenov who was soon to leave for China. On his return journey he stopped in Moscow to talk with Gorbachev. Immediately upon his return the cabal swung into action and on 10 November, the day after the Berlin Wall was breached, Zhivkov resigned.

9

Post-communist
Bulgaria

DISMANTLING THE APPARATUS OF TOTALITARIANISM,
NOVEMBER 1989–DECEMBER 1990

Zhivkov's fall was the work of the party hierarchy; it was a palace coup rather than a revolution, and 'people power' in Bulgaria was to be more the consequence than the cause of the change of leadership.

Soon after 10 November a number of new political organisations appeared. Some of these had lived a shadowy, semi-legal half-life in the final years or months of the old regime and were now assuming a full and open existence; some were entirely new creations; and others were reborn versions of historic parties, amongst which were the social democrats, and the agrarians who, to distinguish them-selves from the collaborators of the post-1947 years, reverted to the name of Petkov's agrarians: the Bulgarian Agrarian National Union – Nikola Petkov (BANU–NP). On 14 November fourteen of the non-communist political groups came together in a federation which called itself the Union of Democratic Forces (UDF). As its leader the UDF chose Zheliu Zhelev, an academic philosopher who had incurred the displeasure of the old regime.

Meanwhile, the new leader of the BCP, Mladenov, had arranged for a central committee plenum which met from 11 to 13 December. It expressed contrition for the mistakes of the past and promised that in future there would be more party democracy, and that there would be real parliamentary life rather than the stage-managed show it had been since 1947. It also revealed the hard fact that the foreign currency debt stood not at the $3 billion figure admitted by Zhivkov, but at $12 billion.

Even before he had called for a plenum Mladenov had apologised for and repudiated the regenerative process which was formally abandoned in a decree of 29 December. This provoked a fierce reaction. On 7 January thousands of protesters arrived in Sofia from all over Bulgaria, obviously with the connivance of local party officials who alone could have sanctioned the use of so much rationed petrol. People power, it was clear, could be on the side of reaction as well as revolution. Counter-demonstrations in favour of the decree were held a week later but the most important effect of the 7 January events was that they precipitated the formation of a social council with representatives of the BCP, the UDF, the Turkish minority and the Bulgarian nationalists. This, in effect, was Bulgaria's round table.

Almost everyone agreed that the apparatus of totalitarianism had to be destroyed. It was the round table's function to determine how this should be done. It had to decide how to secure the withdrawal of the party from its position of political and social dominance, to separate the party bodies from the social and political ones it had penetrated and subdued for over forty years. The first priority had to be to end the leading role of the party, and particularly the power of the primary party organisations in the workplace. In December 1989 some of these had disbanded themselves, and the Union of Journalists banned them from its ranks at the end of January. On 24 January the politburo dissolved those in the military and in places of work. Other changes followed rapidly. In February the old trades union central council was abolished and the unions entirely separated from any political organisation; a new body, the Confederation of Independent Trade Unions in Bulgaria (CITUB), was established under the leadership of Krûstiu Petkov, an academic sociologist. A few days later another prominent landmark of communist Bulgaria disappeared when the communist youth organisation dissolved itself; its successor organisation played a much less prominent role. At the end of March the Fatherland Front underwent its dose of restructuring to emerge as the Fatherland Union. Most importantly, after tense debate, the constitutional provision allowing the BCP its leading role was amended.

At the end of January the BCP called its fourteenth congress. It enacted a drastic restructuring of the party. Both the politburo and the central committee were replaced by larger bodies which were to be more responsible to the membership; the old regime, said Mladenov, had been a dictatorship over the party as well as over the people, and to underline his point it was announced that Zhivkov was to be arrested on charges which included embezzlement, the misuse of power, and incitement to racial hatred. Mladenov also declared that the economy was to be restructured on the basis of privatisation, decentralisation and demonopolisation; that a multi-party democracy was to be introduced; and that there was to be complete separation of party and state, in conformity with which he relinquished his post of party chief which went to Aleksandûr Lilov, Mladenov remaining head of state. At the same time a new government was formed with Andrei Lukanov as prime minister. The agrarians, embarrassed at their collaborationist record, did not join the new administration; ironically, the collapse of totalitarianism had produced the first purely communist government in Bulgaria's history. It was communist only in name, and not even that for long because at the beginning of April the BCP changed its name to the Bulgarian Socialist Party (BSP).

The attempt to separate the party from the state and from society involved the further extension of individual liberties and fundamental social and economic reform. The most significant move to extend individual liberties was the abolition of the sixth department of the ministry of the interior, the old secret police. Between February and April private agriculture was legalised and there were decrees lifting restrictions on the employment of labour and allowing free enterprise in retailing, the service industries and tourism. On 6 March strikes were legalised, after compulsory arbitration and mediation, though they were not to be permitted in the army, the police, the ports, the medical services and the power industry. There were also further concessions to the ethnic minorities; on 5 March the sûbranie accepted a bill allowing free choice of names for all citizens.

The fourteenth congress of the BCP and discussion of issues such

as ethnic minorities had delayed movement towards full constitutional revision. So too had a number of disagreements between
the BCP and the UDF in the round table, but these were resolved
at the end of March when it was agreed that a Grand National
Assembly should be called to redesign Bulgaria's political system.
Concessions had to be made by both sides before it was finally
agreed that half the GNA's 400 deputies would be elected by
proportional representation and half by the first past the post
system.

The elections were held on 10 and 17 June 1990 and were
pronounced by Zhelev to have been 'free but not fair'. They were
not fair because the BSP had a much more extensive infrastructure
of offices, phones, faxes, etc., and because it used unfair
propaganda amongst the rural voters who were dominated by local
party bosses. The results gave the BSP 211 seats, the UDF 144, the
predominantly Turkish Movement for Rights and Freedom (MRF)
23, and the agrarians 16. Lukanov remained prime minister.

The meeting of the GNA should have marked the beginning of
the phase of constitutional construction, but it did not. The
ceremonial opening, in Tûrnovo, was attended by noisy demonstrations by anti-Turks angered by the presence of the MRF, and
when the assembly moved to Sofia students and others staged
protests against the failure to investigate alleged electoral irregu-
larities. Early in July the protesters revealed a video tape which, they
said, showed Mladenov urging the use of tanks against demonstrators in December 1989; Mladenov resigned and Zhelev
succeeded him as president with Petûr Beron, a zoologist, becoming
leader of the UDF. Mladenov's fall was not the end of the protests.
Calls which had been heard for months for the ending of communist
domination over the media and other aspects of national life
continued and at the end of August led to the burning of a section
of the party's headquarters in the centre of Sofia.

The fire induced a more sober mood but real progress towards
change was still not possible. There had to be an emergency packet
of economic reforms but Lukanov wanted these to be passed by a
coalition government because that would give the appearance of
full national backing for them. The UDF refused to be drawn,
replying that as the socialist/communist leadership had caused the

mess it should clear it up and take the consequences. And mess it was. The harvest of 1989 had been poor, not least because of the disruptive effects of the exodus of the Turks, many of whom worked on the land or in the distributive processes; in September food rationing was extended from the provinces to Sofia. In the first seven months of 1990 production was 10 per cent below the poor levels of 1989; inflation in May and June alone had reached 108 per cent; unemployment was rising at a rate which seemed to be almost beyond calculation; established trading patterns had collapsed with the virtual disintegration of Comecon; and above all there was the Gulf crisis. Bulgaria adhered rigidly to the UN sanctions on Iraq but it did so at great national cost. Iraq was Bulgaria's largest debtor and agreement had only recently been reached that its debt should be repaid in oil, 600,000 tons of which were due for delivery in 1990. The situation was made worse because in March Lukanov had suspended repayment of Bulgaria's foreign debt, and in June he did the same to interest payments. This made hard-currency loans much more difficult to secure. Despite this American advisors helped Lukanov draft a reform programme; but the opposition refused to give it parliamentary support.

By November the political impasse was producing social unrest. Demonstrations had been a constant feature of Bulgarian political life since 1989 and once more the streets filled with protesters, many of them students. Towards the end of the month both CITUB and Podkrepa declared strikes and on 29 November Lukanov resigned, chased from office by public action on the streets rather than by due parliamentary process. On 20 December a new administration took office under the premiership of Dimitûr Popov, a non-party lawyer.

CONSTRUCTING THE APPARATUS OF DEMOCRACY, DECEMBER 1990–OCTOBER 1991

Between November 1989 and December 1990 most of the apparatus of totalitarianism was dismantled. Many communist-appointed officials were still in place but the old order had been discredited by its political arrogance and its economic ineptitude. And in foreign relations Bulgaria was presenting a new face to the

Plate 9.1 The fire in the Bulgarian Socialist Party (former
Communist Party) headquarters, August 1990

world; the close links with the USSR were gone and diplomatic
relations had been established with Israel, Chile and South Africa.
But if the mechanisms of totalitarianism had been dismantled those
of democracy had not yet been constructed. This was in part
because no workable consensus could be found within the GNA or
perhaps within the nation.

It was the task of the Popov government to find that consensus.
It called itself 'a government to guarantee the peaceful transition to
a democratic society', and as a condition of its taking office insisted
that the major parties must agree to a peaceful and orderly
transition. Given this consensus the Popov government could set
about rescuing the political process from the streets and returning it
to constitutional channels; having accomplished this it could allow
the GNA to redesign those channels. It would also have to draw up
and impose economic reforms.

Initially the latter took precedence. There was no pretence that
the task would be easy but help came from the trade unions and
the managers/employers who on 8 January 1991 signed, with the
government, a tripartite agreement on social peace. The trade
unions accepted a 200-day moratorium on strikes in return for

which government and the managers agreed to handle the economic transition with as much sensitivity as possible. The social peace hit an immediate rock when the government introduced its first round of real economic reform. On 1 February 1991 the prices of many goods were deregulated and those of controlled goods greatly increased. February also saw a bitter sûbranie battle in which the government finally prevailed in its efforts to enact laws for the decollectivisation of agriculture and the privatisation of small businesses. In the summer there was a second stage of economic reforms, for which the trade unions agreed to a second 'social peace'. The reforms included making the Bulgarian National Bank accountable to parliament rather than to the government, and also further price deregulation.

Both sets of reforms had been painful but they did prove Bulgaria's reforming intent and this reassured some western politicians and bankers. Early in March Bulgaria was one of the beneficiaries of aid released by the European Community for reconstruction in Eastern Europe, and in August a major loan of $250 million was granted by the World Bank.

In addition to the dislocative effects of economic reforms there were also ethnic tensions. In February the minister of education had announced that in Turkish areas there was to be four hours of teaching per week in Turkish if that was what the local population desired. There was a swift reaction. Teachers in the affected areas, especially Razgrad, Kûrdjali and Shumen, went on strike whilst Bulgarian parents demonstrated and withheld their children from school. The UDF claimed that those opposing the reform were those who had been responsible for the regenerative process in the 1980s but whether this were the case or not, the government deemed it prudent to postpone the introduction of the plan until the beginning of the new academic year in September.

When the GNA was not discussing economic or ethnic issues it found other problems to divert its attention from the constitutional debate. There were stormy scenes when the question of police files and the relationship of GNA members to the former political police were discussed. One casualty of this conflict was Beron, who resigned after admitting to having played a minor role as an informant on foreign academic visitors; his successor as leader of the UDF was Filip Dimitrov. When the constitutional debate did at last begin there were still a series of distractions. A number of UDF deputies argued that a constitution drawn up by a communist-dominated assembly could not be trusted, and in June thirty-nine of them staged a hunger strike on this issue. There was also a delay when it was decided to hold a national referendum on the future nature of the Bulgarian state, a euphemism for asking whether or not the monarchy should be restored. After the question had taken up almost two weeks of GNA time the referendum was cancelled.

Eventually, however, the GNA did address itself to the new political structure it was meant to define and on 12 July the new constitution was approved. Bulgaria was to be a democratic state subject to the rule of law with complete separation of powers. The head of state was to be a president elected by direct vote for a five-year term of office, and all candidates for the presidency had to have been resident in Bulgaria for five years, this restriction being introduced to prevent King Simeon presenting himself for election as president. A constitutional court was to be established, and the legislature was to be a sûbranie of 240 members. The elections to the sûbranie, it had already been decided, would be according to proportional representation and there would be an electoral threshold of 4 per cent of the national vote to achieve representation in the assembly.

The first elections under the new system were held on 13 October, but only after the right of the MRF to stand had been challenged, unsuccessfully, on the grounds that it contravened a law of 1990 stating that no party might be formed on the basis of ethnic or religious affiliation. Thirty-eight parties eventually entered the contest, but only three managed to cross the 4 per cent hurdle and the result produced was agonisingly close. The UDF had the most votes, but only just, their share of the poll being only 1 per cent greater than that of the BSP. The UDF emerged with 110 seats, the BSP with 106 and the MRF held the balance with 24. The agrarians, true to tradition, had damaged themselves by splitting. More than one in five of the votes cast were for parties which did not gain representation in the sûbranie because they had failed to cross the 4 per cent threshold.

THE UDF GOVERNMENT, OCTOBER 1991–
OCTOBER 1992

After the election a new government was formed by the leader of the UDF, Filip Dimitrov. His cabinet consisted mainly of UDF members but the MRF, on whom he relied for his parliamentary majority, declined to enter a coalition lest this alienate public opinion from the new administration. Also, outside the cabinet the MRF would enjoy greater freedom of action.

Lilov resigned as leader of the BSP at the end of 1991, to be replaced by the 32-year-old Zhan Videnov. At the beginning of 1992 presidential elections reaffirmed Zhelev as head of state though he was surprisingly taken to a second round of voting.

The Dimitrov government was to stay in office for just under a year. It continued the process of economic reform. In February a law was passed on private and foreign investment which allowed foreign ownership of Bulgarian enterprises and the export of profits. More banking reform was enacted and after considerable delay a privatisation law was passed in April. In the same month the sûbranie, despite opposition from the BSP, passed a law restoring to its former owners property confiscated by the authorities during the years 1947 to 1962. In the previous month a land privatisation law had decreed that all agrarian collectives must be dissolved by 1 November 1992.

The economic reforms, driven to a considerable decree by pressure from western financial institutions, endangered the social consensus created under Popov in 1990–1. In January 1992 the general price level was 500 per cent higher than a year before; unemployment, even by official figures, had reached 402,000; and inflation in that month alone was 30 per cent. And still there was the knowledge that things would get worse before they got better. In protest CITUB staged a symbolic general strike on 8 January to demand higher wages and pensions, better protection for workers during the privatisation process, and more measures to combat unemployment. The general strike, although it evoked only a lukewarm response, was but one indication of the declining effectiveness of the three-way agreement between government, unions and employers/managers; in April the agreement collapsed.

Plate 9.2 President Zheliu Zhelev

By mid-summer social and industrial unrest were widespread. There were strikes by civil servants, on Sofia's transport network and, despite the provisions of the 1990 law, in the ports, and in the medical services. The government was forced to grant a 26 per cent wage increase to all state employees.

After the collapse of the tripartite agreement in April one of the supporters of that agreement, Dimitûr Ludjev, was sacked from the cabinet. He had been Bulgaria's first civilian minister of defence since 1934 and had pensioned off 750 officers, including 10 generals. Most of them had reached retirement age but there was an element of lustration, or punishment of the former regime, in Ludjev's action. Lustration was also evident in September with the sentencing of Zhivkov to seven years in prison; Zhivkov was the first of Eastern Europe's former leaders to be tried and convicted but he was to be allowed to serve his time under house arrest rather than in gaol. Tough attitudes towards former communists were also reflected in the Penev law which banned from administrative posts in the universities or academies anyone who had held party office under the old regime.

The effect of the lustration process on the Bulgarian Orthodox church produced a drama which was both tragedy and farce. On 9 March 1992 Patriarch Maxim was sacked; a report by the parliamentary commission on religious faiths said that his election in 1971 had been improper and there was gossip that he had been a 'collaborator'. In May his opponents elected Metropolitan Pimen as acting chairman of the holy synod. In June, however, the constitutional court declared that it was the removal of Maxim which had been wrong because this was an unlawful intrusion of the government into ecclesiastical affairs. The supporters of Pimen refused to accept the judgement or to vacate the holy synod building, and the Orthodox church, the founding father of the nation, was reduced to the degrading spectacle of its priests fighting on the steps of the Aleksandûr Nevski cathedral. Not even a visit by the Oecumenical Patriarch from Istanbul could mend the breach. The sacking of Maxim was seen by many as the right thing done in the wrong way; a proper end achieved by improper means. Many, including even the president, held the Dimitrov government responsible for the tragedy.

Plate 9.3 Cartoon by Georgi Chaushov showing the loss of
public respect for the Bulgarian Orthodox church; the
drawing appeared in December 1992; the church had split
disastrously earlier in the year

There were few successes which the Dimitrov government could
set against its failures. The successes were to be found mainly in
foreign affairs. One was the admission of Bulgaria to the Council
of Europe in May 1992. There were also significant improvements
in official relations with Turkey. A military agreement was signed
on 20 December 1991, in March 1992 Ludjev became the first
Bulgarian minister of war to visit Turkey since 1917, and in May a
treaty of friendship was signed. Equally importantly, Bulgaria
played a full part in negotiations aimed at establishing the Black Sea
Free Trade Zone, an idea first put forward by Ankara in 1988.

One foreign issue which could never be far from Bulgarian
politics was Macedonia. Soon after 10 November 1989 those in
Bulgaria who regarded themselves as Macedonian had attempted to
establish a Macedonian party in Bulgaria, to be called 'Ilinden', but

this was refused recognition. The collapse of the Yugoslav state and the proclamation of independence by the Skopje government posed considerable difficulties for Sofia but on 16 January 1992 Bulgaria became the first country to recognise the Macedonian state, though it was explicitly said that this recognition was of a separate Macedonian state and not of a separate Macedonian nation. Both Zhelev and the government were criticised for this decision, but it was one made in an attempt to preserve the fragile stability of the southern Balkans, and it was one which caused much anger in Greece which had until then been a keen supporter of Bulgaria's attempts to draw closer to the European Community.

President Zhelev had made the running over the recognition of Macedonia and the government, despite its misgivings, had not in the end frustrated him. But relations between the two were bad. There had been intermittent skirmishing over issues such as the control of the intelligence services but in the late summer of 1992 the president launched an outright attack on the government. Gratuitous aggression on its part, said Zhelev, had not only caused social deprivation but had alienated the trade unions, the press, the non-parliamentary parties, and even the church. The UDF fought back with equal vigour but it now had an added cause for concern because Ahmed Dogan, the leader of the MRF, upon which the government relied for its majority in the assembly, sided with the president. The MRF itself faced grave difficulties. The government's economic reforms had hit the Turkish areas even harder than the rest of the country, and many ethnic Turks believed the land privatisation programme was discriminating against them; they responded by emigrating. If this second wave of emigration were to continue the Turkish population might be so depleted as to deprive the MRF of the 4 per cent of the national vote it needed for representation in the sûbranie. In September the MRF, to prove its muscle, drove the chairman of the sûbranie from office.

In October relations between Dimitrov and Zhelev deteriorated even further when it was alleged that one of the prime minister's advisors had been involved in attempts to sell arms illegally to Macedonia. Dimitrov denounced the rumours as a smear spread by the chief of the intelligence services acting in concert with some of the president's advisors. This was yet another round in the dispute over control of the intelligence services and it was also the final nail in Dimitrov's prime ministerial coffin. On 28 October he resigned after losing a vote of confidence in the sûbranie.

The president then asked each major political faction in turn to try and form or sponsor a government. The bargaining continued for over a month until a cabinet sponsored by the MRF took office. It was led by Liuben Berov, a professor of economic history, and consisted mainly of non-party, technical experts.

The Dimitrov government had few positive achievements to its name but the fact that it entered and left office entirely by due constitutional process was proof that Bulgaria had successfully negotiated an important part of the transition to representative democracy.

THE BEROV GOVERNMENT, DECEMBER 1992–SEPTEMBER 1994

Shortly before the Berov government was formed the European Union announced that it would sign an interim trade agreement with Bulgaria. If this created hopes of a new dawn for Bulgaria such hopes were soon dashed. Wranglings within the EU prevented implementation of the agreement until December 1993. It was symbolic of the disappointments that were to characterise the Berov administration.

Berov's first priority was to tackle the economic problem and to try and push forward the flagging reform process. He produced an economic 'plan of action' in February 1993 but it failed to command widespread support. The UDF condemned it as a return to the old-fashioned and discredited nostrum of economic planning and this, said the UDF, was only one sign of a drift back towards the bad old days. Another, it was alleged, was the replacement of those in the media, especially in radio, television and the official news agency, who were critical of the government. The worst of the many reactionary steps, said the UDF, was the judiciary bill introduced into the sûbranie in October 1993 and given parliamentary approval the following February. This stated that no one might serve as a judge or a public prosecutor unless they had had five years experience in such a post. This would mean that only those who had held such high office under the communist regime would be eligible, and that figures such as the current chief prosecutor, Ivan Tatarchev, who had pursued former communist *prominenti*, especially Zhivkov, with a relentless passion, would have to stand down. The bill was submitted to the constitutional court.

The judiciary bill was one of the few occasions on which the Berov government showed any resolution. A major problem for the cabinet was its lack of clear support in the sûbranie. The government had been sponsored by the MRF which had held the balance in the assembly but early in 1993 defections from the party ranks robbed it of that power. Sûbranie and national politics were made more complicated by the formation in March 1993 of the New Union for Democracy from amongst disaffected UDF deputies; in June the Civil Alliance for the Republic appeared taking members from both the UDF and the BSP. The new factions only encouraged the intensification of politicking which seemed by the summer of 1993 to have replaced government in Bulgaria. And there was little improvement in 1994, partly because in the spring of that year Berov himself was incapacitated and had to undergo heart surgery.

The lack of firm government made itself felt most notably in the continued inability first to enact proper economic reform and, second, to contain the mounting wave of crime. In the economic sector Berov's plan of action produced little effect. By the summer of 1994 the privatisation of land was way behind schedule and in the industrial sector there had been only one major privatisation; meanwhile the International Monetary Fund (IMF) had twice expressed concern at the lack of economic reform, and had criticised Berov's plan for allowing too high a government spending deficit. And the foreign debt problem had become even worse. In March at a meeting in Frankfurt the London Club of Bankers, who held most of the credits, had offered a remission of 38 per cent of the total debt, but this the Berov government had refused, holding out instead for 50 per cent. In this it was eventually successful, though agreement on the amount of debt to be repaid also meant that repayments had to begin.

The economic troubles of Bulgaria were not solely attributable to the lack of firm government at home. They had been made immeasurably more difficult by the imposition of full UN sanctions on Serbia and Montenegro. Bulgaria held fast to the UN line but, as with the sanctions against Iraq, the cost was horrendous. The rail and road routes through the former Yugoslavia were some of the chief arteries for Bulgarian trade, particularly for the export of perishable products, and the only available alternatives, through Romania or by sea, were slow and congested; the Romanian route was even partially closed by a rail strike in August. By September the cost of sanctions was calculated at $2.71 billion, and one estimate put the total cost of all sanctions, i.e. those against Iraq and Libya as well as against Serbia, at $13 billion or the equivalent of Bulgaria's total foreign debt. At the end of 1993 the UN had approved a transit arrangement for Bulgarian goods but it was limited in extent and so beset with bureaucratic regulations that it was almost useless.

Sanctions were also very much responsible for the growth of crime in Bulgaria. The end of the communist regime had seen a decline in respect for the police and a consequent burgeoning of prostitution, theft, mugging and other forms of petty crime. Much more serious, however, was large-scale crime in which were involved, according to popular belief, many new business conglomerates, some of which were run by former communist apparatchiks or industrial managers. Whether or not this is true is impossible to establish, but there is little doubt that many organis-ations took advantage of sanctions to smuggle goods into Serbia and Montenegro. These operations could not have been carried out without the connivance of local customs officials and border police and it is difficult to see how high officials in Sofia were not also implicated when the sums involved were so large: one operator smuggling petrol by the lorry-load into Serbia said that although he made 10,000 deutschmarks from one run the customs officers made 12,000. Sanctions busting, it was argued, spread crime and corruption within the administrative system.

BULGARIA SINCE SEPTEMBER 1994

The Berov government, undermined by popular disillusion over economic stagnation and rising crime, finally collapsed in

September 1994 and a caretaker administration under Reneta Indjova, Bulgaria's first woman prime minister, was appointed. When elections were held in December the BSP secured an outright victory. The previous administration's failure to combat economic drift and rising crime were important reasons for this victory but they were not the only ones. The previous five years had been perceived as years dominated by the UDF, and even though the UDF had been in office for only one of those five years it was that group's ideology which was believed to have dominated the period. The UDF were in effect held responsible for the failure to produce proper economic reform, for the social crisis which the transition from totalitarianism had produced, and for the general lack of morale which affected the whole country.

The December 1994 elections made the BSP the first party since 1989 to enjoy an overall majority in the sûbranie. The BSP had won 52.08 per cent of the votes and 125 seats; the UDF had 28.65 per cent of the votes and 69 seats; the MRF took 6.25 per cent of the votes, giving it 15 seats. Also represented were the Popular Union (PU) which took 7.5 per cent of the votes and had 18 seats, and the Bulgarian Business Bloc (BBB) which had 5.42 per cent of the vote and 13 seats. The main constituent elements of the PU were the Democratic Party and BANU–NP, both of which had left the UDF in September. The BBB, as its name implies, represented commercial interests and its electoral image was enhanced by its exotic leader, Georgi Ganchev, a former fencing star who had taught at Eton. After the elections Dimitrov resigned as leader of the UDF and was replaced by a former finance minister, Ivan Kostov.

The return to a socialist government did not produce any change in the commitment to economic reform. Videnov's new government, in which were included some extra-parliamentary agrarians, was committed to economic reform at an accelerated pace and promised rapid privatisation on the Czech coupon model, one which could be interpreted as passing ownership to the mass of workers, not shareholders. On the issue of the land the new government took a clear step back towards the old system when it attempted to restrict the right to buy and sell privatised land; the president insisted that this bill be referred to the constitutional court. Another return to previous attitudes and policies was seen in the new cabinet's readiness to restore closer relations with Russia. There were also fears that the appointment of the historian Ilcho Dimitrov as minister of education heralded a return to a tougher attitude towards the Turkish minority; Dimitrov had held the same post in the 1980s and was said to have been closely involved in the regenerative process.

Since 1989 Bulgaria has had three general and one presidential election. It has clearly established the mechanisms of parliamentary rule and individual liberties have by and large been respected. It has experienced minority government by the BSP, government by the UDF, and government by two non-party technocratic cabinets. Now it has majority government by the BSP. That government will be judged by how it tackles its three main responsibilities: to try and introduce economic restructuring which satisfies foreign money lenders without producing ruinous social dislocation; to contain crime; and to carry out the next general election by the prescribed rules at the prescribed time.

CONCLUSION

At the time of writing over half a decade has passed since the fall of communism in Eastern Europe. The 'post-totalitarian' era has seen its own brand of cynicism and disillusion as the hopes for rapid material advance were disappointed and economic reform exacted a heavy social price: one Bulgarian friend recently greeted me in Sofia with the words, 'Welcome to post-democratic Bulgaria.' But in Bulgaria there is an extra dimension to the puzzlement and disillusion of post-totalitarianism.

It is significant that in this half decade and more of post-totalitarianism the Bulgarians have not been able to agree upon a new state emblem. There is, it would seem, a sense of doubt as to their national identity and their place in the contemporary world. There have been many articles and books dealing with this issue. An excellent example is Ivan Elenkov and Rumen Daskalov's compilation, *Zashto nie sme takiva; v tûrsene na bûlgarskata kulturna identichnost*, published in Sofia in 1994. The title means 'Why are we as we are? In search of Bulgaria's cultural identity', and the book is a collection of fifty articles written by nineteen authors and published in Bulgarian journals between 1898 and 1943. All the articles try and define what it means to be Bulgarian, what is specific about 'Bulgarianness'. At a time when the future is possibly bleak, almost certainly daunting, and inevitably obscure, it is to the past that many present-day Bulgarians look for clues as to their true identity, for grid references to plot their position in an increasingly unstable and unsure world. What, then, can their own history tell the Bulgarians of their national identity and their place in the contemporary world?

One of the themes in Bulgarian history is the dichotomy between an eastward and a westward orientation. This we can see in the great debates over whether to align with the western or the eastern branch of Christendom. In later centuries early nationalists debated the merits of relying on Russian or central/west European assistance, and this debate was continued in intensified form in the fierce and frequently violent political struggles between the russophobes and russophiles of the Bulgarian state after 1878.

Inevitably the debate over external orientation was linked, consciously or subconsciously, with the process of modernisation. Somewhat paradoxically, both traditionalists and extreme radicals could find role models in Russia, the former primarily in the church and the latter in revolutionary movements from the narodniks to the bolsheviks. For the newly emerging bourgeoisie and intelligentsia, however, the west had more to offer. Economic and trading ties with Russia were weak. Russia and Bulgaria exported similar commodities and therefore there was little trade between them; both also looked to central and western Europe for capital to rebuild and modernise their economies. But it was not only for economic help that the Bulgarians looked westward. Before the first world war, Bulgarians knew that they had to adapt to western manners and customs if they were to integrate into that world. One of the most famous of Bulgarian literary creations is Aleko Konstantinov's Bai Ganiu, a peasant who visits the wider world, an encounter which produced bemusement and puzzlement on both sides but in which Bai Ganiu's raw, peasant cunning served him well. It was in order to distance themselves from the unsophisticated Bai Ganiu image that those few Bulgarians who could afford to do so sent their children to be educated abroad; but very few of those children went to Russia and most went to Germany or France. Of the nineteen authors in Elenkov and Daskalov's compilation, one did not go to university at all, three did so in Bulgaria, one studied in both Russia and the west, one in Russia alone, and thirteen in the west.

In the political arena decisions on whether to align with Russia or its adversaries could and did prove critical. In 1913 and 1915 and again in 1941 Bulgaria chose to defy Russian interests with ultimately catastrophic consequences for Bulgarian aspirations towards full national unification. After 1944 Bulgaria's rulers opted for close relations with Russia at enormous cost to the political liberty of the Bulgarian citizen, as well as to the long-term economic and environmental well-being of the country. In the immediate aftermath of the changes of 1989 Bulgarian foreign policy swung around full circle. Close association with the EU became the ultimate goal of Bulgaria's foreign-policy-makers and there was a wave of intense pro-American feeling. A malign fate meant that just when Bulgaria was making its most concerted effort ever to integrate with the states of central and western Europe, it was cut off from those states by economic sanctions against Serbia and Montenegro; a new curtain descended over the Balkans and as far as many western Europeans were concerned Bulgaria seemed to have dropped off the edge of the map.

This might prompt the feeling that Bulgaria would be better off developing links with the Middle East, North Africa and the states of the Black Sea littoral. There is a historical precedent for this, though few Bulgarians would welcome it. The economic revival of the Bulgarian communities in the nineteenth century was based mainly on the expansion of trading relations not with central and western Europe but with the rest of the Ottoman empire, that is with European Turkey and Anatolia. Liberation in 1878 meant exposure to what the Bulgarians of the day would have called 'European' competition, bringing widespread economic dislocation and the destruction of much of the existing industrial system: and here is another obvious parallel with the post-1989 situation.

Despite the setback of sanctions and notwithstanding the historical precedents, Bulgaria's cultural identity lies within the legacy of the European, Christian world. In terms of contemporary policy, membership of the EU remains the ultimate goal but since its electoral victory in December 1994 the Bulgarian Socialist Party has attempted to restore some of Bulgaria's previous links to Moscow, and it has fallen out with the president over the question of membership of NATO about which the government is distinctly dubious. Once more the dichotomy between Russia and the west presents itself.

The dichotomy is in fact an inevitable consequence of Bulgaria's geographic position and its historical development. These two factors have dictated that Bulgaria will always be on the edge of both the east and the west and occupies a nodal position between the end of Europe and the beginning of Asia. In the present world that could be a distinct advantage. If land transportation between Asia and Europe is to continue developing as the planners seem to intend – witness the building of the second Bosphorus bridge and the plans for a rail connection between European and Asiatic Turkey – then Bulgaria will be a crucial link in the European-Asiatic transportation chain. Three other projects will reinforce Bulgaria's importance in the world's trading and transportation structure. The first is the plan to build a highway from Durres on the Adriatic through Macedonia and Bulgaria to Istanbul, which will provide the first new east–west route across the Balkans since the Romans built the Via Ignatia. The second is the intended new road leading from the Greek frontier northwards through Bulgaria to a new bridge to be built over the Danube to Romania, once Sofia and Bucharest can agree on the crossing point. And the third is the pipeline which will take Russian oil from Burgas to the Greek port of Alexandropoulis. In these circumstances neither Russia nor the other European states, nor indeed the nations of the Middle East, could afford an isolated or an unstable Bulgaria. Europe will then need Bulgaria just as Bulgaria will need Europe.

If Bulgaria is to be integrated into Europe it will have to continue to conform to the democratic practices established in the post-totalitarian years. Does an examination of Bulgarian history give reason to believe that this will be the case? Is the capacity to build and sustain a democracy part of Bulgaria's cultural identity?

If a healthy respect for education is a qualification for democracy then Bulgaria is strongly placed. The national revival of the nine-teenth century would have been impossible without the development of a network of schools both at primary and more advanced levels. Any westerner reading the memoirs of Bulgarians who attended schools in centres such as Istanbul, Salonika, Sofia, Plovdiv and Varna cannot but be impressed both by the range of subjects taught and by the dedication of teachers and pupils alike. To judge from the quality of students coming from Bulgaria to

western universities in recent years that tradition has certainly
survived, in no small measure thanks to the specialist gymnasia
which have for generations been a prominent feature of Bulgarian
secondary education. There are threats to that educational structure
and tradition. A depressing number of students abroad, for quite
understandable individual reasons, conclude that life outside
Bulgaria has more to offer them than a return to their native land.

When the modern Bulgarian nation emerged from Ottoman rule
in the final quarter of the nineteenth century Bulgarian society was
largely homogeneous. The pre-conquest aristocracy had been
destroyed and differentiations of wealth had been slow to appear.
On the land, in the late nineteenth century, even the most pros-
perous, with few exceptions, tilled their own plots; their work was
not qualitatively different from that of their poorer co-nationals
and fellow-villagers. In the towns and the manufacturing communities production, before and for many years after the liberation
of 1878, was almost entirely based on traditional processes
organised along traditional lines. Here the guilds played a major
role. The guilds, of course, with their hierarchical structures, did see
differentiations of wealth and influence, but the guilds retained
a sense of collective responsibility in which the wealthy had
obligations to the less fortunate. This lack of social and occupational divisions created a system and a mentality in which there
was equality of opportunity for all and education provided the
medium through which that opportunity could be realised.

In 1879 the Bulgarian nation was given a political system which
reflected this egalitarian society. How effectively did that society
manage its new democracy? The record is not entirely reassuring,
though it is probably no worse than other states of similar age
which emerged from similar backgrounds. It is true that political life
in Bulgaria soon contracted the disease of corruption and clientism;
but so, too, did the political life of Greece, Serbia, Romania and,
dare one suggest it, the trading of political support for contracts or
other favours was not entirely unknown in the United States at
the end of the nineteenth century. In the early years of the state the
executive established an increasing control over the legislature, a
process which weakened democratic impulses and smoothed the
way for royal authoritarian rule and, after it, the totalitarianism of

the communists. The post-totalitarian era has seen few signs that this undesirable phenomenon might manifest itself anew. In 1990 the reformers defeated the ex-communists' proposal that the sûbranie should elect the president; separate elections for parliament and president should help maintain the separation of powers. President Zhelev himself has shown a robust determination not to be dominated by the assembly. When the Union of Democratic Forces, the party he had once led, was in office he broke openly and fiercely with it and its leader, Filip Dimitrov. And since the socialists have been in office the president has engaged in a series of healthy disputes with the government, not least over Bulgaria's relationship with NATO.

Another dispiriting feature of Bulgaria's political past which has, mercifully, failed to reappear is the propensity towards political violence. Three prime ministers or ex-prime ministers were assassinated between 1895 and 1923 and there were a number of other killings; in the 1920s and 1930s violence was widely practised both by the government and the various Macedonian factions, whilst after 1944 the communists indulged in an orgy of retributive murder, official and unofficial.

In modern Bulgarian history the military have played a major role. One faction within the army was responsible for the initial deposition of Alexander Battenberg in 1886; his short-lived return to Bulgaria would have been impossible without another group of soldiers. Prince Ferdinand, that master craftsman of political calculation, made sure of his control of the ministry of war and the officer corps before he moved against Stambolov in 1894. In 1923 and 1934 the army was the instrument of major political upheaval; the overthrow of the old regime on 9 September 1944 was also a military coup but this time against the background of enormous international and domestic upheaval. At present, however, there seems little likelihood of military action against the civilian power. Despite demoralisation engendered by the collapse of the Warsaw pact and by fierce budgetary restraint, the army has remained loyal, allowing its grievances to be given occasional public utterance through the new officers' organisation, the Rakovski Legion. A propensity for military coups may not be the most desirable of historical traditions but it has not prevented Greece, Spain or

Portugal from gaining full membership of the European Union; nor are the histories of modern France and Germany without their military figures.

Since the signature of the treaty of Berlin in 1878 the national question has never been far from the surface of Bulgarian politics. The loss of much of San Stephano Bulgaria, and above all of Macedonia, burnt deep into the Bulgarian national psyche. Most of the great decisions over external policy since 1878 have hinged on the Macedonian issue. In 1912 an alliance was concluded with Serbia to redeem much of lost Macedonia and in the following year the disastrous second Balkan war was fought and lost in an effort to prevent Serbia and Greece from taking too much of the coveted land. In 1915 it was the hope of retrieving lost Macedonia which, above all, persuaded King Ferdinand and his prime minister to commit Bulgaria to the German cause; in 1941, when King Boris came to the conclusion that Bulgaria could no longer remain neutral he sweetened the bitter pill by swallowing most of Macedonia. Internally, for the fifty years from the mid-1880s to the mid-1930s, the Macedonian sore itched and aggravated almost without cessation, and it made a fearful contribution to the growth of political violence in the country. But if a longing for national reunion was a constant feature of Bulgarian history between 1878 and 1944 there is as yet little sign of it re-emerging as a powerful factor in the political life of post-totalitarian Bulgaria. The recognition of the Macedonian state, though not the nation, disappointed many Bulgarians but reassured other governments. And with the weight of immediate social, economic and environmental problems pressing upon them, the majority of the Bulgarian people have shown few signs of wishing to relaunch the drive for territorial expansion, though it is impossible to predict what would happen if the Macedonian state were to be destabilised or to collapse.

There is another trend in Bulgarian history which looks neither to the east or the west and which shows no interest in territorial expansion. This is the tradition of introspection, an introspection at times so intense that it engendered disdain for or even rejection of the entire world of politics. The patron saint of the Bulgarians, Ivan Rilski, was a hermit, and the tradition of hermitism was strong in mediaeval Bulgaria. The bogomils, of course, took this much further and rejected not merely external alignments but the entire structure of the temporal state. During the long centuries of Ottoman rule Bulgarian culture survived primarily in the small, often self-sufficient villages and in the monasteries which were by definition distanced if not divorced from society and the official apparatus of the state.

Some observers believe that this tendency towards withdrawal into the inner self was in part responsible for the apparent lack of Bulgarian involvement in the struggle for political independence from Ottoman rule and against later examples of political oppression. We have seen how few Bulgarians responded to the call to arms in 1876, nor should it go unnoticed that when the delegates of the powers met in Berlin to devise the treaty which was so harmful and hurtful to Bulgarian aspirations and sensibilities, there were no Bulgarians in the German capital to lobby the ambassadors or influence the press; the Bulgarians, it seemed, hoped or even assumed that the Russians could be relied upon to do the job for them. In the early years of the life of the reborn Bulgaria no family could ignore the state because it insisted on receiving their taxes, educating their children, and conscripting their sons; yet there was a massive political apathy reflected particularly in very low turn-outs at elections. In the second world war there was little in the way of resistance to the regime until allied bombing began to make an impact and the prospect of a Soviet advance into the Balkans became a reality.

Under the communists Bulgaria became a by-word for acquiescence and conformity with the Soviet model. There was no Bulgarian equivalent of the independent policies pursued by the other communist regimes in the Balkans, nor of Berlin 1953, Budapest 1956 or Czechoslovakia 1968; the word dissident was not uttered in public in Bulgaria until 1978. We now know that there was more opposition to communist power, particularly in the early years and amongst the peasantry, than was previously believed, whilst both the attempted military coup of 1965 and Liudmila Zhivkov's assertion of Bulgarian cultural identity showed that not all Bulgarians were content with complete subjugation to Moscow. Nevertheless, it was the case that Bulgaria's reputation for conformity and quietude was, at least on a comparative basis, justified.

There are some obvious explanations for this. The party's grip on the state and on society was strong and, at least in the years up to about 1970, the regime, quite literally, delivered the goods. But perhaps the placidity of Bulgaria was not simply the result of police power and increasing material well being. Perhaps it was also to some degree a modern resonance on the string of disassociation from worldly affairs, a contemporary reassertion of the long cultural tradition which rejects the temporal world as tainted, transitory and tawdry. If this is the case, what seems like compliance with existing authority is just conformity with that national tradition which rejects political authority as irrelevant.

It would, however, be dangerous for Bulgarians to dwell too fondly on this theme. Rejection of the state was possible for a mediaeval monk, for the inhabitants of a small, self-sufficient mountain village in the days of Ottoman rule, or even for a disaffected intellectual under German or Soviet domination; it is scarcely a wise prescription for the creation of a functioning, modern representative democracy; and without such a democracy Bulgaria will not secure the admission to the European community it desires.

Apathy towards or withdrawal from political affairs contains another danger for post-totalitarian Bulgaria. A major factor in Germany's success since the second world war has been *Bewältigung der Vergangenheit*, the ability to come to terms with and to overcome the past. Bulgaria's past contains nothing to compare with the horrors of the final solution. The saving of the Jews from Bulgaria proper during the second world war was an achievement of almost the entire nation in which the entire nation takes justifiable pride. In the past Bulgaria had also provided a safe refuge for Armenians threatened with persecution and worse in Turkey; in recognition of this the Armenians in Bulgaria formed their own military detachment to fight with the Bulgarians in the Balkan wars. On the other hand, the Bulgarian national state did place some pressure on its Turkish minority. In the early years after liberation that pressure was cultural and perhaps unintentional to the extent that what the Bulgarians regarded as natural celebration of national independence and cultural liberation, the Turks saw as an intolerable alteration to their traditional way of life. There could be no compromise in such circumstances, but for the most part the Turks who left Bulgaria after 1878 did so voluntarily.

If the Bulgarians have to face a problem in overcoming their past it is less in the way they have treated other peoples than in the way they believe foreign domination has affected them. There is still a tendency amongst many Bulgarians, particularly when an outsider points out a shortcoming, to relapse into a regressive fatalism, a fatalism expressed most often in phrases such as 'Five hundred years of Ottoman rule . . . ' This is an unhelpful attitude. It is using the past to escape from the present and more so from the future. Furthermore, the Bulgarians are not alone in having suffered long centuries of foreign domination. That domination was without doubt at times extremely repressive but the Bulgarian nation, the Bulgarian church and the Bulgarian language survived. When the Ottomans departed from Bulgaria the Bulgarians still spoke Bulgarian and Bulgarian manufacturing had flourished as a supplier to the Ottoman state army; when British rule ended in southern Ireland the Irish language was almost dead and Irish industry had been stifled to prevent competition with British manufacturers. Past oppression is inevitably a part of national consciousness and respect for those who suffered is a proper sentiment, but that oppression should not be used as an excuse for present failings or for a lack of commitment to rectifying them. Bulgarian history has better things to offer the Bulgarian nation than a lack of confidence in its own ability to adapt and survive.

Bulgarian monarchs

KHANS

Asparukh	681–700
Tervel	700–721
Kormisosh	721–738
Sevar	738–753/4
Vinekh	753/4–760
Telets	760–763
Sabin	763–766
Umor	August–September 766
Toktu	766–767
Pagan	767–768
Telerig	768–777
Kardam	777–803
Krum	803–814
Omurtag	814–831
Malmir	831–836
Pressian	836–852

KINGS OR TSARS: FIRST KINGDOM

Boris I	852–888
Vladimir	888–893
Simeon 'the Great'	893–927
Petûr I	927–970
Boris II	970–971
Roman	971–997
Samuil	997–1014

Gavril-Radomir	1014–1015
Ivan-Vladislav	1015–1018

KINGS OR TSARS: SECOND KINGDOM

Petûr II	1185–1187
Ivan Asen I	1187–1196
Petûr II (restored)	1196–1197
Kaloyan	1197–1207
Boril	1207–1218
Ivan Asen II	1218–1241
Kaliman I	1241–1246
Miahil II Asen	1246–1256
Kaliman II	1256–1257
Konstantin Asen	1257–1277
Ivailo	1277–1279
Ivan Asen III	1279
Georgi Terter I	1279–1292
Smilets	1292–1298
Chaka	1298–1300
Todor Svetoslav	1300–1321
Georgi Terter II	1321–1323
Mihail Shishman	1323–1330
Ivan Stefan	1330–1331
Ivan Alexander	1331–1371
Ivan Shishman	1371–1395
Ivan Stratsimir	1395–1396

PRINCES AND KINGS OF MODERN BULGARIA

Alexander Battenberg	1879–1886
Ferdinand	1887–1918
Boris III	1918–1943
Simeon II	1943–1946*

* King Simeon II left Bulgaria after a referendum in September 1946. The legality of the referendum has been questioned.

Prime ministers of Bulgaria, 1879–1996

Todor Burmov	July–November 1879
Metropolitan Kliment	
(Vasil Drumev)	November 1879–March 1880
Dragan Tsankov	March–November 1880
Petko Karavelov	November 1880–April 1881
Johan Kazimir Ehrenrot (Russian)	April–July 1881
No prime minister	July 1881–June 1882
Leonid Sobolev (Russian)	June 1882–September 1883
Dragan Tsankov	September 1883–June 1884
Petko Karavelov	June 1884–August 1886
Metropolitan Kliment	
(provisional government)	9–12 August 1886
Petko Karavelov (provisional government)	12–16 August 1886
Vasil Radoslavov	August 1886–June 1887
Konstantin Stoilov	June–August 1887
Stefan Stambolov	August 1887–May 1894
Konstantin Stoilov	May 1894–January 1899
Dimitûr Grekov	January–October 1899
Todor Ivanchov	October 1899–January 1901
Racho Petrov	January–February 1901
Petko Karavelov	February–December 1901
Stoyan Danev	December 1901–May 1903
Racho Petrov	May 1903–October 1906
Dimitûr Petkov	October 1906–February 1907
Dimitri Stanciov	February–March 1907

Petûr Gudev	March 1907–January 1908
Aleksandûr Malinov	January 1908–March 1911
Ivan Geshov	March 1911–June 1913
Stoyan Danev	June–July 1913
Vasil Radoslavov	July 1913–June 1918
Aleksandûr Malinov	June–November 1918
Teodor Teodorov	November 1918–October 1919
Aleksandûr Stamboliiski	October 1919–June 1923
Aleksandûr Tsankov	June 1923–January 1926
Andrei Lyapchev	January 1926–June 1931
Aleksandûr Malinov	June–October 1931
Nikola Mushanov	October 1931–May 1934
Kimon Georgiev	May 1934–January 1935
Pencho Zlatev	January–April 1935
Andrei Toshev	April–November 1935
Georgi Kioseivanov	November 1935–February 1940
Bogdan Filov	February 1940–September 1943
Dobri Bozhilov	September 1943–June 1944
Ivan Bagryanov	June–September 1944
Konstantin Muraviev	2–9 September 1944
Kimon Georgiev	September 1944–November 1946
Georgi Dimitrov	November 1946–July 1949
Vasil Kolarov	July 1949–January 1950
Vûlko Chervenkov	January 1950–April 1956
Anton Yugov	April 1956–November 1962
Todor Zhivkov	November 1962–July 1971
Stanko Todorov	July 1971–June 1981
Grisha Filipov	June 1981–March 1986
Georgi Atanasov	March 1986–February 1990
Andrei Lukanov	February–November 1990
Dimitûr Popov	December 1990–November 1991
Filip Dimitrov	November 1991–December 1992
Liuben Berov	December 1992–September 1994
Reneta Indjova	October 1994–January 1995
Zhan Videnov	January 1995–

SUGGESTIONS FOR
FURTHER READING

Adanir, Fikret. *Die Makedonische Frage: Ihre Entstehung und Entwicklung bis 1908* (Wiesbaden 1979)

Barker, Elisabeth. *Macedonia: Its Place in Balkan Power Politics* (London, 1950)

Beaman, A. Hulme. *Stambuloff* (London, 1895)

Bell, John D. *Peasants in Power: Alexandŭr Stamboliski and the Bulgarian Agrarian National Union, 1899–1923* (Princeton, NJ, 1977)

The Communist Party of Bulgaria from Blagoev to Zhivkov (Stanford, California, 1986)

Black, C. E. *The Establishment of Constitutional Government in Bulgaria* (Princeton Studies in History, 1, Princeton, NJ, 1943)

Boll, Michael M. *The Cold War in the Balkans: American Foreign Policy and the Emergence of Communist Bulgaria, 1943–1947* (Lexington, KY, 1984)

Boll, Michael M. (ed.) *The American Military Mission in the Allied Control Commission for Bulgaria, 1944–1947: History and Transcripts* (Boulder, CO, and New York, 1985)

Brailsford, H. N. *Macedonia, its Races and their Future* (London, 1906)

Brown, J. F. *Bulgaria under Communist Rule* (London, 1970)

Browning, Robert *Byzantium and Bulgaria: A Comparative Study across the Early Medieval Frontier* (London, 1975)

Chary, Frederick B. *The Bulgarian Jews and the Final Solution, 1940–1944* (Pittsburg, 1972)

Clarke, James F. *Bible Societies, American Missionaries and the National Revival of Bulgaria* (New York 1971, reprint of Harvard Ph.D., 1937)

Constant, Stephen. *Foxy Ferdinand, Tsar of Bulgaria* (London, 1979)

Corti, Egon. *Alexander of Bulgaria* (London, 1954)

Crampton, Richard J. *Bulgaria 1878–1918: A History* (Boulder, CO, and New York, 1983)
  A Short History of Modern Bulgaria (Cambridge, 1987)
  'Bulgarian Society in the Early Nineteenth Century', in Richard Clogg (ed.), *Balkan Society in the Age of Greek Independence* (London, 1981)
Dimitroff, Pashanko. *Boris III of Bulgaria (1894–1943): Toiler, Citizen, King* (Lewes, Sussex, 1986)
Dimitrova, Ekaterina. *The Gospels of Tsar Ivan Alexander* (London, 1994)
Feiwel, George R. *Growth and Reforms in Centrally Planned Economies: The Lessons of the Bulgarian Experience* (New York, 1977)
Friedrich, Wolfgang-Uwe. *Bulgarien und die Mächte 1913–1915* (Stuttgart, 1985)
Genchev, Nikolai. *The Bulgarian National Revival Period* (Sofia, 1977)
Groueff, Stephane. *Crown of Thorns: the Reign of King Boris III of Bulgaria, 1918–1943* (Lanham, MD, New York and London, 1987)
Hatschikjan, Magarditsch A. *Tradition und Neuorientierung in der bulgarischen Aussenpolitik, 1944–1948* (Munich, 1988)
Hoddinott, R. F. *Bulgaria in Antiquity; An Archaeological Introduction* (London and Tonbridge, 1975)
Hoppe, Hans-Joachim. *Bulgarien – Hitlers eigenwilliger Verbündeter* (Stuttgart, 1979)
Hupchik, Dennis P. *The Bulgarians in the Seventeenth Century: Slavic Orthodox Society and Culture under Ottoman Rule* (Jefferson, NC, and London, 1993)
Hupchik, Dennis P. (ed.) *The Pen and the Sword: Studies in Bulgarian History by James F Clarke* (Boulder, CO, and New York, 1988)
Isusov, Mito (ed.) *Problems of Transition from Capitalism to Socialism* (Sofia, 1975)
Jelavich, Charles. *Russian Policy in Bulgaria and Serbia, 1881–1897* (Berkeley, CA, 1950)
  Tsarist Russia and Balkan Nationalism: Russian Influence in the Internal Affairs of Bulgaria and Serbia, 1876–1886 (Berkeley, CA, 1958)
Karpat, K. H. (ed.) *The Turks of Bulgaria: The History, Culture and Political Fate of a Minority* (Istanbul, 1990)
Kiel, Machiel. *Art and Society of Bulgaria in the Turkish Period* (Maastricht, 1985)
Kostov, Vladimir. *The Bulgarian Umbrella: The Soviet Direction and Operation of the Bulgarian Secret Service in Europe* (London and New York, 1988)

Kuhne, Victor. *Bulgaria Self-Revealed* (London, 1919)

Lampe, John R. *The Bulgarian Economy in the Twentieth Century* (London, 1986)

Lang, David Marshall. *The Bulgarians from Pagan Times to the Ottoman Conquest* (London, 1976)

Lory, Bernard. *Le Sort de l'héritage Ottoman en Bulgarie: l'exemple des villes bulgares 1878–1900* (Istanbul, 1985)

Macdermott, Mercia. *The Apostle of Freedom: A Portrait of Vasil Levski against a Background of Nineteenth-Century Bulgaria* (London, 1967)
  Freedom or Death: The Life of Gotse Delchev (London, 1978)

Markov, Georgi. *The Truth that Killed* (translated by Liliana Brisby with an introduction by Annabel Markov, London, 1983)

McIntyre, Robert J. *Bulgaria: Politics, Economics and Society* (London, and New York, 1988)

Meininger, Thomas A. *Ignatiev and the Establishment of the Bulgarian Exarchate, 1864–1872: A Study in Personal Diplomacy* (Madison, WI, 1970)

Miller, Marshall Lee. *Bulgaria during the Second World War* (Stanford, CA, 1975)

Mocsy, A. *Pannonia and Upper Moesia* (London, 1974)

Moser, Charles A. *A History of Bulgarian Literature, 863–1844* (The Hague, 1972)
  Dimitrov of Bulgaria: A Political Biography of Dr Georgi D. Dimitrov (Ottawa, IL, 1979)

Muir, Nadejda. *Dmitri Stancioff: Patriot and Cosmopolitan, 1864–1940* (London, 1957)

Nestorova, Tatyana. *American Missionaries among the Bulgarians: (1858–1912)* (Boulder, CO and New York, 1987)

Nicoloff, Assen. *The Bulgarian Resurgence* (Cleveland, OH, 1987)

Obolensky, Dmitri. *The Bogomils: A Study in Balkan Neo-Manichaeism* (Cambridge 1948, reprinted New York 1979)
  The Byzantine Commonwealth: Eastern Europe 500–1453 (London, 1971)

Oren, Nisssan. *Bulgarian Communism: The Road to Power, 1934–1944* (New York, 1971)
  Revolution Administered: Agrarianism and Communism in Bulgaria (Baltimore and London, 1973)

Padev, Michael. *Dimitroff Wastes No Bullets: the Inside Story of the Trial and Murder of Nikola Petkov* (London, 1948)

Perry, Duncan. *The Politics of Terror: The Macedonian Revolutionary Movements, 1893–1903* (Durham, NC, and London, 1988)
  Stefan Stambolov and the Emergence of Modern Bulgaria, 1870–1895 (Durham, NC, and London, 1993)

Rachev, Stoyan. *Anglo-Bulgarian Relations during the Second World War (1939–1944)* (translated by Stefan Kostov, Sofia, 1981)

Rothschild, Joseph. *The Communist Party of Bulgaria: Origins and Development, 1883–1936* (New York, 1959)

Runciman, Steven. *A History of the First Bulgarian Empire* (London, 1930)

Sanders, Irwin T. *Balkan Village* (Lexington, KY, 1949)

Simsir, Bilal N. *The Turks of Bulgaria (1878–1985)* (London, 1988)

Slavov, Atanas. *The 'Thaw' in Bulgarian Literature* (Boulder, CO and New York, 1981)

With the Precision of Bats (Washington, DC, 1986)

Stoyanoff, Zachary. *Pages from the Autobiography of a Bulgarian Insurgent* (translated by M. W. Potter, London, 1913)

Sumner, B. H. *Russia and the Balkans, 1870–1880* (Oxford, 1937)

Swire, Joseph. *Bulgarian Conspiracy* (London, 1939)

Thracian Treasures from Bulgaria; A special exhibition held at the British Museum January–March 1976 (London, 1976)

Todorov, Kosta. *Balkan Firebrand: the Autobiography of a Rebel, Soldier and Statesman* (Chicago, 1943)

Todorov, Nikolai. *The Balkan Town, 15th–19th Centuries* (Seattle, WA, 1983)

Troebst, Stefan. *Mussolini, Makedonien und die Mächte 1922–1930* (Cologne and Vienna, 1987)

Vazov, Ivan. *Under the Yoke: A Novel* (translated by Marguerite Alexieva and Theodora Atanassova, Sofia, 1976)

Velkov, A. *Cities in Thrace and Dacia in Late Antiquity* (Amsterdam, 1977)

Velkov, A. (ed.) *Roman Cities in Bulgaria: Collected Studies* (Amsterdam, 1980)

Todor Zhivkov: Statesman and Builder of the New Bulgaria, (Oxford, 1982) In the second edition (Oxford, 1985) references to the Turkish minority and its rights have been excised.

Ludmila Zhivkova, Her Many Worlds (Oxford, 1982)

INDEX